# Bodhisattva Awakening

## TIBETAN CLASSICS

Presenting translations of essential and practical works extracted from the riches of *The Library of Tibetan Classics*, the *Tibetan Classics* series aims to make these seminal works more broadly accessible.

*Essential Mind Training*

*Wisdom of the Kadam Masters*

*The Mind of Mahāmudrā*

*Ornament of Precious Liberation*
Gampopa

*Clarifying the Sage's Intent*
Sakya Paṇḍita

*Bodhisattva Awakening*
Thokmé Sangpo

# Bodhisattva Awakening

*An Explanation of Śāntideva's Guide*

Thokmé Sangpo

Translated by
Julia Stenzel

Edited and introduced by
Thupten Jinpa

Wisdom

Wisdom Publications, Inc.
132 Perry Street
New York, NY 10014 USA
wisdom.org



*Library of Congress Cataloging-in-Publication Data*
Names: Thogs-med-bzang-po, Rgyal-sras, 1295–1369 author | Stenzel, Julia, active 21st century translator | Thupten Jinpa editor
Title: Bodhisattva awakening: an explanation of Śāntideva's guide / Thokmé Sangpo; translated by Julia Stenzel ; edited and introduced by Thupten Jinpa.
Description: First edition. | New York: Wisdom Publications, 2026. | Series: Tibetan classics | Includes bibliographical references and index.
Identifiers: LCCN 2026009832 (print) | LCCN 2026009833 (ebook) | ISBN 9798890700667 paperback | ISBN 9798890700766 ebook
Subjects: LCSH: Bodhisattvas | Śāntideva, active 7th century. Bodhicaryāvatāra. English | Bodhisattva (The concept) | Religious life—Buddhism
Classification: LCC BQ4695 .T46 2026 (print) | LCC BQ4695 (ebook) | DDC 294.3/4213—dc23/eng/20260521
LC record available at https://lccn.loc.gov/2026009832
LC ebook record available at https://lccn.loc.gov/2026009833

30 29 28 27 26 5 4 3 2 1

ISBN 979-8-89070-066-7 ebook ISBN 979-8-89070-076-6

Cover image: Indian teacher Śāntideva, Eastern Tibet, 1900–1959. Ground mineral pigment on cloth. Photo by Matthieu Ricard c/o Shechen Archives.
Cover and interior design by Gopa & Ted2, Inc.

Printed on acid-free paper that meets the guidelines for permanence and durability of the Production Guidelines for Book Longevity of the Council on Library Resources.

Printed in the United States of America.

# Publisher's Acknowledgment

The publisher gratefully acknowledges the generous help of Tsadra Foundation and the Hershey Family Foundation in sponsoring the production of this book.

# Contents

# Preface

It is a profound joy for me to see an English translation of the master Thokmé Sangpo's commentary on Śāntideva's *Guide to the Bodhisattva Way* in this special volume. I still recall the first time I came face to face with this important Tibetan work. It was in January 1977, when I had the opportunity to visit Bodhgaya, where His Holiness the Dalai Lama was scheduled to give a series of teachings and to conduct a ceremony for generating the awakening mind. At one of the makeshift bookstalls near the sacred Mahabodhi Temple, I purchased two texts in modern book format, both Tibetan commentaries on Śāntideva's *Guide*, which I had by then memorized as a young monk. One of those commentaries was Thokmé Sangpo's text translated here, the other a lengthier commentary by Gyaltsab Darma Rinchen. Today, nearly half a century after first holding this text in my hand in Bodhgaya, to be able to share Thokmé Sangpo's text with contemporary readers in English feels like coming full circle.

Thokmé Sangpo, the fourteenth-century author of our volume, is profoundly admired for his mastery of scripture and for embodying the bodhisattva ideal. Among the many Tibetan commentaries on Śāntideva's celebrated text, the one featured in this volume is not only one of the most famous, it is also deeply revered for having been penned by a great bodhisattva. The translation of Thokmé Sangpo's work featured here is drawn from The Bodhisattva Ideal: Selected Key Texts (The Library of Tibetan Classics, volume 11), with a new introduction prepared for this special volume and Thokmé Sangpo's detailed outline reproduced as an appendix. The translation for chapters 1–8 and 10 was drafted by Julia Stenzel, with source citations of quotes from scripture drawn from the Tibetan edition published by the Institute of Tibetan Classics. I translated chapter 9, "Wisdom," and also wrote most of the explanatory notes throughout the text and edited the work as a whole.

To the following individuals and organizations, I owe my sincere thanks: to Julia Stenzel for preparing her portion of the translation; to David Kittelstrom, senior editor at Wisdom, for his incisive editing; to my fellow Tibetan editor Geshé Lobsang Choedar for assisting me by sourcing all the citations in the original Tibetan edition of the text; and to the Buddhist Digital Resource Center for providing me access to its immense digital library of Tibetan texts.

Finally, I would like to express my deep gratitude to the Tsadra Foundation for its generous funding of The Bodhisattva Ideal, from which this work has been extracted. It is also through the generosity of the Tsadra Foundation that this special volume has been made available. I would also like to acknowledge the Ing Foundation, whose longstanding patronage of the Institute of Tibetan Classics makes it possible for me personally to be devoting much of my time and attention to editing and translation of classical Tibetan texts.

May the experience of engaging with these Tibetan texts moisten the heart of all readers, awakening within them the seed of great compassion and sprout forth the precious *bodhicitta*, the awakening mind.

Thupten Jinpa
Montreal, 2026

## *Technical Notes*

The Tibetan title of the present work is *Byang chub sems dpa'i spyod pa la 'jug pa'i 'grel pa legs par bshad pa'i rgya mtsho* by Thogs med bzang po (1295–1369). The source text for this translation was the edition in *Rgyal sras kyi spyod pa'i chos skor*, volume 11 of the *Bod kyi gtsug lag gces btus* series (Delhi: Institute of Tibetan Classics, 2006), 9–188. This English translation also appears in volume 11 of *The Library of Tibetan Classics* series, *The Bodhisattva Ideal: Selected Key Texts* (New York: Wisdom Publications, 2026), 51–247.

The titles of all texts referred to in the translation are rendered in English, regardless of whether translations of those texts have been published in English. Tibetan titles can be found in the bibliography.

The chapter and verse numbers from the *Guide to the Bodhisattva Way* that Thokmé Sangpo is commenting on are indicated in brackets—for example, [1.3] for chapter 1, verse 3.

The conventions for phonetic transcription of Tibetan words are those developed by the Institute of Tibetan Classics and Wisdom Publications. Sanskrit diacritics are used throughout.

## *Abbreviated References*

These frequently cited works are referenced in the following abbreviated forms in the notes. See the bibliography for details on each entry.

| | |
|---|---|
| *Bodhicaryāvatāra* | Śāntideva, *Guide to the Bodhisattva Way*, Toh 3871. |
| Kṛṣṇapa | Kṛṣṇapa, *Exposition of Guide to the Bodhisattva Way* (*Bodhicaryāvatāravivṛtipañjikā*), Toh 3873. A.k.a. the *Exposition*. |
| Kṣemadeva | Kṣemadeva, *Excellent Exposition on Guide* |

| | |
|---|---|
| | *to the Bodhisattva Way* (*Bodhisattvacaryāvatārasaṃskāra*), Toh 3874. |
| Prajñākaramati | Prajñākaramati, *Extensive Commentary on Guide to the Bodhisattva Way* (*Bodhicaryāvatārapañjikā*), Toh 3872. A.k.a. the *Great Commentary*. |
| Vairocanarakṣita | *Commentary on the Difficult Points of Guide to the Bodhisattva Way* (*Bodhisattvacaryāvatārapañjikā*), Toh 3876. |

# Introduction

Śāntideva's *Guide to the Bodhisattva Way* (*Bodhicaryāvatāra* in Sanskrit) is perhaps the most influential and beloved classical Indian Buddhist work among Tibetan Buddhists.[1] As a guide to entering (*avatāra*) the "bodhisattva way" (*bodhicaryā*), it focuses on the so-called bodhisattva ideal, an expression that embraces the entire course of the bodhisattva, starting with its basis in the awakening mind (*bodhicitta*). Briefly put, a *bodhisattva* is one who seeks to attain buddhahood to best benefit all beings. While *bodhi* means "enlightenment" or "awakening," the *sattva* carries multiple meanings, including "being," "essence," or "hero." In Tibetan, the *sattva* in *bodhisattva* is uniformly translated as *sems dpa'* (pronounced *sempa*), consisting of two distinct words, *sems* (mind, thought) and *dpa'* (hero, courageous being). Understood this way, a bodhisattva is not simply one who aspires to become a buddha but, more importantly, one who does so with a heroic attitude dedicated to the welfare of all beings. And the hallmark of this heroic intention to alleviate the suffering of all beings is a pursuit of it even if it means deferring one's own nirvāṇa, or liberation.

The present volume is an authoritative Tibetan commentary on Śāntideva's *Guide* composed by Thokmé Sangpo, a fourteenth-century master who was a key figure in the transmission both of Śāntideva's text and of the associated Tibetan "mind training," or *lojong*, teachings.

## *Śāntideva's Guide*

Written entirely in verse, the *Guide* is structured in ten chapters:

1. The Benefits of the Awakening Mind
2. The Confession of Negative Actions[2]
3. Upholding the Awakening Mind
4. Conscientiousness
5. Guarding Awareness
6. Forbearance
7. Diligence
8. Meditation
9. Wisdom
10. Dedication

True to its title, the structure of the text reflects the approach of a guide, leading the aspirant right from the generation of awakening mind. The awakening mind, or *bodhicitta*, is defined by two distinct aspirations: an aspiration to secure the welfare of others and an aspiration to attain buddhahood to that end. The first aspiration is the main cause, while the second is a key condition. In brief, it is a state of mind whose *primary concern* is the welfare of others, whose *objective* is enlightenment, and whose *mode of engagement* is that of an earnest wish. The core of the aspiration to secure others' welfare is *great compassion*. The "great" indicates that the compassion here is very different from ordinary compassion. The "great" connotes its extraordinary scope, embracing the entirety of sentient beings. It also connotes extraordinary courage when faced with the suffering of others. And when this great compassion is combined with an earnest wish to become a buddha for countless others' sake that emerges effortlessly, awakening mind has then arisen. Thus, as the first step in his guide, Śāntideva extolls the virtues of this awakening mind, inspiring the aspirant to make a strong emotional investment in it.

In so doing, Śāntideva clearly has in mind odes to the awakening mind found in the great Mahāyāna sutras, such as this one in the *Array of Trees* (*Gaṇḍavyūha*) *Sūtra*:

> O child of the family, the awakening mind is like the *seed* of all the attributes of the buddha. It is like the *field* that produces a bountiful crop of meritorious deeds for all beings. Since the world of beings depend on it, it is like *earth*. Since it cleanses the stains of afflictions, it is like *water*. Since it moves the world, it is like the *wind*. Since it incinerates the grasping of views, it is like *fire*. Since it lights up the abodes of all sentient beings, it is like the *sun* . . . Since all bodhisattvas ride on it, it is like a *mount*. Since it leads one to enter the deeds of a bodhisattva, it is like a *door*. Since, with it, one resides in the house of concentration, it is like a *mansion* . . . Since it protects all beings, it is like a *haven* . . . Since it precedes the thorough upholding of the Great Vehicle, it is like the *trailblazer*. Since it heals the ailment of the afflictions, it is like a *medicine*.[3]

Since a bodhisattva is defined simply by whether the awakening mind has arisen within them, the opportunity to become a bodhisattva is open to all beings, not just humans. Hence Śāntideva declares in 1.9:

> When the awakening mind has arisen in him,
> a wretch, captive in the prison of cyclic existence,
> he is straightaway hailed as a child of the sugatas,
> to be revered in the worlds of gods and humans.

Chapter 2 and chapter 3, up to verse 21, present what is known as the *seven-limb worship*, an important Mahāyāna Buddhist rite for creating merit consisting of, as the name indicates, seven elements. They are (1) making offerings to the objects of veneration, such as the Three Jewels, (2) prostrating and going for refuge to those objects of veneration, (3) confessing and purifying negative karma, (4) rejoicing in all beings' good deeds, including one's own, (5) requesting the buddhas to turn the wheel of Dharma, (6) supplicating the buddhas not to enter into nirvāṇa, and (7) dedicating merits. In the rest of chapter 3, stanzas 3.22–23 present the actual rite for generating the awakening mind. This is followed by taking joy in having generated this precious mind, and reinforcing one's promise to uphold the mind based on single-pointed conviction that this altruistic awakening mind indeed is the most precious thing in the universe.

Chapter 4, "Conscientiousness," and chapter 5, "Guarding Awareness," together present how best to ensure that the awakening mind, once generated, is never compromised. This means leading a life that accords with the vow one has made, which brings us to the bodhisattva's six perfections, the core of training on the bodhisattva path. Of the six perfections, these two chapters present the perfection of morality, which here includes guarding the precepts one has pledged to uphold. As to the specific precepts, Śāntideva advises the reader of the *Guide* to "definitely and repeatedly read" (5.105) his other major work, the *Compendium of Training.*[4] The practice of the first perfection, that of generosity, is presented in parts of chapter 5 as well as in the final chapter, "Dedication."

Each of the remaining four perfections—forbearance, diligence, meditation, and wisdom—has a chapter bearing its name. Of these, the lengthiest are those on forbearance (134 verses), meditation (186 verses), and wisdom (167 verses). It is in chapter 8, on the perfection of meditation, that the text presents the heart advice for cultivating awakening, through the methods of "equalizing self and others" and "exchanging of self and others." By far, the text of the ninth chapter, "Wisdom," presents the most challenging read, presuming a measure of familiarity with key ontological questions and debates within classical Indian philosophy.

The final chapter, "Dedication," conveys a series of aspirations that sentient beings everywhere, whoever they are, may be free from sufferings—many of which Śāntideva specifies—and achieve happiness. Toward the end of this chapter, in verse 55, appears the lines that His Holiness the Fourteenth Dalai Lama has said are the greatest source of inspiration in his own life:

> For as long as space remains,
> for as long as sentient beings remain,
> may I too remain
> and dispel the miseries of beings.

Legend has it that the *Guide* originated in a live teaching Śāntideva gave at Nālandā Monastery sometime in the eighth century. Because of his monastic peers' perception of him as someone with only three concerns—eating, relieving, and sleeping—his peers had mockingly arranged for him a high throne with no ladder to mount it! When the time came for him to deliver the discourse, however, he magically rose up to the throne and began narrating the entire text that latter came to be the *Guide*. The legend continues that, as he reached the difficult ninth chapter, he began to slowly hover in the air, ascending ever higher, finally disappearing into thin air.[5] Regardless of the veracity of this origin story, no one can dispute that, in composing his *Guide*, Śāntideva penned one of the most important works on the bodhisattva ideal.

## *Thokmé Sangpo and His Legacy*

Since Śāntideva's *Guide* occupies such a special place in the hearts of Tibetans, it has attracted numerous commentaries across generations. The qualities that made the *Guide* so appealing are its deeply personal tone, the lucidity of the language, its practicality of approach, and its incisive insights into a range of human behaviors and their underlying psychology. Even as a thirteen-year-old monk, when I memorized the text and chanted it many times, sometimes in the fields while guarding sorghum crops against marauding parrots, I felt the power of those verses. Although the *Guide* was translated into Tibetan as early as in the ninth century,[6] its widespread popularity in Tibet is probably thanks to the Bengali Buddhist master Atiśa, who came to Tibet in the middle of the eleventh century and spent his final twelve years in the country.[7] Not only did Atiśa quote from Śāntideva's *Guide* liberally in his teachings, many of his aphorisms that later became the basis for the Tibetan mind training (*lojong*) teachings draw on the *Guide*. For example, the Tibetan *tonglen* practice—imaginatively taking away the suffering and afflictions of others and offering to others your own happiness, virtue, and strength—is a direct offshoot of Śāntideva's "exchanging of self and others" instruction presented in chapter 8. It is no wonder that the *Guide* is the most-quoted Indian work in the Tibetan mind training texts.[8]

The author of our commentary, Thokmé Sangpo, was born in 1295 in the Tsang province of Tibet, in a place not far from Sakya. With the tragic deaths of both his parents in his infancy, he was raised by his maternal grandmother, Achi Chönyi. From early childhood the young boy, then named Könchok Sangpo, displayed great tenderness of heart, especially toward suffering animals. Once seeing a leaf carried away by a gust of strong wind, the boy is said to have cried out "Alas! An insect is being blown away!" At age eleven, he received his novitiate vows and was given the name Sangpo Pal. At the age of fourteen, he formally joined Bodong É Monastery, where he began his studies with special focus on Asaṅga's *Compendium of Abhidharma*. It was his mastery of Asaṅga's text at such a young age that earned him the nickname Thokmé, the

Tibetan rendering of Asaṅga.[9] Thokmé himself would come to embrace and use it before his monastic name, Sangpo, thus forming his established name Thokmé Sangpo. At Bodong É, in addition to the *Compendium of Abhidharma*, he studied Maitreya's *Ornament for the Clear Realizations* and his *Ornament of Mahāyāna Sūtras*, Nāgārjuna's texts on the Middle Way philosophy of emptiness, and Śāntideva's *Guide* and his *Compendium of Training*. At Sakya too, the young monk studied the foundational texts of Buddhist logic and epistemology by Dignāga and Dharmakīrti. His confidence in the mastery of Dharmakīrti's thought was such that the young Thokmé Sangpo is said to have uttered:

> Difficult is it indeed to comprehend Dharmakīrti's
> thought,
> and out of laziness, I did not strive too hard.
> And yet, when my intellect encountered his thought,
> the words and their meanings converged in my
> understanding.[10]

At age twenty-two, Thokmé Sangpo sat for his formal debates at the various centers of learning in the Tsang province, attracting the admiration of many scholars. He took his full ordination vows when he was twenty-nine, and at the age of thirty-one, he assumed the abbotship of Bodong É, leading the monastery in that role for seven years. During his abbacy, he is said to have principally taught six Indian Buddhist texts: Maitreya's *Ornament for the Clear Realizations*, Dharmakīrti's *Exposition of Valid Cognition*, Asaṅga's *Compendium of Abhidharma*, Maitreya's *Ornament of Mahāyāna Sūtras* and his *Sublime Continuum*, and Śāntideva's *Guide to the Bodhisattva Way*. While at Bodong É, Thokmé Sangpo composed his commentaries on major Indian Buddhist texts—his authoritative commentary on Maitreya's *Ornament of Mahāyāna Sūtras* at the age of thirty-seven, followed by commentaries on the *Sublime Continuum* and Śāntideva's *Guide* (the text in this volume), and annotations on Maitreya's *Ornament for the Clear Realizations* and Asaṅga's *Compendium of Abhidharma.*

As attested to in his Tibetan biographies, Thokmé Sangpo studied under numerous Tibetan teachers of the time, including especially the famed Pang Lotsāwa Lodrö Tenpa (1276–1342). It was from his teacher Sherab Bum (fourteenth century), who was in turn a student of Butön Rinchen Drup (1290–1364), that Thokmé Sangpo received many of the Vajrayāna teachings, including especially the six yogas of Kālacakra tantra and meditative practices pertaining to Avalokiteśvara. However, it was Sönam Drakpa (1275–1345), known as a bodhisattva, that Thokmé Sangpo considered the crown jewel among his gurus. It is from this master that he received the transmissions of the lojong teachings, such as the *Seven-Point Mind Training* of the Kadampa master Chekawa (1101–75), various shorter instructions connected with Master Atiśa, and the mind training instruction on how to take both happiness and suffering into the path.

When he turned forty-two, Thokmé Sangpo left for the mountain retreat of Ngulchu Chözong, where for over twenty years he remained in single-pointed meditative practice. Following this period of retreat, Thokmé Sangpo began teaching both monastics and the laity, focusing on lojong and Śāntideva's *Guide*. It is said that once when the master was teaching the *Guide*, flowers rained down from the sky. In response, Thokmé Sangpo remarked, "I do not possess the qualities for such a thing to happen. This surely indicates the profundity of the teaching itself."[11] According to one source, in response to questions from his students, Pang Lotsāwa declared, "When it comes to mastery of the *Guide* in Tibet, there is no one more versed than Götsangpa and Guru Thokmé. All the points of the *Guide* are present within their mental continuums."[12]

While at the Ngulchu retreat, Thokmé Sangpo penned numerous shorter practical instructions, often in verse, including a series of "self-exhortations," as well as rituals for generating the awakening mind according to Śāntideva's tradition and according to Atiśa's tradition. He wrote *sādhana* meditation rituals of the deity Avalokiteśvara, including one according to the tradition of Bhikṣunī Lakṣmī used as the basis for *nyungné* fasting practice. He also composed a "guide to the heart of dependent origination," a special instruction stemming from the Kadam founder Dromtönpa that is based on a guru-yoga practice of Avalokiteśvara. It is centered on a guided practice of loving-kindness, compassion, and exchanging of self and others and culminates by resting in an awareness that, ultimately, there are no such dualities as self and other, suffering and happiness, meditation and its object, and so forth.[13] Most importantly, from the perspective of our volume, Thokmé Sangpo authored the famed *Thirty-Seven Practices of the Bodhisattva*. It is said that once, when the master was ill and the monks of Bodong É Monastery requested him for some advice, he responded, "Take my *Thirty-Seven Practices* as my death-bed testimony."[14] He also wrote a work that would come to define the structure and sequence of Chekawa's *Seven-Point Mind Training*, such that some would later even call it "Thokmé Sangpo's Seven-Point Mind Training." In his *Seven-Point Mind Training* instruction, in line with earlier Kadampa masters, Thokmé Sangpo cites key verses from Śāntideva's *Guide*, especially when emphasizing specific aspects of the lojong instructions, such as taking adversities into the path and exchanging self and others.

To offer a glimpse of how Thokmé Sangpo's embodiment of the lojong teachings came to define his presence in the world, let's look at a few verses. In a short self-exhortation, he writes:

> With no enemies to destroy or friends to protect,
> no master to bow to or servants that cater to you,

if in solitude you do not master your own mind,
what else is there for you to do, O Maṇipa!

Similarly:

Now I will enter the hut here in solitude.
Like the grain sack whose rope has been cut,
I will let go of all activities of my body.
Like the fiddle whose strings have snapped,
I will let go of all activities of my speech.
Like the watermill whose river stream has ceased,
I will let go of all activities of my mind.[15]

Elsewhere, he contemplates how to bring illness and so forth into the path:

This illusory body that I cling to as "self,"
if it is sick, I will rejoice that this is so,
for this helps consume past bad karma.
All the varied Dharma activities are in fact
pursued to cleanse the two defilements.

If it is free of illness, I will rejoice that this is so,
for when the body and mind are well, virtuous deeds can
increase.
To endow human life with great purpose
means to apply the three doors to cultivating virtue.

If I lack wealth, I will rejoice that this is so,
for I will be free from the stress and chore of guarding it.
Whatever disputes and fights there are
most certainly stem from attachment to wealth.

If I possess wealth, I will rejoice that this is so,
for I can increase the collection of virtue and merit.
Whatever benefit and happiness there is, immediate or
 long-term,
are most certainly the fruits of one's merit.

If I die soon, I will rejoice that this is so.
Uninterrupted by the obstacles of adverse conditions
and accompanied by good karma that connects [to the
 next life],
I will most certainly be placed on an unerring path.

If I live long, I will rejoice that this is so,
for the harvest of experience can arise
when pith instructions are applied continuously
while they remain warm and moist.[16]

Over time, not only did Thokmé Sangpo come to be revered as a bodhisattva—hence his epithet Gyalsé ("son of the conquerors")—he also came to be viewed as an emanation of Avalokiteśvara himself. In addition to the name Gyalsé Thokmé Sangpo, he is referred to as Bodong Thokmé, because of his association with the monastery, and Ngulchu Thokmé Sango, thanks to his long association with the Ngulchu retreat. His students included, among others, the Sakya hierarch Jamyang Dönyö Gyaltsen, Lama Dampa Sönam Gyaltsen, Lochen Jangchup Tsemo, Drogön Palyé (author of the lengthy commentary on Thokmé Sangpo's guide on the *Seven-Point Mind Training*), and Jetsun Rendawa, the principal teacher of Jé Tsongkhapa. Even the king of Tibet at the time, Jangchup Gyaltsen (1302–64), the first in the Phakmo Drupa dynasty, honored the master by inviting him to Central Tibet.[17] On his way to Central Tibet, Thokmé Sango visited Shalu Monastery and met with Butön

Rinchen Drup, one of the great Tibetan Buddhist luminaries of the fourteenth century.[18]

Thokmé Sangpo's impact and legacy, especially with respect to lojong and the practice of compassion in Tibetan Buddhism, is succinctly summarized in one of the master's biographies:

> Because this precious bodhisattva himself embraced lojong and *nyungné* and so forth based on Avalokiteśvara as meditation deity as the heart of his personal practice, here in this land of Tibet, lojong and *nyungné* practices pervade everywhere with no sectarian differentiation—within Sakya, Ngorpa, Geluk, Nyingma, Jonang, and Dakpo Kagyü—and the source of all of these streams of transmissions lead to Gyalsé Thokmé Rinpoché. That they came to be disseminated from the students of the master is clear from the gurus within their lineages of transmission. So he was truly the master of these two teachings and is thus uniquely a supreme source of blessing.[19]

### *Some Key Elements*

Written in a succinct style, one unique value of Thokmé Sangpo's commentary is the way he cites variant readings by four major Indian commentators—Prajñākaramati, Kṣemadeva, Kṛṣṇapa, and Vairocanarakṣita. None of these commentaries have been published in any contemporary language (the last three are no longer extant even in Sanskrit), so Thokmé Sangpo's commentary here offers a rare opportunity for English-language readers to benefit from their diverse interpretations. By indicating variant readings, Thokmé Sangpo's commentary is unique. Other Tibetan commentaries on the *Guide* tend to adopt the canonical version uncritically.

Among the Indian commentaries, the one by Kṛṣṇapa merits

special mention for two features. As mentioned in note 2, he has nine chapters, as opposed to the standard ten, due to fusing of the second and the third chapters into one called "Adopting the Awakening Mind." The second unique feature is where he places an extensive section on cultivating the awakening mind. In the canonical version, whose structure matches Prajñākaramati's commentary, these appear as verses 90–173 in the "Meditation" chapter, but Kṛṣṇapa includes them in the "Diligence" chapter, as a feature of the bodhisattva's perfection of diligence because of its focus on equalizing self and others. Kṛṣṇapa criticizes those who insist on placing this passage in the "Meditation" chapter, saying it goes against the very wish of Śāntideva, whom Kṛṣṇapa refers to as "Master Akṣayamati, who received Mañjuśrī's special attainment."[20]

I have also drawn attention in the notes to important elements of the commentary, but I highlight a few specific points here.

The first pertains to the topic of the awakening mind, a central concern of the *Guide.* In chapter 1, Thokmé Sangpo gives a careful reading of Śāntideva's differentiation between "aspiring" and "engaging" awakening minds, where he employs the metaphor contrasting the state of mind of a person setting an intention to go with that of a person actually going. On the same topic, the opening of chapter 2, under the heading "General Points," gives an overview of the awakening mind, including its most well-known definition, from Maitreya's *Ornament for the Clear Realizations*, its types, and other important aspects of generating the mind and taking the bodhisattva vow. And in chapter 3, Thokmé Sangpo reads verses 22–23 as presenting a ritual for generating aspiring awakening mind and taking the bodhisattva vow simultaneously. He also offers an alternative reading whereby, with a slight modification, one can first generate the aspiring mind based on verse 22 and then follow it with taking the bodhisattva vow based on verse 23.

The rite for generating the awakening mind appears to have been a topic of enduring concern for Thokmé Sangpo. In addition to its treatment in the present commentary, he gives it a lengthy treatment in his commentary on *Ornament of Mahāyāna Sūtras*. Later too, while at the Ngulchu retreat, he would compose two separate texts on the topic: a short one on the rite according to Master Atiśa's tradition, and a second, lengthy one according to Śāntideva's tradition. The latter text ends by dedicating:

> Through this presentation on the rite of bodhisattva
> vows
> based on what is found in the bodhisattva Śāntideva's
> scriptures,
> may the Conqueror's teaching flourish, and may all
> beings
> enter the way of the bodhisattva.[21]

The second element of the commentary I would like to draw the reader's attention to is how Thokmé Sangpo understands verse 9.2, which differentiates and defines the two truths—the ultimate truth and the conventional truth—in particular, the line (9.2cd) "The ultimate is not an object of the intellect, for the intellect is accepted to be a concealer." Part of the challenge of reading 9.2 in the Tibetan tradition is the use of the word *blo* (*buddhi*), here rendered "the intellect" but which can also be rendered more generally as "cognition" or "mind." If read in the latter way, an unavoidable consequence is that ultimate truth cannot be an object of consciousness. The reading of 9.2 and its implication for the definition of the two truths, and whether ultimate truth is beyond human knowledge, would come to occupy the minds of many commentators of the *Guide* in Tibet.

The final element to highlight here is Prajñakāramati's assertion that 9.49–51 might be a later addition by a different author.

Thokmé Sangpo suggests that if one takes these three stanzas to be by Śāntideva himself, they must be placed later to ensure greater logical coherence. To my knowledge, this suggestion is unique among the commentators on the *Guide.*

Tibetan commentators developed a tradition of mapping Indian Buddhist texts with thematic outlines, and Thokmé Sangpo's commentary is a classic example of this, with a comprehensive framework of headings and subheadings. Thus a key benefit of reading the *Guide* through the lens of this commentary is for its map of the entire terrain of Śāntideva's text.[22] This map reveals how Thokmé Sangpo understands the structure and content of the text, including especially how he understands the relationships among various parts. Except for the philosophically dense ninth chapter, Thokmé Sangpo stays very close to the text, rarely venturing into any digression, such as complementary citations from relevant sources. And when he does unpack a particular point, his approach is to marshal the readings of the Indian commentaries and not scriptures or other treatises that could add to the length of the text of his own commentary. His own contribution is typically in the form of concluding summaries.

## *How to Read This Book*

Given the multitude of competent translations of the *Guide* now available in English, we have chosen not to insert a translation into Thokmé Sangpo's commentary, which paraphrases the root text in prose in the course of his explanation. To help the reader easily correlate the commentary to the root text, we have supplied the relevant chapter and verse numbers in brackets, e.g., [1.25] for chapter 1, verse 25. We recommend having a translation of the *Guide* to consult as you read Thokmé Sangpo's text.

Clearly, the best way to read the *Guide* with the help of this important commentary is to carefully read the *Guide* as it was written, from the beginning, and follow along the with the commentary in the same way. Reading the entire text sequentially will offer the best way to deeply engage with the *Guide* and let the teaching and insights of the text infuse your mind.

If pressed for time, or if you wish to sample the text, here is what I would suggest. Read the first chapter in its entirety, then jump to chapter 3. After this, read chapters 4 and 5, which together present instructions on how to live according to the precepts of someone who has generated the awakening mind. These two chapters also present what one today might call "everyday mindfulness"—strategies for regulating our emotions, especially those that may lead to destructive behavior. Then read the second half of chapter 8 (8.89–158), which presents the heart of the cultivation of awakening mind, including the method of "equalizing and exchanging self and others." Finish by reading the final chapter, the dedication, to strengthen earnestly felt altruistic aspirations.

You could also choose to read chapters specific to your interests. For example, you could focus on chapter 6 on forbearance to delve into Śāntideva's analysis of the psychology underlying anger and his strategies for dealing with anger. Or you could focus on chapter 7, "Diligence," if your interest is to understand the psychology behind laziness—especially its three main forms: procrastination, avoidance through indulging unhealthy habits, and discouragement—and what techniques Śāntideva recommends to generate enthusiasm and sustain it over a long time. You could also choose to focus on the eighth chapter, especially the second half, if your main interest is to understand Śāntideva's teaching on cultivating the awakening mind through "equalizing and exchanging self and others." Or, if your primary interest is understanding the content of wisdom—especially emptiness, the ultimate nature of reality—then you could use chapter 9 as a textbook to investigate the Middle Way philosophy of emptiness that Śāntideva, like Nāgārjuna, upholds as the key to liberation.

Finally, another approach is to use Thokmé Sangpo's outline as a detailed table of contents and then chose specific topics that interest you and build your understanding of the text that way.

In brief, there is more than one way to engage with Śāntideva's *Guide*, a living and breathing ancient text that has been the source of profound inspiration and insights for Tibetans for centuries. I'll end my introduction with two verses from the master's own dedication:

> May those who have entered the Sugata's doctrine
> be free from the bondage of indolence and distraction and,
> abiding in discipline, always engage their three doors
> in meaningful ways through listening, reflection, and
> meditation.
>
> May the rains of the heavens fall in a timely manner;
> may the great earth be richly adorned with grains, pulses,
> grasses, and trees;
> may the people enjoy happiness and be kind to each other;
> may they always engage in the ten virtuous deeds.

# An Ocean of Excellent Discourses

## *A Commentary on "Guide to the Bodhisattva Way"*

Thokmé Sangpo
(1295–1369)

# Homage

Homage to the noble Avalokiteśvara!

I bow to you, O son of Śuddhodana, who out of compassion for all beings engendered the awakening mind, vast as an ocean,
exuding warm air of the two accumulations. From this arises massive heaps of clouds, the three bodies whose nature is nonabiding nirvāṇa.
A bountiful rain of Dharma nectar descends from them ceaselessly, free from the proliferations of no-self and the other extreme views,
dousing the flames of beings' defilements. You multiply the harvest of their welfare and happiness beyond all limitations.

I bow to the protector Avalokita.
The mere touch of your name's light waves
entering the ears' pathway
dissipates the darkness of mind.

I bow to Mañjughoṣa, who teaches ultimate reality, devoid of the elaborations of self and no-self,
and conventional reality, where actions are carried out and accumulated based on "I" and "mine"; you dissipate the dark delusion inherent in such views.

Skillfully you teach the pure conduct of surrendering one's
    own happiness for the sake of others,
thereby helping all beings accomplish the twofold benefit,
    for self and other, making them Dharma kings.

I bow to Śāntideva, the son of the Victor.
Leaving your kingdom behind forever,
you displayed the excellent conduct of bodhisattvas
and propagated the teachings of the Victorious One.

In the lotus garden of sacred teachings,
I have consumed the honey of his excellent discourses.
Here I will lay them out for the sake of those
who practice the conduct of bodhisattvas.

# 1. The Benefits of the Awakening Mind

THIS EXPLANATION of *Guide to the Bodhisattva Way*, which presents a faultless teaching on the complete Mahāyāna path, has two sections: the title and the text itself.

## THE TITLE

In the Indian language, the treatise's title is *Bodhisattvacaryāvatāra*.[23] Translated into Tibetan, *bodhi* is awakening, *sattva* is heroic being, *caryā* is conduct or way of life, and *avatāra* means introduction or guide. Titles are applied according to certain criteria. They may reflect the subject matter, the range of topics, the function of the text, the location, the audience, or the time, or they may employ metaphors. The title of this text belongs to the first category.

What is the purpose of giving texts titles? Generally speaking, applying names to objects is necessary to understand them. The *Descent into Laṅkā Sūtra* says:

> If things were left unnamed,
> people would remain ignorant.
> To remove their ignorance,
> the Protector gave names.

Regarding this specific text, since the title accords with the subject matter, an intelligent person will, just by reading the title, gain a basic understanding of the content. In addition, by reciting in Sanskrit, we develop a disposition for the language; we acknowledge the text's authentic origin and remember the kindness of the translators and scholars. By reciting the title at the beginning, all our endeavors become easy to achieve. Since the text belongs to the teachings of the Sūtra collection, the translators inserted the salutation imposed by royal command: "Homage to all buddhas and bodhisattvas!"

## The Text

Master Kṣemadeva[24] said, "This treatise can be summarized in terms of virtue in the beginning, in the middle, and at the end. In progressive order, these three are the verses of homage, from there up to the dedication, and the dedication itself."[25] Master Kṛṣṇapa[26] said, "The text can be subsumed under three points—the reasons behind its origin, the explanations of the six perfections, and the respectful expression of gratitude. As for the perfections, the first three chapters starting from 'leisure and opportunity' [1.4a][27] together with the dedication chapter are said to teach generosity. The chapters on conscientiousness and on guarding awareness are said to teach morality."[28]

This commentary explains the treatise by way of three key points: the way the author proceeds to compose the text, the nature of the practice being engaged in, and the concluding points.

## The Way the Author Proceeds to Compose the Text

The first section has two topics: the actual point and the purpose and interrelatedness indicated.

## The actual point

The actual point, in turn, has three parts: the homage, the promise to explain, and an expression of humility.

## The homage

[1.1ab] The first [Śāntideva's homage] is explained as follows. According to Vairocanarakṣita,[29] since they are well (*su*) gone (*gata*), *sugatas* means those who have gone to bliss. The adverb *well* designates, for example, a form that is *well* shaped, an epidemic that is *thoroughly* cleared away, or a jar that is *completely* filled.[30] Applied here, the sugatas, since they have eliminated all the afflictions and other obscurations, are *excellently* gone. Since they have dissipated the ignorance that obscures suchness, they are *irreversibly* gone. Since they have purified all latencies, they are *perfectly* gone. Thus the term is explained in the sense of elimination. Kṣemadeva adds that the epithet *sugata* is given because they have realized everything one can possibly realize.[31] In sum, they are sugatas because they have completely perfected elimination and realization; they have gone to the stage of supreme bliss. The *Bodhisattva Ground* too states, "Having gone to the very superior level without regression, they are called well gone."[32] This [the word *sugata*], then, refers to the Buddha Jewel.

"Dharmakāya" [in the homage] is explained by the *Sublime Continuum* as follows:

> The dharmakāya should be understood as twofold:
> the utterly stainless dharmadhātu
> and its corresponding cause, the teaching—
> the principles of profundity and diversity.[33]

This means that the dharmakāya that is realized is inseparable from the dharmadhātu possessing the two kinds of purity[34] and from primordial awareness free of stains. The "teaching" consists of all the profound and manifold discourses of the Buddha on the two truths—the ultimate and the conventional. They constitute the Dharma Jewel. And since the sugatas are endowed with this [dharmakāya, Śāntideva] says that they have "mastered" it.

The "children" or "heirs" [mentioned in the homage] are explained by the *Sublime Continuum*:

> Devotion for the supreme vehicle is the seed,
> wisdom is the mother of the Buddha and Dharma,
> the womb is meditative bliss, and the wet nurse is
>   compassion.
> Out of these are born the followers of the Sage, his
>   children.[35]

The noble bodhisattvas are his children because they are born into the family of the sugatas and have the capacity to uphold the lineage. They are the Sangha Jewel. To these three objects of refuge, Śāntideva respectfully pays homage with his three doors [that is, with his body, speech, and mind]. He also pays respect to all those who, although not objects of Mahāyāna refuge, are nonetheless worthy of veneration by virtue of their excellent qualities, such as śrāvakas and pratyekabuddhas, the learned and wise ones.

The word "and"[36] should be related to what comes after, where he announces his intention to compose the treatise. The purpose of paying homage in such a way is as explained in the *Sūtra of Praise of the Buddha's Qualities*:

> Whoever offers praise to the Teacher,
> the Sugata, ever so small,
> will traverse the happiness of humans and gods
> and attain supreme immortality.[37]

In other words, the purpose is to attain temporary and ultimate happiness.

### The promise to explain

[1.1cd] Second, Śāntideva announces his intention to teach on the discipline of the Sugata's children, which consists of abstaining from harm, gathering virtue, and engaging in ethical behavior that brings about the welfare of sentient beings. How to accomplish these will be taught in the ten chapters. In what way [are they taught]? Just as they are explained in the scriptures—the sūtras and the treatises. Some might think, "Since they were already taught in the scriptures, there is no point in teaching them here." But there is no fault [of redundancy], because here we present in an organized way what remains unorganized, clarify what remains unclear, bring together what remains scattered [in the scriptures], and present in distilled form the content of a multitude of treatises. The purpose of making a promise to explain is this: Since sublime ones never shun their obligation to fulfill a pledge, making such a promise ensures successful completion [of the composition].

### An expression of humility

[1.2–3] Śāntideva expresses the third point in the following manner: "Nothing that has not already been said in the sūtras or other texts will be taught here; nor am I uniquely skilled in composition. For these two reasons, it is not for others' benefit that I have composed this treatise. Why have I done it then? I have written the treatise to cultivate the awakening mind in my own consciousness."

"In that case," some might ask, "it would have been enough to understand it; why compose a text?" [Śāntideva responds:] "To grow accustomed to virtue and the awakening mind, I compose this teaching according to my own understanding, and for now my faith will increase and become more durable." The masters Kṣemadeva and Vairocana say that the expression "for now" indicates that benefitting others is indeed a condition [for composing the text].[38] "How so?" some might ask. [Answer:] "In the event that other people who are similar to me—namely, those who aspire for the bodhisattva way and are unbiased—see this text, their mind of awakening will be strengthened. Then they, too, would benefit from it." This expression of humility shows that the author's pride is minimal, so if errors are found [in the work, readers] will be forgiving.

## The purpose and interrelatedness indicated

This next topic has three elements. First is the natures of the individual factors.[39] The *subject matter* is illustrated by the phrase "to enter the discipline of the Sugata's children" and refers to the lineage of the Great Vehicle, its path, and the result in their entirety; most importantly, it consists of the trainings of the bodhisattva. The *purpose* is to generate understanding of the subject matter on the basis of this text. That such understanding is dependent upon the treatise is the *interrelatedness,* while the result to be achieved through the practice of what is understood is the *ultimate goal.*

Second, the purpose of the teachings, is for wise people to understand that the treatise does indeed possess a purpose and so forth and, on that basis, engage with the text.

Third is how the treatise indicates its purpose. Kṛṣṇapa's *Clarification of the Difficult Points* says, "As for its purpose and so forth, they are indicated by the treatise's title itself."[40] Kṣemadeva states that the line "To enter the discipline of the Sugata's children" indicates the subject matter, while benefit for self and others is the purpose, and the fact that the treatise and its purpose relate to each other as a means and its end constitute their interrelatedness.[41]

### The nature of the discipline being engaged in

This has three parts: (1) the person who engages in the discipline, the basis, (2) the intention of the person engaging in the discipline, and (3) the practices by which the person engages [in the discipline].

### The person who engages in the discipline, the basis

The first topic has two parts. [1.4] Of these, the first is explaining how human existence endowed with leisure and opportunity, which is the basis, is difficult to obtain:

> Being born in the hells, a hungry ghost, an animal,
> a barbarian, or a long-lived god,
> holding wrong views, being born when there is no
> buddha,
> or being born deaf and mute.[42]

To be free of these states is called *leisure*.

> Born human, in a central land, with sense faculties intact,
> having not transgressed the bounds of karma, with faith
> in the [enlightened] state,
> in a world where a buddha has appeared and taught the
> Dharma,
> where the Dharma is alive and there are followers and
> benefactors.[43]

The five opportunities that pertain to oneself are to be a human with either male or female organs, to be born in a central land, to have sense faculties such as the eyes intact, to not have transgressed the bounds of karma through committing one of the five heinous acts, and to have faith in the state—that is, in the discipline of the Tathāgata's Dharma. The five opportunities that pertain to others are that (1) a buddha has appeared in the world and (2) has taught the Dharma. (3) The teachings remain because there are people who have seen the truth. (4) Since their instructions accord with the realizations of the āryas, there are followers of the Dharma. And (5) there are benefactors offering support, and therefore there is mutual kindness and compassion. These ten conditions define *opportunity*. A human existence characterized by these eighteen advantages is difficult to obtain. In the *Array of Trees Sūtra*, in the chapter on the liberating story of Jayoṣmāyatana, it says that it is difficult to avert the eight unfavorable circumstances. Excellent perfect leisure is also difficult to find.[44]

Human life with leisure and opportunity has the potential to fulfill a person's aims, whether a higher rebirth or the highest good, so at this juncture, when we have obtained such a life, we should practice virtue diligently. If we fail to cultivate virtue, which benefits both self and others, when will we ever find such an excellent existence of leisure and opportunity in the future? Never! Therefore Śāntideva instructs us to not let this life become meaningless. A sūtra says, "This being the case, waste not this existence of leisure and opportunity."[45] And the *Letter to a Student* says:

> That which when obtained can help cross the ocean of
> saṃsāra
> and plant the seed for supreme enlightenment,
> that which is superior even to a wish-grating gem—
> such is human existence; who would waste such a thing?[46]

[1.5] The second topic is how the mental basis that is the meritorious thought is so rare. Its occurrence is comparable to a flash of lightning, which on a dark cloudy night may illuminate everything for an instant. Likewise it is rare that worldly beings, engulfed in the thick of suffering caused by their unwholesome deeds, develop even momentarily, through the power of the buddhas, the idea to do good. These thoughts do not arise frequently, and neither do they last. Therefore we should strive to generate and increase our intentions to practice acts of goodness.

> Though we possess the two wings of leisure and
> opportunity,
> and eyes capable of distinguishing good from bad, virtue
> from wrongdoing,
> yet if we are caught in the net of desire for gain and honor,
> would we not be trapped in the cage of negative karma?[47]

## The intention of the person engaging in the discipline

The intention of the person engaging in the discipline has two parts: the benefits of generating the awakening mind and the way to uphold it.

## The benefits of generating the awakening mind

The first point has three parts: the actual benefits, the proof that there are indeed such benefits, and praising individuals who have generated the awakening mind.

## The actual benefits

The first, in turn, is twofold: the general benefits, and the specific benefits.[48]

## The general benefits

This has five parts. [1.6] The first [benefit] is the elimination of negative karma. Given that the basis [human existence] and the intention are difficult to acquire and quickly pass, the virtuous behavior that acts as an antidote [to negative karma] is always fragile. Its strength is perpetually weak. On the other hand, the causes of nonvirtue assemble very easily. Negative karma is strong and utterly inexhaustible. It wells up in an unceasing stream. To overcome it, we have to generate virtue, and what virtue could eliminate bad karma as efficiently as the perfect awakening mind, whose nature is wisdom and compassion? So you should generate this mind! The *Array of Trees Sūtra* states, "Mice are overpowered by the gaze of a cat's eyes; it is unbearable for them. Likewise, the mice of karma and afflictions are overpowered by the eyes of the precious mind of omniscience. They cannot bear it."[49]

The second [benefit] is the creation of well-being and happiness. [1.7] For many eons—namely, during "three uncountables"—the lords of the sages thoroughly contemplated and examined the various ways to benefit beings. They saw that the awakening mind is singularly beneficial for beings because it is the only way that all beings, infinite in number, can easily achieve supreme happiness and unsurpassable enlightenment.

The third [benefit] is the fulfillment of wishes. [1.8] Those who wish to overcome the hundreds of sorrows of their lives and put an end to the unhappiness of all others, those who wish for all—themselves and others—to experience a multitude of joys, should never forsake the mind of awakening because it is certain that all wishes will be fulfilled by it.

The fourth benefit is the change of name and status. [1.9] In the prison of saṃsāra, bound by the chains of karma and afflictions, beings are tormented by overwhelming sorrow. If these beings develop the awakening mind, then from that moment on, they will be called "children of the sugatas." The [name] change entails a change in status, too, since they become persons venerated both by gods and by humans of this world.

The fifth, praising the benefits, is presented through six analogies. [1.10] The first analogy is that of the alchemical transformation into gold, whereby an inferior substance is transformed into an excellent one. Like the most excellent elixir of alchemy, the awakening mind transforms our naturally impure body into the priceless body of a victorious one. Therefore hold fast to the mind of awakening, which is endowed with such capacities. The *Array of Trees Sūtra* uses the analogy of one unit of a mercury-like substance that resembles gold and can transform one thousand units of iron into gold:

> Likewise, the mercury element of generating the mind aspiring for omniscience, imbued with the wisdom of the universal dedication of the roots of virtue, will entirely eliminate the iron element of karmic and afflictive obscurations and turn it into one with the color of knowledge of all phenomena. The awakening mind, however, the sole element that can turn into omniscience, will never be degraded by the iron of karma and afflictions. They do not have the power to afflict it or to eliminate it.[50]

[1.11] The second analogy is that of a jewel and indicates how the awakening mind is difficult to find and is of great value. The unequaled Buddha is the only guide who can lead all wandering beings to the city of liberation and bring them to enjoy a wealth of qualities. With his wisdom, he understands all there is to know. Since no one else has the capacity to assess, examining all phenomena with his immense mind, he sees the rarity and preciousness of the awakening mind and thus its great value. The *Array of Trees Sūtra* states:

> Among all jewels, the wish-fulfilling "mighty king" gem (*cintārāja*) is the most precious. Likewise, the preciousness of the "mighty king" gem of the mind of awakening cannot be matched, no matter how long one searches with omniscient wisdom among all the objects of the ultimate expanse in the three times, including all the roots of virtue, both the exhaustible and the inexhaustible, of all the gods, humans, śrāvakas, and pratyekabuddhas.[51]

Therefore all beings who wish to be free from painful situations should hold firmly to the precious mind of awakening.

[1.12] The third analogy is that of a tree, and it indicates how the fruits of the awakening mind will multiply rather than becoming exhausted. All other kinds of virtue, all those not sustained by the awakening mind, will be exhausted after having produced their results, like a banana tree. Alone, the tree of the awakening mind will continue bearing fruit forever. It is not exhausted but grows ever more fertile. The *Jewel Casket Sūtra* says:

> Mañjuśrī, it is like this: The various kinds of trees grow because they are sustained by the four elements. Mañjuśrī, similarly, also the roots of virtue grow when they are sustained by the awakening mind and dedicated to omniscience.[52]

[1.13] The fourth analogy, of a bodyguard, teaches that the awakening mind protects from the consequences of unwholesome actions. Even if you have committed unwholesome actions such as harming the Three Jewels, just like relying on a brave bodyguard can protect you from a deep fear of enemies, relying on the awakening mind will immediately free you of the fully ripened result of a severe, unwholesome action. Why would a reasonable person not entrust themself to the awakening mind? They should indeed do so. The *Teachings of Akṣayamati Sūtra* says:

> Child of noble family, it is like this: When you have a brave person to rely on, you are not afraid of any enemy. Similarly, a bodhisattva has the guardian that is the awakening mind to rely on and therefore does not fear the enemy of evil action.[53]

[1.14] The fifth analogy, of fire, illustrates that the awakening mind completely destroys negativity. The fire at the end of time—or, more precisely, at the end of an eon—will burn the entirety of the universe below the realm of the first meditative absorption.[54] Similarly, all the extremely negative actions, including the five acts of immediate retribution, will be burned up by the awakening mind in a single moment. They will be annihilated down to their roots. The *Array of Trees Sūtra* says, "It is like the fire of the eon that burns up all evil."[55] As Kṣemadeva interprets this, a single moment of the great patience leaves nothing to hold on to, [so all evils are] definitely burned off.[56] You might object that this analogy and the previous one are incongruous, for previously, negativity was said to be [merely] suppressed, whereas in this analogy, it is completely eradicated. Is it not a contradiction to define a single moment of the awakening mind by two contrary characteristics? However, this is not the case, because when the awakening mind reaches increasingly superior levels, its benefits and advantages grow too and become ever more exalted.

The sixth is how other benefits are mentioned in the sūtras. The incalculable benefits of this awakening mind are explained by the wise Lord Maitreya to Sudhana in the *Array of Trees Sūtra*. Sudhana, a child of enduring wealth from a city called Source of Happiness (Dhanyākara), generated the awakening mind in the presence of Mañjuśrī. He then traveled to various places to seek out instructions on the bodhisattva training. He found Lord Maitreya in the south, by the sea, in a multistory palace called Essence Adorned by the Ornaments of Vairocana (Vairocanavyūhālaṃkāragarbha). He was teaching the Dharma to an entourage as large as an ocean. Upon seeing the Lord, Sudhana made prostrations. Maitreya pointed him out to his entourage, saying:

> Look upon this one who has a pure motivation,
> Sudhana, a child of enduring wealth,
> who is in search of the sublime bodhisattva conduct—
> this wise person has come before me.

He then asked:

> Did you come well, you who emerged from compassion and love?
> Did you arrive well into the wide circle of lovingkindness?
> Did you arrive well, you who brings peace to those who gaze at you?
> Are you not wearied from engaging in the hardships of practice?
> Come here and welcome, you who have a pure motivation.[57]

Addressed with such words, Sudhana replied: "O Noble One! I have set upon the unsurpassed enlightenment, but as for how to engage in the bodhisattva training and how to do so with dedicated effort, I have no knowledge. So please do teach me."

Maitreya replied:

> Child of the family! You have been thoroughly accepted as a disciple by many spiritual friends. Why is that so? Child of the family, the awakening mind is like the seed of all the attributes of the buddha. Since it gives the bountiful crop of meritorious deeds of all beings, it is like a field. Since it supports all beings individually, it is like the earth. Since it ends all poverty, it is like the wealth god Vaiśravaṇa. Since it protects all the bodhisattvas, it is like a father. Since it helps to accomplish all aims, it is like the sovereign wish-fulfilling jewel. Since it fulfills all wishes, it is like the excellent treasure vase.[58]

From this point up to where it says, "Child of noble family, the awakening mind possesses these qualities and also countless other specific benefits,"[59] in words such as these, [the benefits of the awakening mind] are explained extensively.

## The specific benefits

This has three parts: the divisions [of the awakening mind], their difference in terms of nature, and their difference in terms of benefits.

[1.15] The first is as follows. The awakening mind should be understood to be of two kinds. The *Array of Trees Sūtra* states, "Beings who aspire to unsurpassable enlightenment are rare. Much rarer still are those who engage [the path to] unsurpassable enlightenment."[60] In accord with this statement,

> There is the aspiring awakening mind
> and the engaging awakening mind.

[1.16] The second is [their difference in terms of nature]. As in the example of wanting to go to some place, the thought that wishes to attain buddhahood for the sake of others is the aspiring [awakening mind]. In contrast, like the example of actually going to that place, entering the path that leads to buddhahood with the wish to cultivate that path is the engaging [awakening mind]. Just as one understands the difference between the two examples, the wise who wish to accomplish the aims of self and others should understand the difference between the two referents and their sequence.

[1.17] The third is [their difference in terms of benefits]. The aspiring aspect of the awakening mind produces great results for those living in cyclic existence. The *Array of Trees Sūtra* states:

> Child of noble family, even if a piece of diamond is broken, it still outshines all the most exquisite gold ornaments and still does not lose its name as precious diamond. Likewise, with respect to the precious diamond of a mind aspiring to omniscience, O child of noble family, even if it were to be divorced from dedicated practice, it will outshine all the śrāvakas and pratyekabuddhas, which are like the gold ornaments. And, without losing its name "awakening mind," it will dispel the poverty of cyclic existence.[61]

[1.18–19] However, [the aspiring aspect] cannot produce a continuous stream of merit equal to that of the engaging aspect of the awakening mind. From the moment we commit ourselves to liberating the limitless beings in all realms from the bonds of karma and afflictions and the prison of cyclic existence, with a resolve to never turn back from benefitting others until the end of cyclic existence, we have correctly given rise to the engaging awakening mind. From that moment on, and for as long as it remains undamaged, though we may doze off or be distracted many times, uninterrupted streams of merit in manifold aspects and equal to the vastness of the sky continuously pour forth.

## Proof of the benefits of the awakening mind

This is twofold: through scriptures and through reasoning.

[1.20] Regarding the first, the great merit produced by the engaging awakening mind has been explained with proofs and proper reasoning in the *Questions of Subāhu Sūtra*. In that sūtra, to lead all those beings disposed toward the Lesser Vehicle to the Great Vehicle, the Tathāgata himself says:

> Since I have donned the armor for securing benefit and happiness for the limitless hosts of sentient beings, the limitless roots of virtue of focusing on the benefit and happiness of all sentient beings are such that whether I remain attentive or asleep, throughout day and night, in every moment of consciousness, they will increase, be strengthened, and perfected.[62]

The second [proof through reasoning] is twofold: the superiority of the intention and the superiority of the action.

## The superiority of the intention

The first is twofold: the vastness of the intention's object and aspect, and how it surpasses any worldly [intention].

[1.21–22] As to the first, if someone with a compassionate heart were to have the thought "I want to heal a few people's headaches with medicine," this well-intentioned person will earn boundless merit. Some commentators explain this verse by referring to the story of Maitrakanyaka.[63] If a person takes all sentient beings as their scope, wishing to remove the unending unhappiness of each and every one of them and to actively help them realize boundless achievements, it goes without saying that such a person earns boundless merit.

[1.23–25] As to the second, whether father or mother, relative or friend—who possesses an altruistic mind such as this? None of them. Do the gods, sages, or even Brahma have it? They do not. The *Ornament of Mahāyāna Sūtras* states:

> The children of conquerors possess altruistic intentions
> with which they bring all beings to complete maturation.
> Neither father, mother, relative, nor
> son or friend possesses anything comparable.[64]

If such a mind has never before arisen in these beings for their own sake, not even in their dreams, how can it arise for the sake of others? This means that even the intention to bring about their own welfare does not arise in ordinary beings. How then could a mind arise that cares solely for others' welfare, this unique jewel of a mind, unprecedented and awe inspiring?

### The superiority of the action

This is twofold: how the focus and aspect of the action are vast, and how they are the absent in others.

[1.26–27] As to the first, [the action] is the seed of joy in the world and the remedy that dispels the illness of beings' suffering. How can we measure its merit? The *Questions of the Householder Vīradatta* elucidates:

> If the merit of the awakening mind
> were to take material form,
> it would fill the whole of space,
> and still more would be left.[65]

Merely thinking to benefit beings surpasses worshiping the buddhas. As the *King of Meditations* states:

The merit of offering daily and forever
myriad realms filled with infinite multitudes
of offerings of all kinds
cannot compare to that of a loving mind.[66]

How much more so, then, is it surpassed by persistent effort for the complete happiness of every being?

[1.28–30] The second [how they are absent in others] is as follows. Although hoping to escape suffering, they run toward the causes of suffering, acting in unwholesome ways. Although wishing for happiness, they are ignorant and do not know how to find it. Because of this ignorance, they neglect virtue and destroy their own happiness as if it were the enemy. They are starved of happiness and oppressed by many sorrows. Through great lovingkindness, it satisfies them with every happiness. Through great compassion, it cuts away all sorrows. And through great wisdom, it drives off delusion, which is the lack of understanding of the causes of happiness and sorrow. Where would we find a comparable virtue? Where would we find a friend who helps us in such a way? Where would we find something that produces merit such as this?

## Praising individuals who have generated the awakening mind

This is fivefold: [praising them for] how they help others unconditionally, how they are outstanding benefactors, how they are an extraordinary field of merit, how they are not overwhelmed by suffering, and how they are worthy of praise and are a source of refuge.

[1.31] The first is [how they help others unconditionally]. When people return a favor, this is said to be noteworthy. But if such persons are considered worthy of praise, what more can be said about bodhisattvas, who work for others' happiness and welfare with no obligation to do so?

[1.32–33] The second is [how they are outstanding benefactors]. When people give alms to merely a few creatures, just a few times—annually or monthly—just for a short moment, giving mere ordinary food, in a patronizing, condescending manner, and with the mere impact of filling people's bellies for half a day, nevertheless, the world praises them, exclaiming, "What good actions they do!" What more can be said, then, when the recipients are the boundless multitudes of beings; when the duration is long, everlasting, and without interruption; when the gift is the unsurpassable happiness of the sugatas; when the impact is the fulfillment of all aspirations; and when the manner of giving is deeply respectful? According to the commentaries, the term *everlasting* is illustrated by the saying "Even if space and beings come to an end, it [the activity of bodhisattvas] remains inexhaustible."[67] Prajñākaramati applies the term [everlasting] to time, and Kṣemadeva uses it to characterize the object.[68]

[1.34–35a] The third point is [how they are an extraordinary field of merit]. A person who thinks ill of such a bodhisattva and benefactor will remain in hell for eons equal in number to the moments he upheld such evil thoughts. Thus the Mighty One spoke in the *Meditative Concentration on the Miraculous Ascertainment of Peace Sūtra*:

> Mañjuśrī, a bodhisattva who harbors thoughts of anger or contempt against another bodhisattva will remain in hell for as many eons as there were such thoughts, and so needs to armor themself for that period of time![69]

On the other hand, for a person who has deep faith in the bodhisattva, the result of this faith will be far more powerful than that of an evil mind. In the *Sūtra Evaluating Whether Progress Is Certain or Uncertain*, it is said:

> Imagine that all beings in the world's ten directions were to lose their eyes, and imagine that some noble sons and daughters, with hearts full of love, restored their vision. Mañjuśrī, compare this to other sons and daughters of noble family who gazed with a mind filled with faith upon a bodhisattva devoted to the Great Vehicle. The merit generated by this action is incalculably greater than that of the former.[70]

[1.35bcd] The fourth is [how they are not overwhelmed by suffering]. Even when bodhisattvas are confronted with difficult situations, such as intense pain or anguish, negative states of mind like anger do not arise. On the contrary, through those experiences, their virtue increases. The *Condensed Presentation of the Perfections* states:

> Even though they experience many intolerable harms,
> the mind of great beings does not waver.
> Through the power of forbearance, they remain most steadfast
> and increase their determination to attain supreme enlightenment.[71]

[1.36] The fifth point is [how they are worthy of praise and are a source of refuge]. In the *Heap of Jewels*, it is said:

> For example, when a king, ruler over a great land,
> has a son whose body is adorned with signs,
> the citizens of his cities and vassals all bow
> as soon as they see the newborn child.
> Likewise, the instant the awakening mind is born,
> to that Conqueror's child most excellent
> the whole world and the gods bow,
> and with minds of admiration, they revere him.[72]

We bow down to those in whom the precious genuine mind has arisen. We take refuge in the bodhisattvas, who turn even an offense into happiness for the harm bringer and who are a source of happiness for all beings. You might object that this contradicts the verse that says "a person who thinks badly about such a bodhisattva" and so on (1.34), but there is no contradiction. In the former verse, Śāntideva taught the outcome of an evil mindstate, but here he reflects upon the awakening mind that cares for and supports the harm bringer in the short and the long term. It is like the example of the king who had such strong altruistic love that he led five *yakṣas* to temporal and ultimate happiness.

> To not be able to see this awakening mind, sun of thousandfold brilliance
> that dispels the darkness of the two obscurations,
> despite possessing the eyes of intellect to view the two extremes
> of permanence and nihilism amid the darkness of ignorance, how very strange!

This concludes the explanation of chapter 1.

# 2. The Confession of Negative Actions

The second chapter explains the correct methods to uphold the mind endowed with such qualities. This has two sections: the general explanations and the explanations in the text itself.

## General explanations

This has two parts: the generation of the awakening mind and its cultivation.

## The generation of the awakening mind

The first is twofold: its defining nature, and its classification. As to its defining nature, a careful examination of the great masters' teachings clearly shows, generally speaking, that all mental states cultivated on the Mahāyāna path are aspects of the generation of the mind. As for the defining nature of the mind being generated in the present context, *Ornament for the Clear Realizations* states:

> *Generation of the mind* is the aspiration to
> perfect and complete awakening for the sake of others.[73]

As for [its classification], if we classify the generation of the mind [of awakening] in a general way according to the [bodhisattva] grounds, there are four stages. Ordinary beings generate the mind through devotion and practice; beings on the seven impure [bodhisattva] grounds generate a pure altruistic mind; beings on the three pure [bodhisattva] grounds generate the fully matured mind; and on the buddha ground, the generation of the mind is devoid of any defilement. These four stages are taught in *Ornament of Mahāyāna Sūtras*:

> The mind generated on the grounds [is classified]
> through imagination, pure superior intent,
> maturation, which is asserted to be distinct,
> and likewise that of the elimination of obscurations.[74]

There is also a classification in terms of the accompanying factors or analogies. Here, *Ornament for the Clear Realizations* states:

> There is that of earth, gold, moon, fire,
> treasure, jewel mine, ocean,
> diamond, mountain, medicine, spiritual friend,
> wish-fulfilling gem, sun, song,
> king, treasury, highway,
> mount, fountain,
> lute, river, and cloud—
> these then are the twenty-two.[75]

If it is classified according to the way it is attained, we can identify two kinds: one by means of signs and the other through the power of the nature of reality. If classified according to their objects, there is ultimate [awakening mind] and conventional [awakening mind]. And if it is classified from the point of view of intention versus action, we have the aspirational and engaging awakening minds. The classification relevant here [in this text] is the last one.

## Its cultivation

This has three parts: how to receive the vow, how to protect it, and how to restore it.

## How to receive the vow

How to receive [the bodhisattva vow] is threefold: the one it is received from, the individual who receives it, and the rite for receiving it. With respect to the first point, *Bodhisattvas' Individual Liberation* says:

> With respect to upholding the vow, too, one should receive the vow from someone who is devoted to the meditative practice of the points of the bodhisattva trainings and who possesses the vow themselves.[76]

The *Twenty Verses* states:

> We should receive it from a teacher
> who abides by the vow, is wise, and is capable.[77]

And here too, in this text, we read:

> Spiritual friends are always
> well versed in the matters of the Great Vehicle
> and exhibit supreme bodhisattva conduct.[78]

However, should we be unable to find such a teacher, the *Bodhisattva Ground* describes how to take [the vow] in front of a support.[79] One should do this as instructed in the *Compendium of Training*:

> In the absence of a spiritual friend, visualize that all the buddhas and bodhisattvas of the ten directions are vividly present and declare, "I shall do my very best" and uphold the vow.[80]

The second [the one it is received from] is as follows. *Lamp for the Path to Enlightenment* states:

> Those who uphold at all times
> any of the seven types of prātimokṣa vow
> have the requisite to receive the bodhisattva vow;
> all others do not.[81]

Although it is stated thus, if the vows of individual liberation were a necessary condition, you might object that bodhisattvas in the pure lands could not obtain it, and that it would be lost at the moment of death. These and other issues have been discussed in the *Exposition*.[82] Taking these issues into consideration, Lord Atiśa, who was an expert in all aspects of the bodhisattva basket, would not maintain categorically this necessity of the prātimokṣa [vow] as the basis. However, there have been people who could not even uphold a fraction of the prātimokṣa vows and yet claimed to possess the bodhisattva vow. And there have been those who thought that the bodhisattva vow was trivial. Many people these days have such thoughts as well. It is to refute these that Atiśa spoke of the prātimokṣa vow as a prerequisite. This is what I think. In his own commentary to *Lamp for the Path to Enlightenment* too, he gives an explanation in terms of an extraordinary basis, but he says that the awakening mind can also arise on the other types of bases.[83] To conclude, the prātimokṣa vows are not compulsory. As long as a person has compassion, faith, and the wish to receive [the vow], it will definitely arise.

The third [the rite for receiving it] is as follows. The *Bodhi-*

*sattva Ground* does not present any rite for the aspiring awakening mind, and Dharmamitra[84] and others maintain that the aspirational awakening does not depend on a rite. However, Lord Atiśa performed the rites for the aspiring and the engaging minds in consecutive stages. What is presented in our text [*Guide to the Bodhisattva Way*], the *Exposition* explains, represents a rite by which one takes the aspiring and engaging minds simultaneously, and it is meant for exceptional individuals.[85] Kṛṣṇapa, for his part, describes the aspiring mind as "generation of the mind" and the engaging mind as a vow, maintaining that our present text presents both methods of receiving them—sequentially and simultaneously. Furthermore, there are many who, like Prajñākaramati, take the aspiring mind to be the mind generation and the engaging mind as the vow.[86] So let me briefly analyze this [question].

Although it is true that there are instances where the aspiring [awakening mind] is not produced through a rite and where it does not constitute a vow, there is no contradiction in it arising through a rite as well. Furthermore, if through such rite the determination to renounce all that should be renounced up until enlightenment is attained, then it is indeed a vow. Our text states:

> When the intention to renounce is attained,
> that is the perfection of morality.[87]

As for the engaging [awakening mind], this consists entirely of a vow. The two minds [aspiring and engaging] can be received either sequentially or simultaneously. Not only *can* there be both of these instances, there is also no objection to there being so.

Generally speaking, the ritual procedure can be carried out in various forms. Here, we explain it in terms of the preparation, the main part, and the conclusion, just as presented in the root text.

## How to protect the vow

To protect the vow, we need to renounce all that ought to be renounced in relation to the awakening mind and engage in all the required trainings. According to the *Bodhisattva Ground*, what we have to renounce are the four acts that entail defeat and the forty-five misdeeds.[88] The *Ākāśagarbha Sūtra* explains eighteen [defeats],[89] which the *Compendium of Training* summarizes as follows:

> Stealing provisions from the Three Jewels
> is accepted as a defeat infraction.
> Forsaking the sublime teaching
> the Sage stated to be the second.
> Even toward a monk who has lapsed morally,
> taking his saffron robe, beating him,
> throwing him in prison,
> or forcing him to renounce his monastic life,
> or robbing someone of life—this is the third.
> Committing [any of] the five acts of immediate
>     retribution [is the fourth];
> holding wrong views [is the fifth].[90]

These are the five that a king can incur. Of these, the first four as well as

> Destroying a village and so on, too,
> the Conqueror stated are the root infractions.[91]

These five a minister can incur.

> Speaking of emptiness
> to beings whose minds are not trained;
> turning away from full awakening

those who have set out to toward buddhahood;
urging others to adopt the Great Vehicle
by totally forsaking prātimokṣa [discipline];
believing that the vehicle of the trainees
does not eliminate attachment and so on
and urging others to believe similarly;
proclaiming one's own virtues
and disparaging others for the sake of
material gain, honor, and words of praise;
saying falsely, "I am someone who can bear the profound";
meting out punishments to a renunciate,
giving away the property of the Three Jewels,
and taking such gifts [intended for the Three Jewels];
discarding tranquil abiding
and giving the provisions meant for those
in meditation retreat to those who merely recite:
these are the root infractions,
causes leading sentient beings to the great hells.[92]

In sum, these are the ten infractions that kings and ministers can incur and eight that beginner bodhisattvas can occur. These, together with giving up the aspiring awakening mind, [Śāntideva] accepts to be the nineteen root infractions. In *Ornament of the Sage's Intent*, these eighteen are condensed into four, just as explained in the *Bodhisattva Ground*.[93] In short, the training consists generally of the vows to renounce what needs to be renounced, to accumulate virtuous qualities by practicing the six perfections, and to engage exclusively in benefitting beings. This is the threefold ethical discipline for the welfare of beings. In other words, the training of bodhisattvas consists of discarding all that is harmful for self and others, including their underlying conditions, and practicing all that is helpful. This practice principle is also described in *Twenty Verses on the Bodhisattva Vow*:

For others and also for yourself,
do what is beneficial even if it is painful.
Do what brings benefit and happiness,
not what is not beneficial, even if it is gratifying.[94]

In that sense, when both the intention and the action are virtuous, [our behavior] is entirely free of infraction, but the opposite entails pure infraction. When the intention is virtuous, then even if the action appears nonvirtuous, this is merely an appearance. The contrast of this case is merely an appearance of there being no infraction.[95]

## How to restore the vow

*Twenty Verses on the Bodhisattva Vow* states:

Take the vow once again.
Confess middling offenses to three [bodhisattvas],
the rest in the presence of one,
and the afflicted and unafflicted [faults] within
one's mind.[96]

The *Compendium of Training* explains:

Confess these in a dream
with Ākāśagarbha in front of you.[97]

And in our text:

Three times, day and night,
recite the *Three Heaps Sūtra*
so that, through recourse to the conquerors and the
bodhisattvas,
the remaining transgressions cease.[98]

## The explanations in the text itself

This has three parts: the preparatory activities, the actual ceremony, and the concluding rite.

## The preparatory activities

Preparatory activities are twofold: purifying the mental continuum and training the mind to benefit others.

## Purifying the mental continuum

The first is composed of eight: offerings, prostration, going for refuge, confessing and purifying negative karma, rejoicing, requesting to turn the wheel of Dharma, supplicating [the buddhas] not to enter nirvāṇa, and dedicating the merit.[99]

## [Offerings]

The presentation of offerings is twofold, general and specific.

[2.1] The first is as follows. The purpose [of making offerings] is to get a hold of the precious mind. We offer to the Three Jewels—that is to say, to all the tathāgatas or "thus-gone ones"; to the Dharma, which is free from the distorted concepts that things are existent or nonexistent; and to the children of the buddhas, the ārya bodhisattvas who have mastered the limitless ocean of qualities. The offering is made in the right way, which means it is accompanied by the aspiration to attain buddhahood, it is for the benefit of beings, it is giving exquisite things, it has purified the three spheres,[100] it is not defiled by unconducive conditions, and it is dedicated to supreme awakening. According to the *Exposition*, our offerings should have these six characteristics.

The specific explanation of offerings has six parts, the offering of (1) unowned objects, (2) the body, (3) objects conjured by the mind, (4) aspirations for the offerings to last, (5) unsurpassable [offerings], and (6) praise. First, the unowned objects are explained in two parts: the objects, and the rationale for offering these.

The *King of Meditations Sūtra* says:

> We should offer the flowers growing in wetlands and plains in all the worlds of the ten directions along with the precious gems and everything not owned by anyone.[101]

[2.2] Just as this text says, we offer as many flowers and fruits as there are in the world, all the different types of medicinal herbs, and the vast array of precious gems. We offer clear and refreshing water that has these eight qualities: it is cool and tasty, light and soft, limpid, and free from impurity; when drunk, it does not harm the stomach nor harm the throat.

[2.3–5] We offer mountains of precious gems, gold, and other [treasures] as well as solitary and delightful forests and [other] places, beautiful fruit trees decorated with the ornaments of their own blossoms, trees with branches bending down under the weight of their delicious fruit, a blend of fragrances of the godly realms and other worlds, incense of agarwood and other substances, wish-fulfilling trees that satisfy every desire, jeweled trees, harvests of crops that grow without the land being tilled and the seeds being sown, and all the other beautiful things that are worthy of being offered, such as lakes and ponds embellished with lotus flowers and resonant with the enchanting melodies of calling geese. [The offerings] extend to the limits of this immense universe; they are boundless.

[2.6] All the things unowned that exist in the pure realms, in Uttarakuru[102] and elsewhere, we bring to mind and present in an excellent manner to the recipients of this offering: the Sage, supreme among beings, and his children. Offering to them produces great results. "May these supreme recipients, the greatly compassionate ones intent on working for the welfare of beings, out of lovingkindness toward us accept these gifts from me."

[2.7] Second, what is the rationale for making these offerings that are not offered in a substantial way? Since I have not acquired merit in the past, I am destitute. I have no other wealth to offer. However, I desire to offer to you! Therefore may the protectors, whose exclusive concern is for the welfare of others, accept these offerings in their great power for the sake of me, the worshiper.

[2.8–9] Next is the offering of the body. To the buddhas, who are the conquerors because they have vanquished the four māras, and to their children, I make a constant and everlasting offering of my own body. I say, "Sublime heroic beings! Please accept me and make me yours! With reverence I devote myself to be your servant and do as you command. Now that I am sustained by you, supported by a great being, I will be undaunted by the sufferings of cyclic existence and ensure I have the capacity to benefit others. Were I to remain full of negativity, I would have no such capacity. I will therefore leave behind my prior negative behavior—that is, I will declare it and never again do another wrong.

The third [offering objects conjured by the mind] is presented in a sequence as a list:

> Baths, towels, clothes, and jewelry,
> perfume, flowers, incense, and food,
> lights, floors, houses, and parasols—
> these twelve offerings are manifested by the power of
> the mind.[103]

[2.10–11] The first offering is bathing chambers, scented with sandalwood and other wonderful fragrances. The crystal floors are transparent and sparkling, perfectly polished. There are beautiful pillars, studded with sparkling gems of every kind. Canopies of gleaming pearls are arrayed above. I will bathe the tathāgatas and their children numerous times with myriad golden vases studded with superb jewels and filled with pleasantly scented water and blossoms and accompanied by songs and music.

[2.12ab] Second, with [towels] of unequaled cloth—soft, immaculate, and perfumed—I will dry them.

[2.12cd] Third, once they are cleansed, I present them with clothes, beautifully dyed in saffron and other colors suitable for a monastic, and I offer them to all those holy ones who live the life of a renunciate. To those who live the life a householder, I offer exquisite and soft garments in myriad colors.

[2.13] Fourth, with choice ornaments—diadems and so forth—I adorn the āryas, who have the direct perception of reality, in particular Samantabhadra, Mañjughoṣa, Lokeśvara, Vajrapāṇi, Maitreya, and all the others who display the signs of a householder for the sake of their disciples.

[2.14] With respect to the fifth [perfumes], the *Treasury of Abhidharma* states:

> The universe consisting of four continents, sun, and moon,
> the central mountain [Meru], and the heavens of the gods
> of the desire realm and of the Brahma worlds—
> all this increased a thousand times describes the
> chiliocosm.
> This multiplied a thousand times is the dichiliocosm,
> which has been described as an intermediary universe.
> And this once more a thousand times increased is the
> trichiliocosm.[104]

These billionfold worlds and all the infinite pure realms are permeated by perfumes. The universe is filled forever with sublime fragrances. With these, I anoint all the sages, whose bodies are blazing with the luster of burnished, refined, and polished gold.

[2.15] Sixth, to all the mighty Sages, the supreme objects of worship, I offer objects that delight the sight, such as the fragrant divine flowers of mandārava, lotus, and utpala, as well as multicolored garlands, beautifully braided with these and with precious jewels.

[2.16] Seventh, I also offer them exquisite incense whose aroma ravishes the mind. Its pungent smoke spreads in all directions. It piles up in clouds that fill all of space.

Eighth, I also offer them all divine delicacies, special foods and drinks, such as white sugar, juices of a hundred fruits, and many more.

[2.17] Ninth, I offer them lights arranged in rows on golden lotuses, studded with jewels, and shining brightly.

Tenth, I offer mosaic floors sprinkled with perfumed water and strewn with lovely flowers.

[2.18] Eleventh, to the lords of compassion I also offer palaces of immeasurable beauty and excellence, delightful with songs of praise chanted by celestial ladies, beautified by hanging ornament tassels made of a multitude of pearls and jewels. There are countless victory banners and other brilliant decorations that emanate light, decorating the sky so as to fill all of space with light.

[2.19] Twelfth is exquisitely beautiful, attractive jeweled parasols, raised on golden shafts, beautifully decorated all around with pearl ornaments, lovely and elegant in shape. Holding them high above, I continuously offer them to the mighty sages.

Next is [aspirations for the offerings to last]. [2.20–21] In addition to the offerings [enumerated] so far, may even more magnificent offerings in great amounts, music and tunes with the loveliest melodies that have the power to soothe and appease the sorrow of beings and inspire them with happiness, appear in clouds and remain present for all the worthy ones. May rains of precious gems and flowers fall in an unceasing stream on volumes of texts that represent the Jewel of the Dharma in its aspects of scripture and realization, on all [stupas,] supports for offering, and on all statues and images of the Buddha.

As to [offering the unsurpassable], [2.22] "Just as Mañjughoṣa and the other great bodhisattvas made offerings to the victorious ones of the ten directions . . ." About their manner [of offering], the *Jewel Torch Dhāraṇī* elaborates:

> Emanating multitudes of flowers, flower canopies,
> and light rays in the shape of flowers,
> and having strewn about various flowers,
> those great beings worship the Conqueror.[105]

I make aspirations that I may also make offerings in just the same manner to the tathāgatas, the protectors, and to all their children.

The sixth [topic in the specific presentation of offerings is praise]. [2.23] To the buddhas and bodhisattvas, these oceans of good qualities, I offer oceans of praise in various melodies. I praise them without end. May clouds of tuneful acclaim ascend unceasingly before those oceans of good qualities.

## Prostration

The second [preparatory activity for purifying the mental continuum] is prostration. [2.24–25] "To the buddhas manifesting in the three times of past, present, and future, to the Dharma, and to the supreme assembly of the sangha, I bow down and offer prostrations as numerous as there are atoms in all buddha-fields. To the buddhas' representations, who arouse the awakening mind, to the collection of scriptures on the awakening mind, based on which it is generated, cultivated, and taught; and to the stupas, the supports for offering, I prostrate. I bow to the preceptors from whom I have received instructions, and likewise to the spiritual masters and all those who strive to perfect their conduct for the sake of liberation."

## Going for refuge

[2.26] This is twofold: [the general meaning and the corresponding verse]. The general meaning consists of the presentation and the practice. The presentation has three parts: the essence, the classification, and the specific natures of each [of the objects of refuge].

First, [the essence of going for refuge] is relying on an object of refuge with the purpose of eliminating a threat.

With respect to classification, there is mundane and supramundane [refuge]. The latter consists of the refuge of the Great Vehicle and of the Lesser Vehicle.

The third, the specific natures of each of the objects of refuge, is as follows. The mundane act of seeking refuge is for people who desire protection from certain types of threat and seek refuge in worldly gods and powers. This is not a superior refuge. The *Banner's Crest Great Sūtra* states:

> Those who are in fear of danger
> seek refuge mostly in the hills, forests,
> parks, or near a tree or a stupa.
> All these are not the best kind of refuge,
> and all who rely on them
> will not be freed from suffering.[106]

The supramundane act of going for refuge means that one goes for refuge to the Three Jewels for the duration of this life in order to be liberated from the suffering of cyclic existence. However, going for refuge in the Great Vehicle means that one wishes to attain buddhahood motivated by great compassion and by the need to free all beings from suffering. Therefore one goes for refuge in the three objects of refuge according to the tradition of the Great Vehicle until one attains buddhahood.

The second point [of the general meaning, the practice,] is as follows. At first, one receives the refuge vows from a spiritual master. In a sūtra, it states:

> One who seeks refuge in the Buddha
> is indeed one who seeks virtue.
> Such a person will never
> seek refuge in other gods.
> One who seeks refuge in the holy Dharma
> would be free of thoughts harmful and destructive.
> One who seeks refuge in the Sangha
> will not turn to the tīrthikas.[107]

In line with the practice explained in this [quotation], rely on the Three Jewels at all times. With deep respect for them, exert yourself in making offerings. Do not inflict harm on beings, and do not keep company with negative friends. By following these and other [rules], you will not damage your refuge precepts. Should the precepts be damaged, take them again. In this way, you will eliminate faults and increase your positive qualities.

Second, the [corresponding] verse of the root text reads [2.26]: In terms of *time*, "I take refuge until the core of enlightenment is reached." The *objects* [of refuge] are all the buddhas and likewise the Dharma and also the assembly of bodhisattvas. As for the *manner*, by saying, "I go for refuge," you imply, "Since I put my trust in you, grant me protection!"

## Confessing and purifying negative karma

This has two parts: the general meaning, and the meaning in the text itself. The first is threefold: (1) the six aspects of negative karma that have to be purified, (2) the four powers of the purifying antidote, and (3) the method of purification, consisting of the preparation, the main practice, and the conclusion.

The first [the six aspects] are distinctions based on the time, the cause, the doors, the act itself, the object, and its type.[108]

As for the [four powers], they are [the powers of] remorse, the support, the antidote, and the resolve to turn away from error. The first is the feeling of remorse that arises when we recognize we have made an error; it is like having drunk poison and realizing the possible outcome. The second power is a support that has the capacity to protect us from these [outcomes], like having the help of a doctor. The third [the power of the antidote] is practicing virtue, which is like taking medicine. The fourth is to not commit [errors] again, even at the cost of our own life, which is like not drinking poison ever again. These [four powers] need to be complete. If they are, the purification is guaranteed. There is thus a significance to the definite number four here. The *Teaching the Four Factors Sūtra* states:

> Maitreya! Bodhisattvas who possess four factors will overcome the misdeeds they have committed and accumulated. What are these four? Thoroughly regretting, relying on the awakening mind, cultivating the antidotes, and turning away from errors."[109]

Third is [the method of purification]. The *preparation* consists of going for refuge and generating the [awakening] mind. The *main practice* is to apply the four powers while reciting the words of the confession and to imagine that they are purified. And in *conclusion*, we meditate that those who received our confession give their blessing, whereby all our negative actions are cleansed; we dedicate [the merit] and so forth. These are the [general] instructions that all gurus give.

The meaning in the text itself consists of four: the power of remorse, of the support, of the antidote, and of turning away from error.

## The power of remorse

The first has two parts: the general teaching on the confession of negative actions, and the confession of especially negative actions against superior objects.

[2.27–29] As to the first, we address the recipients of our confession, the perfect buddhas residing in all directions and the bodhisattvas endowed with great compassion, by holding our hands together [in reverence] and praying, "Throughout the beginningless cycle of existence, in my previous lives and in this life, whatever negative misdeeds I have committed, unknowingly, either personally or by instigating others to carry them out, or whatever negative deeds committed by others that I, under the influence of my stupidity, have rejoiced in, having seen the blameworthiness of this joy, I sincerely confess it to the protectors, hiding nothing."

For the second, [the confession of especially negative actions against superior objects, pray] as follows: [2.30–31] "Whatever mistake or harmful action that I, as the agent, have committed against the object of the Three Jewels, or my parents, or the spiritual teachers, preceptors, or ritual masters—or anyone else—with afflicted intentions and with body, speech, or mind, and moreover, all the extremely negative actions that I, corrupted by many kinds of evil, attachment, and negativity, have done, O guides, I confess them all."

## The power of the support

This is threefold: the person's reason for seeking refuge, the objects of refuge, and what it means to go for refuge.

## The person's reason for seeking refuge

The first has a brief explanation and an elaboration.

[2.32][110] As to [the brief reason for seeking refuge], why should I wholeheartedly confess? If I die without having purified my negative actions, I will go to the lower realms. Therefore, how can I be assured of liberating myself from this negative karma? By quickly going for refuge.

The elaboration has two parts: reflecting on the immediacy of death and generating the thought of going for refuge, and reflecting on the great terror of having to die and generating the thought of going for refuge.

## Reflecting on the immediacy of death and generating the thought of going for refuge

The first, in turn, has a brief presentation, an extensive explanation, and a summation.

First [the brief presentation]. [2.33–34] "Why should I hurry to go for refuge?" we might ask. "[Death] will not come right away," I might say, but that cannot be trusted. Death does not wait for me to finish my work, such as that of purifying negative karma, and he does not consider whether I have finished that work. Whether I am ill or not, he comes suddenly, at any moment. One cannot trust life and say, "I will not die." At death, I will leave behind enemies and friends; I must leave alone. Not understanding this, I have acted in various negative ways so as to benefit friends and harm enemies. This is what [the text] says.

Second [the extensive explanation]. [2.35–37] For the sake of many people, I have acted in negative ways. However, all those I despise will die. Those I love will die. I myself will die. Equally, all beings and all possessions will perish. The negative deeds carried out for them are futile. I might think that the happiness derived from these acts here and now, such as giving joy to my friends, will follow me later and therefore has a purpose. But this kind of happiness, like all things and all present experiences, will fade to memory. It cannot be seen or experienced again. Since it has passed, it is like the happiness experienced in a dream: you will not feel it any more once you wake up. Without even talking about the continuation of lives, even in this life, as I have stood by, many loved and loathed ones have gone. The happiness experienced in their company is, just like the dream experience, gone and cannot be seen any more. But the evil occasioned by them remains intolerable before me as habitual tendencies, in a latent mode.

As to the third, the summation, [2.38–39] just like those others, I am simply passing through. This I have failed to recognize. In delusion, attachment, and aversion, I did evil acts many times. If I wish to be cleansed of it in this lifetime, I must purify it quickly. Day and night, without respite, moment after moment of this life is lost. It never gets any longer. As for me, will I not die? It is certain that I will. It is like a pond whose feeder stream has stopped.

> Like a stream whose source has dried up,
> none can be added, but it keeps ebbing away;
> so if everyone on the road to death . . .[111]

"Who would trust this ephemeral life?"[112] states the *Discourse on Impermanence.*

## Reflecting on the great terror of having to die and generating the thought of going for refuge

This is twofold: a brief and an extensive explanation.

First is [the brief explanation]. [2.40–42] We might think

that while it is true that I must die, when the time comes I will have my companions. But at the moment of death, while lying on my bed surrounded by all my family and friends, it is I alone who will suffer the agonies of dissolution. They will not be affected. In addition, we might also think that they will have the power to protect me when the time comes. But for one seized by the messengers of Death, what good is a relative, what good a friend? They cannot help. What can help me then? At that time, merit alone is a protection, and I have not acquired it. "O protectors," I cry out, "I have been careless, not cultivating virtue and not attending to the defiling elements in my mind. I did not recognize these dangers. For the sake of this transient life, I have acted countless times in negative ways."

For the extensive explanation, [2.43–46] consider the analogy of a criminal who is taken away today to have a limb cut off. He is terrified, his throat is parched, his gaze wretched, and whatever experiences he had previously now appear to him in a completely different light. What need, then, to speak of the fears I will experience myself when Death's utterly terrifying messengers stand over me in their threatening forms and seize me? I will be struck by feverish terror and tormented by sorrow. At that time, I will cry aloud, "Who can guarantee me protection from this great horror?" And with wide eyes glancing fearfully about, I will search for refuge in all four directions. But although I search in every direction, I will find no refuge, and again, I will fall into utter despair. In such a place, where no protection is to be found, what will I do? There will be no escape!

## The objects of refuge

This is in two parts: seeking refuge in the Three Jewels in general, and taking refuge in the bodhisattvas endowed with the great power of aspirational prayer.

The first is as follows. [2.47–48] Since at that time [of dying],

I will have no protection, I will take refuge from today onward in the victorious ones, the protectors of beings, who eliminate all fear because they are endowed with these two characteristics: they perfectly endeavor to protect all beings, and their great power makes them supremely capable of protecting. The *Sūryagarbha Sūtra* states:

> Any sentient being who goes to the buddhas for refuge
> cannot be destroyed through the doings of Māra.
> Even if they are morally flawed and mentally disturbed,
> they will definitely travel beyond the shores of birth.[113]

When I rely on the Dharma that has been realized by the victorious ones, the danger of cyclic existence is destroyed. In the same way, I also wholeheartedly take refuge in the virtue-loving assembly of bodhisattvas.

The second point is [taking refuge in the bodhisattvas endowed with the great power of aspirational prayer]. [2.49–52] Gripped by fear of the hells and other suffering realms, I give myself to the great bodhisattva Samantabhadra, and I give my body to Mañjughoṣa. Terrified, I cry out in sorrowful anguish to the protector Avalokita, whose intentions and conduct overflow with infallible compassion. "I beg you: Please protect me! I have done wrong. I seek refuge in the noble Ākāśagarbha and Kṣitigarbha, in Maitreya, and in all the protectors who possess great compassion and the capacity to eliminate suffering. I cry out from the depths of my heart: Please protect me! I take refuge in Vajrapāṇi, holder of the thunderbolt, the one who instills terror in the messengers of Death and in all other creatures who see him, putting them to flight in the four directions."

## What it means to go for refuge

[2.53] We say, "I have transgressed your command in the past. Now, seeing the danger, terrified, I go to you for refuge. Destroy the danger, quickly!"

## The power of the antidote

This has three parts: (1) the reason for exerting oneself in the antidotes, (2) making an immediate effort, and (3) the manner of exerting oneself.

The first point has two parts, and of those, the first illustrates using the analogy of illness. [2.54–56] Even an ordinary illness caused by wind, bile, or [phlegm] scares me such that I take the medicine the doctor prescribes. And since I am plagued constantly by the hundredfold diseases of attachment and so forth, what need is there to speak of applying the antidotes according to the victorious ones' instructions? The disease here is [my] grave wrongdoings, and it is difficult to obtain the means to remove them. Why is that so? Even just one of the diseases, like attachment, could lead to warfare among the people of this world and could wipe out many, if not all, inhabitants. In all directions, no remedy can be found that could heal these diseases apart from practicing according to the victorious ones' instructions. The Omniscient One is the only one who can heal the diseases of the afflictions, since he is the remover of all pains. The idea of ignoring his advice is therefore stupid and blameworthy.

The second point illustrating [the reason for exerting oneself in the antidotes] is through the analogy of a cliff. [2.57] Even at the edge of a small, ordinary cliff, I have to stand with careful attention so as not to fall down. Standing at the precipice of a thousand-league chasm, from which I could fall into extreme suffering that I would have to endure a long time before becoming freed, it goes without saying that I ought to be attentive.

Making an immediate effort is threefold. First is how one cannot rely on their lifespan. [2.58–59] Perhaps I think, "Although I have committed negative actions and great wrongs, I will be able to confess them later on." But I cannot rest easily thinking that death will not come this very day. For the time approaches relentlessly when I will die and be no more. Who would give me the security that I will not die? Nobody. How can I find an escape from death? There is none to be found. Since it is beyond doubt that I will pass away, how can I possibly enjoy happiness? It is absurd.

Second is how one cannot rely on material resources. [2.60] Compared to the material resources I have enjoyed in the past, which are no more, what other resources are there that would not similarly cease? To [continue to] grasp at material resources and ignore my teacher's advice would be irrational indeed. I should never do so.

Third is how one cannot rely on friends and family. [2.61] Not only my experiences, I will also have to leave behind this world of the living—my friends and my family. Wherever I go, I will go alone. What does it mean then to have people we love and people we dislike? To get attached to them is pointless.

The manner of exerting oneself is twofold: [the intention and the action]. As to the intention, [2.62] since nonvirtue leads inevitably to suffering, we should be concerned at all times, day and night, with nothing other than escaping that nonvirtue once and for all.

And for the action, think as follows. [2.63–64] In my ignorance and delusion, I have done things that are wrong by nature, such as killing somebody. I have also done things that are wrong by commandment, which means actions that are wrong only for those who have taken monastic vows, such as eating after midday. Imagining the protectors being truly present in front of me, I join my palms, and with my mind filled with fear of suffering, I prostrate again and again and confess all that I have done.

### The power of turning away from error

This is [to think] as follows. [2.65] "O guides, I pray, accept my negative and harmful conduct for what it is! Eradicate my harmful behavior! This negative behavior is not good, O protectors. I will not do it again."

This concludes the explanation of chapter 2.

# 3. Upholding the Awakening Mind

## Rejoicing

Rejoicing has two parts: rejoicing in mundane good deeds and rejoicing in supramundane good deeds.

For the first, [think,] [3.1] "I rejoice with delight in all beings' good works. It decreases their suffering in the bad states of existence, temporarily stopping the causes thereof. [I also rejoice] in its fruition, the state of being liberated from suffering and abiding in happiness."

Rejoicing in supramundane good deeds has four parts. [3.2–3] Of these, the first, rejoicing in the virtue of the Lesser Vehicle, is [to think], "I rejoice in the mass of good works that is the cause for the pratyekabuddhas' enlightenment." [The second] is rejoicing in the results: "I rejoice in the liberation of beings from suffering—the attainment of arhatship." [The third] is rejoicing in the virtue of the Great Vehicle: "I also rejoice in the ultimate result, the enlightenment of the protectors, and in the temporary result, the grounds of the bodhisattvas." [The fourth] is rejoicing in the cause: "I rejoice in the ocean of good coming from the generation of the enlightened mind, which aspires to bring happiness to all beings. And I rejoice in the application, the actual work for the welfare of beings."

## Requesting to Turn the Wheel of the Dharma

[3.4] Holding my palms together in reverence, I beseech the perfect buddhas in every direction: "Please show the way by lighting the torch of Dharma for beings in the darkness of suffering. Because they are in a state of darkness characterized by suffering and ignorance, they are confused, unable to understand which way to follow and what to avoid."

## Supplicating the buddhas not to enter nirvāṇa

[3.5] Holding my palms together in reverence, I implore all the victorious ones who wish to enter nirvāṇa: "Pray do not let beings become blind through ignorance! Remain for endless eons without passing into nirvāṇa!"

## Dedicating the merit

Dedication is twofold. First is the *general dedication.* [3.6] Through the good acquired by doing all that has been described, from the offerings up to the prayer to remain, may I relieve all the suffering of every living being.

[3.7–9] The *specific dedication* has three parts. The dedication for the sake of the sick is "For as long as it takes to cure the diseases of sick beings, may I be their medicine, their doctor, and their nurse." The dedication for the sake of the hungry and thirsty is "By bringing down a rain of food and drink, may the pain of hunger and thirst be removed. During intermediate eons of famine, may I become food and drink and possess the power to rid beings of hunger and thirst. Likewise, during intermediate eons of warfare, may I cause rains of flowers to fall." The dedication for the sake of the poor is "Through my activities, may I be an inexhaustible treasure for poor and destitute beings. All the various goods they need, I will spread out nearby and in front of them."

## Training the mind to benefit others

Training the mind to benefit others[114] has two parts: the general presentation of giving away everything, and the specific explanation of giving one's body. The first is twofold, the objects to be given and the reason for doing so. As to the objects, [3.10] "I shall give away my body, my possessions, and all the good acquired by what I have done, am doing, and will do in the three times. To accomplish the benefit of all beings, I intend to give everything, holding nothing back." The reason for doing so is that [3.11] by giving away everything, one attains nirvāṇa, and my mind's goal is to accomplish nirvāṇa for the benefit of myself and others. Given that, at the time of death, I have to give up my body, my possessions, and everything in one go anyway, I might as well give it to other beings now, which is better, for this will bring about great benefit for myself and others.

[The specific explanation on giving one's body] has two parts: giving to those who accumulate karma because of me, and praying that it will become a cause of well-being for everyone. The first, in turn, is twofold: giving without reservation, and dedicating it to becoming a cause of benefit.

[Giving without reservation] is this: [3.12–14ab] "I have already given this body to all beings. So they may use it as they like. Therefore may they continually do whatever pleases them, [even] kill, despise, or beat it. Let them do whatever they want. Let them play around with, tease, or mock my body. Now that I have already given away this body of mine, why should I be concerned about protecting it against harm? I will use it to engage in activities that do not bring harm to them [sentient beings], either in the immediate or in the long run."

[Dedicating to it becoming a cause of benefit] is twofold, [general and specific]. The general presentation is [3.14cd] "May all that is done in connection with me always bring joy, welfare, and happiness to beings and never be meaningless." The specific explanation is twofold. *Dedicating that one's intention may be meaningful* is [3.15] "Whether others develop thoughts of anger or trust toward me, may it always be the cause for fulfilling their desires and objectives." While the root text has the word "thoughts of trust," the *Extensive Commentary* reads it as "distrust" instead.[115] *Dedicating one's action to be meaningful* is [3.16] "Those who insult me to my face or inflict other harm on me or who talk badly about me to others, may they all have the good fortune of reaching enlightenment."

Praying that it will become a cause of well-being for everyone is [3.17–21] "May I be a protector of the unprotected, a guide for those who journey on the road. For those who wish to cross the water, may I become a boat, a ship, or a bridge. For those searching for an island in the water, may I be that island." Some versions of the text include the line "May I be a lamp for those who need a lamp." "May I become a bed for those who need a bed, and a servant for all who need a servant. May I be the wish-fulfilling jewel, the vase of fortune, the words able to conjure whatever is wished, the great medicine that cures all ills, the wish-granting tree that brings forth all that is needed and desired, and the cow of plenty that satisfies all beings' wishes. Just as the four great elements such as earth constitute with space the ground of life for all beings, may I also become the ground that nourishes all the myriad creatures." [3.22] And, "Likewise, for all the realms of beings as far as the limits of space, may I be the ground that sustains them until they all pass beyond suffering." Kṣemadeva and Jitāri[116] accept these verses to constitute the generation of the aspiring awakening mind.

## The actual ceremony

The ceremony [for cultivating the awakening mind] is as follows. We may take it from a spiritual master or from a representation [of the Three Jewels]. We then recite in their presence the prayer "Buddhas and bodhisattvas residing in the ten directions, all of you, please attend to me!" Then, if we take the [vows for] the aspiring and engaging [awakening mind] separately, we recite the following three times:

> Just as the sugatas of the past
> generated the awakening mind,
> likewise, for the benefit of beings,
> I shall generate the awakening mind."[117]

With this [we vow to uphold] the aspiring mind. And then:

> Just as the sugatas of the past
> abided in the bodhisattva training,
> through a step-by-step process
> I too shall proceed step by step
> in the practice of the training.

By reciting this verse three times, we take the [vow of the] engaging [awakening mind]. If we take both [vows] together, we do so by reciting the verses just as they are given in the text itself. [3.23–24] For this, the text says, "Just as the sugatas of the past generated the awakening mind, wishing to attain buddhahood for the sake of others, and just as they practiced the activities of the bodhisattva training in progressive stages and embodied them, in the same way shall I, for the benefit of beings, generate the awakening mind, and in the same way shall I practice the progressive stages of the training."

### The concluding rite

The concluding ritual has two parts: a transitional statement and the actual ritual. The [transitional statement] is: [3.25] In this way, the wise ones take hold of the awakening mind with deep confidence. Even if one has generated and engages in it, one should not let it deteriorate but enhance it. For this purpose, one encourages and praises the [awakening] mind.

The actual ritual is twofold: developing joy within oneself and engendering joy in others. The first, in turn, has two aspects. *Developing joy because one has accomplished one's own purpose* is [3.26–28] "Today my life has come to full fruition. How so? This human existence has excellently fulfilled its purpose. Today I am born into the family lineage of the buddhas, and I have become their child. And therefore I will in all situations behave with my three doors in ways that befit such a family lineage. I will be pure in the beginning, the middle, and the end and act in such a way that this faultless and venerable family lineage will not be stained by the blemish of negative behavior. To give an analogy: I am like a blind man who has found a jewel in a heap of dust. Likewise, by chance or miracle, the awakening mind has arisen in me. This is indeed a miracle."

*Engendering because of accomplishing others' welfare* is [3.29–33] "This awakening mind is the supreme elixir of immortality since it conquers death in the world. It is the inexhaustible treasure that alleviates the poverty of all people. It is also the supreme medicine that cures the mental and physical diseases of all beings. It is a tree that offers relief in the cool shade to suffering wanderers staggering along the road of existence. It is the universal causeway or bridge that saves all beings from the lower existences. It is the rising moon of the mind eliminating the obscuration of mental defilements that torment beings. It is the brilliant sun clearing away the obscuring mist of ignorance that veils beings. It is the fresh butter that surfaces from churning the milk of the true Dharma. For beings, travelers on the road of existence, hungry for the enjoyment of happiness, this awakening mind is a banquet of supreme happiness that will satisfy many great beings and guests with contentment."

On engendering joy in others, [3.34] the text says, "Today,

in the presence of all saviors, who will be my witnesses, I invite beings to the ultimate happiness of the sugatas, the buddhas, and meanwhile to temporal happiness. Gods, demigods, and all beings, rejoice!"

This concludes the explanation of chapter 3.

# 4. Conscientiousness

## The practices by which the person engages [in the discipline]

The correct manner of carrying out the practices generally refers to the six perfections.[118] In this text, however, generosity is not presented as a separate topic. Of the remaining five[119] such as morality, in relation to the first [the perfection of morality], there are two parts: conscientiousness and meta-awareness.

## Conscientiousness

The defining nature of *conscientiousness* is the careful implementation of the principle of adopting and rejecting. The *Compendium of Abhidharma* says:

> What is conscientiousness? Based on nonattachment, nonhatred, and nondelusion and accompanied by diligence, it is what habituates the mind to virtuous factors and guards the mind against factors that are contaminating.[120]

This is a means to [cultivate] all virtues. The *King of Meditations* states:

> It is conscientiousness that has been explained
> to be the very root of all virtuous qualities.[121]

To explain this [conscientiousness], there are three parts: a brief presentation, a detailed explanation, and a summation.

The first is as follows. [4.1] The children of the victorious ones who have firmly adopted the awakening mind in such a way, having carried out the preparations, the actual ritual, and the subsequent [activities], should not neglect it even for an instant, but always exert themselves never to transgress the training.

The detailed explanation has three parts: (1) conscientiousness with respect to the training, the object of cultivation, (2) conscientiousness with respect to one's existence endowed with leisure and opportunity, the basis, and (3) conscientiousness with respect to the afflictions, which are to be discarded.

## Conscientiousness with respect to the training, the object of cultivation

The first is threefold: why we should not forsake [the awakening mind], the negative consequences of forsaking it, and hence the advice not to forsake it.

[Why should we not forsake it?] [4.2–3] If we started an action carelessly, without proper consideration, or if we analyzed too briefly, without properly thinking it through, then even though we might have already given a promise, it is right to examine once again and ask, "Should I do it or should I leave it?" Here, however, this is not the case, because the buddhas and their children, with their profound insight, have already examined it, and before taking the vow, I also have examined it. As this mind generation has been properly examined, why should I procrastinate in its training? There is no good reason to.

The negative consequences of forsaking it are threefold: (1) How, as its fruitional effect, one will fall to the lower realms, (2) how one's altruistic activity will be undermined, and (3) how one will be obstructed from the fruit, the attainment of liberation.

The first [falling to the lower realms], in turn, consists of three parts. First, [4.4–5] if at the time of generating the [awakening] mind, we gave the solemn promise to liberate all beings, yet if through the actions of our three doors we do not pursue this, we would be deceiving all those sentient beings. So what would be our future birth? There would be no chance of any other than birth in the lower realms.

Second is the reason [why the consequence is so extreme]. [4.6] If a person who had made the intention in his mind to offer something, even if it were a small and insignificant thing like giving a bit of food, but does not actually do it, this would be a cause for rebirth in the hungry ghost realm. The *Application of Mindfulness Sūtra* states that if one does not give after having a slight intention to do so, one will be born as a hungry ghost. If one makes a pledge to do so and does not give, one will be born in hell.[122] Accordingly, if we were to deceive all those beings after having invited them with great sincerity to temporary happiness and to the unsurpassable happiness of a buddha, how could we then attain a happy rebirth? It would not be possible.

The third, refuting objections against this, is [4.7] "[It is stated in the sūtra, for example,] that when the noble Śāriputra engaged in the way of a bodhisattva, a malevolent demon came and asked him to give his right hand. Cutting off his right hand, [Śāriputra] offered it to the demon with his left hand. [Considering this a disrespectful behavior,] the demon insulted him harshly. As a result, [Śāriputra] became upset and discarded the awakening mind. He nevertheless became an arhat. The *Account of Kanakavarṇa* tells the story of a man who practiced the way of a bodhisattva for forty eons before he gave it up. But as soon as he did that, he turned into a pratyekabuddha.[123] Wouldn't what you said earlier contradict these statements?

[Answer:] The way karma works—in this case, how certain people who have abandoned the awakening mind come to attain liberation—cannot be comprehended by ordinary beings. Only the omniscient ones can understand this. We do not. This is how Vairocana and the *Exposition* interpret [these lines]. Kṣemadeva, on the other hand, explains that although [Śāriputra] abandoned the [the awakened mind] in terms of its method aspect, since he embraced it in a perfect way, he liberated sentient beings.[124] Vibhūticandra says that although he discarded the conventional awakening mind, he did not discard the ultimate awakening mind.[125] This is correct, for even though he abandoned the altruistic intention, he did not abandon the wisdom that understands no-self. Therefore he did not go the lower realms. This is what I think. That said, why tire oneself in relation to something inconceivable!

The next point is [how one's altruistic activity will be undermined]. [4.8–11] Abandoning the awakening mind is the most severe of all the bodhisattva infractions. The *Condensed Perfection of Wisdom* states:

> If, after practicing the ten paths of virtue for millions of eons,
> one engenders the wish to become an arhat or a pratyekabuddha, then one's ethical discipline has become degenerate.
> Generating such an attitude is more severe than a root infraction.[126]

This is so because if bodhisattvas err in such a way, they weaken their capacity to benefit every being. And any person who prevents or interferes ever so briefly in the merit of bodhisattvas—that is, in their generation of the [awakening] mind—will diminish those bodhisattvas' activity for the good of all beings. Since such troublemakers diminish the capacity of [bodhisattvas], they will undergo endless bad rebirths. This is the reasoning: If I destroy the happiness of just one being, I actually hurt myself. If I obstruct the virtuous activity of one bodhisattva, I am destroying the happiness of all beings, who are infinite as space itself. Therefore it goes without saying that I would be reborn in the lower realms. The *Meditative Concentration on the Miraculous Ascertainment of Peace Sūtra* states:

> Suppose someone were to kill all the beings in Jambudvīpa and rob them of all their possessions. Then compare that act to that of one who was to create obstacles for a bodhisattva's virtue, be it no more than hindering the giving of a single morsel of food to an animal. This latter act would create immeasurably more negativity than the former. And why? Because it would interfere with the virtue that causes a buddha to appear.[127]

The next point is [how one will be obstructed from the fruit, the attainment of liberation]. [4.12] If we are swinging back and forth between two [attitudes], alternately under the sway of transgressions or the power of the awakening mind, it will take a long time to reach the first [bodhisattva] level and the ones that follow.

[Hence the advice not to forsake the awakening mind] is as follows. [4.13–14] Therefore I must diligently fulfill what I have promised at the time of generating the mind [of awakening]. If I make no effort today, I will sink lower and lower in the realms of inferior existence. I might think that this cannot happen because the buddhas are there to protect me. However, innumerable buddhas have [come and] gone in the past, working for the happiness of all beings. Through my own fault of transgressing the precepts, I was beyond the reach of those buddhas' healing care. They might save me later, I might think. But if I still act as I have in the past, I will repeatedly experience the same kind of suffering. As such, I will have to bear the suffering of the lower existences. And even if I am reborn in higher existences, I will have to experience sickness, death, severed and broken limbs, and much more.

### Conscientiousness with respect to one's existence endowed with leisure and opportunity, the basis

This has three parts: the difficulty of obtaining it, the disadvantages of not obtaining it, and forswearing making no effort after having obtained it.

The first is as follows. [4.15–16] When will I find these rare circumstances again, such as the appearance of the tathāgatas, faith in the objects [of refuge], the human birth, the possibility to cultivate virtue—in brief, an existence endowed with the eighteen factors of leisure and opportunity? I will not find them again. At times like the present, I have obtained [such a human existence], in that I live my days free of sickness and in favorable circumstances, having enough to eat and not under the threat of a disaster. But this life is not trustworthy, not even for a single moment. It is deceptive, for this body is like an object on loan. We do not control it.

[The disadvantages of not obtaining it] has two parts: the actual point and the substantiation. The [actual point], in turn, consists of two, of which [the first is that] *virtue remains unachievable in the lower realms*. [4.17–18] If I continue to act as I do at present, I will fail to achieve the human state ever again. Instead, I will fall into the lower existences. If I cannot attain the human state but live in a lower existence, I will lack the power to do good and will act in exclusively negative ways. If now, even though I have the capacity to do good, I do not act virtuously, what then will I do later on, when stupefied by the suffering of the lower realms? There will be no possibility [for me] to do virtuous deeds.

Second, *hence one will not obtain rebirth in the higher realms*: [4.19] By not engaging in virtuous deeds and instead heaping up negative karma, I will not even hear the word "happiness" for hundreds of millions of eons, much less attain it.

[The substantiation] is twofold, starting with *the substantiation through scripture*. [4.20] For the very reason [mentioned above], the Blessed One stated how, as in the illustration of a turtle poking its neck through the hole of a yoke floating on the mighty ocean, obtaining human existence is extremely difficult. In the *Connected Discourses*, [the Buddha] said:

> "Monks, imagine that this great earth is [covered by] a great ocean on which floats a wooden yoke with a single hole, moving here and there, wherever the wind pushes it. A blind turtle living [in that ocean] raises its head [above the water] once every hundred years. Would it be easy for this turtle to find its head inserted in the hole of this yoke drifting on the immense ocean?"
>
> "Blessed One, it would not."
>
> The Blessed One proclaimed, "Monks, in comparison, it is much more difficult to find a human existence."[128]

Next is *the substantiation through logical reasoning*. [4.21–22] Through an act of evil committed in a single instant, we have to endure an eon in the Avīci hells. The commentaries explain that in case of a [crime] such as the [five] acts of immediate retribution, the "single instant" refers to the time required for the completion of that action. But if the recipient of the action is exceptional and the motivation particularly negative, it refers to the [shortest possible] duration of time. Since we have accumulated such negativity in saṃsāra since beginningless time, it is evident that we will have no access to happy existences and will rather descend to the lower realms. And even after having experienced the result of the previous negativity, we will still not be released from suffering, because throughout the experience, we will continue to commit further evil, which serves as the cause of further suffering. Thus [the negativity] reinforces itself.

[Forswearing] making no effort after having obtained it is twofold: a general presentation and its explanation.

As to the first, [4.23] if I do not cultivate virtue now that I have found such leisure, there will be no greater waste than this, no greater folly.

Its explanation has three parts: reflecting on the results of such foolishness and ignorance, criticizing the course of action itself, and examining the cause thereof.

The first is as follows. [4.24–25] If, despite understanding the mistake of transgressing the precepts, I nevertheless remain stupidly inactive and do not put effort into the training, then at the moment of my death, regret and great sorrow will overcome me. And once I am dead, my body will burn in the intolerable fires of hell while my tormented mind will certainly burn in the intolerable fires of remorse.

The second is criticizing the course of action itself. [4.26–27b] Although I have attained, somewhat inexplicably, this favorable state of leisure and opportunity that is so difficult to obtain yet provides the power to do much benefit, and although I do understand the difference between virtues and flaws, between positive and negative qualities, I still act in negative ways. Therefore I will be drawn into the hells again. So, just like a person bewitched by spells, I too am being mindless here in this context.

As to the third point [examining the cause thereof], [4.27cd] What is it that makes me so foolish that I deceive myself? There must be something in the past that I have not understood. What is within me that causes me to be this way? If I examine this question, it can be nothing other than the afflictions.

## Conscientiousness with respect to the afflictions, which are to be discarded

This third point [above], therefore, indicates the need for conscientiousness with regard to the afflictions, which must be discarded. This has three parts: examining the afflictions that must be discarded, developing the determination to discard them, and generating the enthusiasm that enables us to discard them.

## Examining the afflictions that must be discarded

The first is twofold: reflecting on the faults [of the afflictions], and making up our mind not to embrace them. The first, in turn, has three parts: how they harm us even though this should not be the case, how they cause great harm, and the advice to not embrace them.

As to the first, [4.28–29] anger, craving, and so forth are enemies that lack arms, legs, or other limbs. They are not warriors endowed with zeal and the like, nor are they clever geniuses. How is it that they enslave me, deprive me of my self-control? It is because they live inside my mind. They use me at their own pleasure, shamelessly. And I am not even upset about it but bear it with patience. [However,] this is forbearance directed toward the wrong object, something to be condemned by those with true forbearance.

The second is how they cause great harm. [4.30–32] The harm [caused by afflictions] is enormous in scope. Even if all gods, demigods, and other beings were to rise up against me as enemies, they could not drag or push me into the fire of Avīci hell. However, [my] powerful afflictions are enemies that propel and thrust me instantly into Avīci's flames—a blaze that incinerates absolutely everything in its path, reducing even Mount Meru to ash. They are also long-lived: my afflictions have been my enemies for a very long time—in fact, for beginningless eternity—while all other enemies have not survived that long.

Third is the advice to not embrace them. [4.33] With a conciliatory attitude and obliging behavior, we might bring others around to being well disposed and helpful, but these afflictions, when willingly obeyed, only give great suffering and harm in return.

Next is making up our mind not to embrace them. [4.34–35] For a very long time, indeed from time without beginning, the afflictions have continuously and unceasingly been a destructive enemy. They are the sole cause for the development of all [my] damaging [behavior]. Those afflictions, the enemies, are deeply entrenched in my heart. Since that is so, is it acceptable that I am leading a carefree, hedonistic life in saṃsāra? It certainly is not. Moreover, these afflictions are the jailors in the prison of saṃsāra who prevent liberation. They are the Lord of Death's slaughterers in the hell realms. If they lie within my mind, in the net of clinging, how can I be happy? Thinking this, I make up my mind.

### Developing the Determination to Discard the Afflictions

This has three parts: donning armor by abandoning the afflictions, not becoming disheartened by suffering, and persisting with the antidotes.

The first is as follows. [4.36] I will not let go of my effort until these afflictions, my enemies, are definitively destroyed. Consider this analogy: When people feel hurt by an "ordinary enemy," even if it was only a minor aggression, they are enraged, and inflated with pride, they do not rest until that enemy has been crushed. How much more energy should I invest then into crushing the enemy of the afflictions!

Not becoming disheartened by suffering is threefold: (1) the faults of what is to be abandoned, (2) the beneficial qualities of the antidotes, and (3) ensuring, through contemplating one's pledge, that one does not become disheartened.

First, [the faults of what is to be abandoned]: [4.37–38] Even if they do not resort to killing, my enemies, [driven by] afflictions, are destined by nature to suffer death. They rather deserve my compassion. When [soldiers] fight in the battlefield, they fiercely desire to overcome their enemies, ignoring the pain of being wounded by spears, arrows, and other weapons or even of being mortally wounded. They will not turn around to escape. Why not then me, when I am striving to overcome my natural enemies, who by their mere existence will always bring me suffering? Even if I am harmed and suffer many hundred kinds of pain, what reason would I have to feel disheartened, depressed, discouraged, or dejected?

Second, the beneficial qualities of the antidotes: [4.39–40] People display the wounds and scars that unimportant enemies have inflicted on their bodies in battle, as if they were adornments that prove they are heroes. Why then, when I am giving my full energy to the great cause of all beings, do I think that pain will harm me? And moreover, fishermen, *cāṇḍālas*—that is, butchers—farmers, and the like work with their minds set on earning a living, enduring cold and heat and all kinds of drudgery. Should we not endure the same for the happiness of all beings? We should indeed, says [Śāntideva].

Third, ensuring, through contemplating one's pledge, that one does not become disheartened: [4.41–42b] I have promised to liberate from their afflictions all beings [living in] the ten directions, up to the limits of space. At the same time, I myself am not freed from the defilements. Speaking without knowing the limitations of my mental and physical capacities—is it not madness? It does look like madness, indeed. And therefore, so as to lead others to liberation, I need to bring about my own liberation. This is the meaning.

Next is persisting with the antidotes. [4.42c–4.44] As a consequence, I will always work toward overcoming the afflictions, never turning back. With passion I will pursue the elimination of afflictions. With hostile intentions toward the afflictions, I will fight them and defeat them. "Given that all the afflictions are to be eliminated," one might ask, "how can one employ passion and hostility [in combating them]?" [Answer:] Temporarily, these aspects that are part of the destroyer of afflictions are not included among the aspects of affliction that should be abandoned. For now, I will not discard them. However, they too must ultimately be discarded. This [interpretation] is clear in the commentaries. This accords with how, in relation to the phrase "except for those that are not part of the afflictions," the *Extensive Commentary* says, "They appear as if they are afflictions, but they are not."[129] Though I be burned to death or my head chopped off,[130] I will not bow down to my enemies, the afflictions. I will not succumb to their power.

## Generating the Enthusiasm That Enables Us to Discard the Afflictions

[4.45] When you banish ordinary enemies from a country, they will settle in another country, appropriate it, and build up their power. Then, quite possibly, they will return and inflict harm again. It is not the same with my enemies the afflictions. Once they have been uprooted, they cannot return.

How do we discard them? [4.46] By examining these afflictions, they are easily overcome. Therefore we call them disparagingly *affliction* or *defilement*. The *Extensive Commentary* glosses the term with, "Since these afflictions are devoid of a foundation, simply by seeing the suchness that is the ultimate truth, they are cleared away. Hence, they are called *afflictions*."[131] The *Exposition*, on the other hand, explains simply, "these afflictions such as attachment . . ."[132] They [the afflictions] will be relinquished by looking at them with the eyes of insight—that is, with an understanding of no-self. Once I clear my mind of them, where could they go? They have no place to go. Where could they stay to build up the power to come and hurt me again? They will not come. This shows that it is only my weak mind and my lack of effort that has made their elimination impossible.

[4.47] How should we examine them with eyes of insight? The afflictions neither dwell in the sense objects, such as forms and so on, nor do they dwell in the collection of sense organs, such as the eyes and so forth. Afflictions arise independently of them. They do not dwell in the space between the objects and the sense organs, and there is nowhere else for them to dwell. They cannot be seen anywhere. Nevertheless, these afflictions harm all beings whenever they are present. When we look at them [directly], they cannot be established as harm-doers, yet they appear as harm-doers. They are an illusory play! To the heart that thinks itself incapable of discarding them because they appear without being real, [Śāntideva] says, "Let go of your fear and maintain your diligence so that you may develop wisdom! Why would you not do this and instead needlessly be tormented in the hells and other such realms? To act like that makes no sense!" Therefore, [Śāntideva] adds, do not act like that.

## The summation[133]

[4.48] Having reflected in this way on the meaning of practicing conscientiousness according to the explanations given here, I resolve to strive for conscientiousness in order to accomplish the training of a bodhisattva, as it is taught in the sūtras and the treatises. If I ignore this, I would be acting like a sick person in need of medicine who refuses to follow the doctor's advice. Who could expect to be cured [when behaving in such a way]? No one! And likewise, there would be no deliverance from the disease of the afflictions and of suffering. The *Compendium of Training* advises:

> Here, understand the key points
> by means of which you will not incur infractions:
> your body, your possessions, and
> your virtue engendered over the three times—
> giving these away to all sentient beings
> and protecting, purifying, and enhancing them.[134]

Just as stated above, we are being advised that it is most appropriate to strive with the greatest effort.

This concludes the explanation of chapter 4.

# 5. Guarding Awareness

## Mindfulness and meta-awareness

Now, the text presents mindfulness and meta-awareness.[135] Here, *mindfulness* refers to the remembering of what we have promised—namely, what to eliminate and what to cultivate. *Meta-awareness*, on the other hand, refers to being skilled in the pursuit of the activities of such elimination and cultivation. These are presented here in the text. This presentation has three points: guarding the mind as the means to protect the precepts, guarding mindfulness and meta-awareness as the means to guard the mind, and exhorting oneself to relate these [practices] to one's own mind.

## Guarding the mind as the means to protect the precepts

This has two parts. First, a brief presentation: [5.1] Wishing to maintain our training without deterioration, we must scrupulously guard against the mind going in the wrong direction. Failing to control the mind, we will be incapable of protecting the precepts.

Next, the extensive explanation has four parts: the rationale for guarding the mind, the way to guard it, the benefits of guarding it in this way, and the need to strive in guarding the mind.

### The rationale for guarding the mind

This has three parts, the negative consequences of not guarding the mind, the benefits of guarding it, and the summation of the points.

The first is as follows. [5.2] The elephant of the mind goes the wrong direction when it is let loose, causing great harm such as that of Avīci hell. Even wild elephants in a rage do not cause that much devastation.

The second, the benefits of guarding the mind, is twofold. First is a brief presentation. [5.3] If that roaming elephant, the mind, is tethered to a virtuous object by the rope of mindfulness, every danger subsides, and all virtuous actions come [naturally].

[Second,] the extensive explanation has two parts: avoiding the dangers and cultivating virtue.

### Avoiding the dangers

The first, in turn, is twofold: the actual point and the substantiation of that point. The first is as follows. [5.4–5] As for the tigers, lions, elephants, bears, and snakes, as well as all the antagonists, all the guards of hell, ogresses, evil spirits, and demons—with respect to all of these, it is by tethering our own mind alone that all these harbingers of harm can be tethered. Simply by taming this mind, all of them will be tamed. The *Garland of Birth Stories* says:

> Because of his compassionate nature,
> [the animals] were calmed as if moistened [by
> compassion].
> Free from the harmful intent of preying on each other,
> even the fierce animals began to live like hermits.[136]

Second, the substantiation of that point: [5.6] All dangers and fears, and the countless external [environmental] sufferings, too, stem from the mind that has gone wrong. This, the Truth Speaker declared. The *Jewel Cloud Sūtra* says:

> If you gain control over your mind, you will have control over all phenomena.

And:

> Virtue or negative karma,
> all has been produced by the mind.[137]

Also, the *Perfectly Gathering the Teachings Sūtra* says that all phenomena depend on the mind.[138]

[5.7–8] Moreover, who is the creator, the one who diligently forged the weapons of hell to torture beings? Who made the burning iron ground? From where do the "female beings" on the mountain of the sword-leaf forest emerge? This is how the *Extensive Commentary* and Vairocana[139] explain it. Kṣemadeva[140] too reads it as female beings. So the version that has "heaps of fire" (*me tsogs*) is erroneous. Thus one should read this word either as "female beings" (*bud med*), as found in the commentaries, or as "hosts of females," as Pang Lotsāwa renders it, which is better.[141] In sum, all those [visions] have arisen from a negative mind, the Sage taught.

> The mind is the greatest of all enemies.
> No enemy exists apart from our mind.[142]

So it is stated in sūtras such as the *Application of Mindfulness*. Therefore, in the three worlds, nothing is to be feared other than the mind itself. And for this reason, the mind must be tamed.

## Cultivating virtue

The virtues of the bodhisattvas consist of the practice of the six perfections. To indicate that in relation to these too the mind is primary, the text has six parts.

The first is [the perfection of generosity]. [5.9–10] If the perfection of generosity meant the elimination of the poverty of all beings, then how could all the saviors of the past have attained the perfection of generosity? Did they not attain this perfection? Because there are still impoverished beings. How then is [the perfection of generosity attained]? [Answer:] By giving away all our possessions, outer and inner, together with the virtue that results from these acts, our habituation to giving to every being will come to be perfected; it is through the state of mind free of miserliness that the perfection of generosity is attained. This is as stated in the *Teachings of Akṣayamati*:

> What is the perfection of generosity? It is this: a mental state intent on giving away all possessions together with the [karmic] result of that act. Hence it is a state of mind.[143]

Second is the perfection of morality. [5.11] If ending harm constituted the perfection of morality, then the saviors of the past would not have attained the perfection of morality. This is because harm to animals, such as fish and turtles, to the property of other people, to women, or to any other beings, such as through killing or forcibly abducting them, has not been eradicated, and violent people committing these still exist. Therefore, while they yet persist, to attain the mental state free of violence toward all is the perfection of morality, for as the sūtra says:[144]

> What is the perfection of morality? It is the state of mind that renounces harming others.[145]

[5.12–14] As for the third, likewise, [the perfection of] forbearance does not mean stopping enemies or their aggression, because wicked people are infinite as the sky, and suppressing them all would be endless. But subduing my own angry mind is the equivalent of subduing all enemies. Take the following analogy: How could I find leather enough to cover the whole earth? However, just covering the soles of my feet is tantamount to covering the entire world. Similarly, I cannot fend off all external harms. However, if I guard my own mind against aggression, what need is there to control others? Once I have perfected forbearance, there is no such need.

[5.15] Likewise, for the fourth, [the perfection of] diligence, the mind is also primary. One single, short moment of "a clear mind," encompassed within the discipline of meditative absorption as interpreted by the *Exposition*,[146] which Kṣemadeva interprets to mean [a state of mind] free of activities of body and speech, generating a single instant can result in being born in the Brahmā realm[147] and so forth. Some say this is analogous to the sūtra statements where one is reborn in the Brahmā realms through generating the mind of lovingkindness. If, in contrast, [such actions] are not connected with strong mental states, then, owing to the feebleness of the mental activity, the physical and verbal actions could not bring about such a result [of being born in the Brahmā realms].

[5.16] Likewise, for the fifth, [the perfection of] meditative absorption, it is the state of mind that secures it. The Buddha, knower of the nature of all things, explained that the recitations of the mantra and the other paths, and all physical austerities, even if practiced a long time, are futile when carried out with a mind distracted elsewhere. They have but little value. In the *Distillation of Meditation*, [the Buddha] declares, "Monks! As for austerities and recitations undertaken with a mind distracted by desire, they will be fruitless."[148] The *Mother Perfection of*

*Wisdom* states that with a distracted mind, one will not accomplish [even] one's own self-interest.[149]

[5.17] The sixth, [the perfection of] wisdom, is as follows. The real meaning of things is secret and is empty in nature. As to the word *secret*, the *Extensive Commentary* says, "Since it is not within the domain of the childish, it is secret,"[150] while the *Exposition* says, "The suchness that is selflessness needs to be hidden in the depth of one's mind."[151] Those who do not know this may well wish to experience happiness and overcome suffering, but their wishes are futile, and they will [continue] wandering meaninglessly through saṃsāra. In a sūtra, it says:

> Beings are caught in confusion, like wild animals in
> a trap.
> Understanding this, the wise ones move like birds
> through the sky.[152]

This shows that for wisdom, the mind is primary. Similarly, the *Array of Trees Sūtra* says, "All the practices of the bodhisattva depend upon one's own mind."[153]

As for [establishing the perfections of] method, aspiration, power, and gnosis, given that they are aspects differentiated from wisdom, the mind is primary for these as well.

Next is the summation: [5.18] For all these reasons, I will bring my mind under control by means of mindfulness, and I will guard it by means of meta-awareness. As long as I do not control my mind, what use are my many other practices? They are futile.

## The way to guard the mind

[5.19–20] If I were to find myself amid an agitated crowd, distracted and chaotic, I would need to be very cautious and attentive with any wound [I may have]. Similarly, if I do not guard the wound that is my mind when in the company of bad people who trigger many negative emotions in me, much suffering will ensue. Therefore I need to control [the mind] constantly. If fear of the physical pain of a minor wound makes me anxious and conscientious, why then would I not protect myself against the fear of being crushed between the great mountains of hell, and against the injury of my mind thus inflicted? Therefore I need to control [the mind].

### The benefits of guarding the mind in this way

[5.21] If I maintain a lifestyle by which the mind is guarded in the way described, then even when among evil people or surrounded by [alluring] women, I will observe my vows and discipline, and my conscientiousness will not degenerate.

### The need to strive in guarding the mind

[5.22] [The text says to] let my gains such as alms, my honor such as homage [from others], even my body and my life as well as my other virtues perish. This "other virtues" Vairocana interprets to mean letting even the virtue accumulated for the benefit of others and myself disappear.[154] But never let the mind perish. "The mind" here Kṣemadeva interprets in terms of "I will never let these ten aspects of the awakening mind perish," while the *Extensive Commentary* glosses on it [simply] as "this virtuous mind."[155] In brief, the phrase "other virtues" could be understood to refer to karmic actions of body and mind. This is just as stated in the following in the *Advice to a King Sūtra*:

> I will give away my wealth and protect my body.
> I will give away wealth and body and protect my life.
> Giving away wealth, body, life, and everything else,
> I will protect the Dharma.[156]

## Guarding mindfulness and meta-awareness as the means to guard the mind

This has three parts: (1) an exhortation to guard mindfulness and meta-awareness, (2) the negative consequences of not guarding them, and (3) the method for guarding them.

The first is as follows. [5.23] [Here the text says,] I strongly encourage all those wishing to guard their mind to maintain these [disciplines] at the cost of their own lives: mindfulness, which means not forgetting which [attitudes] to adopt and which to reject, and meta-awareness, which means examining one's flow of consciousness and supervising the [process of] adopting and rejecting.

The negative consequences of not guarding them has three parts: the negative consequences of not guarding both, of not guarding meta-awareness, and of not guarding mindfulness.

The first is as follows. [5.24] People troubled by illness do not have the strength to move around or carry out any work. Similarly, a mind troubled by ignorance about [the principle of] adopting and rejecting does not have the strength to carry out any virtuous deed. This analogy describes the negative consequence of lacking meta-awareness, according to the *Exposition*, or lacking both, according to the *Extensive Commentary*.[157]

The negative consequences of not guarding meta-awareness is twofold. First, *it allows knowledge to go to waste*. [5.25] When my mind lacks meta-awareness, it cannot retain the knowledge attained through listening, reflecting, and meditating. What I have learned through these activities does not stay in my memory, just like a cracked jar will not hold the water I pour into it. It will be forgotten, according to the *Exposition*, or not clearly experienced, according to Kṣemadeva.[158] Second, *this leads to the degeneration of morality*. [5.26] I may be highly educated, devoted, and extremely diligent, and I may carry out the various aspects of the training with deep respect. However, lacking the meta-awareness of [observing] the fine details of my conduct, I make mistakes, thereby incurring infractions.

The negative consequences of not guarding mindfulness are as follows. [5.27–28] The afflictions, accompanied by a lack of meta-awareness, [are] thieves who sneak in when mindfulness is slacking. They steal the merit I have accumulated. When it is gone, I will go to the lower realms. The afflictions, this band of robbers, multiply and look for an opportunity to do harm. When they have found one, they steal all virtuous deeds, destroying the chance of attaining rebirth in a happy existence. The *Extensive Commentary* adds that the reason for this is the extinction of the provisions of virtue.[159]

### The method for guarding mindfulness and meta-awareness

[This is in two parts: Guarding mindfulness, and guarding meta-awareness. The first] has three parts: the method for guarding mindfulness, the causes that give rise to mindfulness, and the effects of having guarded mindfulness.

The first is as follows. [5.29] Without guarding mindfulness, I will make a lot of mistakes. Therefore I will never withdraw mindfulness from the door that leads to the inner home of my mind. This [interpretation] follows the *Extensive Commentary*. And further, in the event [mindfulness] leaves its station, I will remind myself of the consequences—that is, the various sufferings of the lower realms. This will reinstate it once again.

Second is the causes that give rise to mindfulness. [5.30–32b] By associating with teachers and friends practicing authentic Dharma, I will receive instructions from them and from preceptors and so forth on how to engage in the practices that I should adopt and avoid the behaviors that I should reject. I would feel ashamed about any transgression. Fearing that, I will wholeheartedly engage in the proper training, and mindfulness will easily arise. In addition, by thinking that I will always be in the presence of all the buddhas and bodhisattvas, who possess all-penetrating vision seeing all there is to be known in the three times, I will feel a sense of shame, deep respect for the training, and the fear born of embarrassment.[160] Because of this I will reflect in such ways and act with mindfulness. The *Garland of Birth Stories* says:

> If you do something negative, even if no one sees it,
> it is like eating poison. How could this lead to happiness?
> There is nothing that the pure eyes of the gods
> and humans with yogic power do not see.[161]

Third is the effects of having guarded mindfulness. [5.32c–5.33] Having contemplated in this manner, I will bring the buddhas to mind. Without any effort, they will appear again and again. When mindfulness is stationed at the door of the mind to guard it against intruding afflictions, then also meta-awareness comes effortlessly. Even if it leaves [occasionally], it will return once again.

## Guarding meta-awareness

The method for guarding meta-awareness has three parts: bringing meta-awareness prior to acting, simultaneous application, and a concise definition of guarding meta-awareness.

The first is as follows. [5.34] Each time, before acting, I first examine the mind. If afflictions are present, the mind is flawed. Once I recognize this, I hold still, as if I were a block of wood, remaining in the fire agitated by the afflictions.

Simultaneous application has four parts: (1) examining the state of the three doors, (2) having examined them, bringing them under control, (3) having brought them under control, training in practices that purify the mind, and (4) the elements of a perfect training.

## Examining the state of the three doors

The first is threefold: examining activities of the body, examining activities of the mind, and indicating situations where one could remain at ease.

The first is [examining activities of the body]. [5.35] I will never allow my gaze to wander purposelessly. With a mind firmly settled in the principle of adopting and rejecting, my eyes will always gaze downward, as far as the length of a yoke. [5.36] When feeling tired from doing that, I may occasionally look to the horizon to relax the eyes. And if someone appears within my field of vision, I will look at them and greet them. The commentaries all state that it says, "Look at them with a welcoming expression." This is the explanation given here, too. [5.37] When traveling on the road, I verify whether I have taken the wrong path or check for dangers such as robbers by slowly looking in every direction. Should I feel the need to look repeatedly or quickly in the four directions, I will, so as to avoid the negative effects of agitation, look only after having taken a pause of relaxation, turning the body around and then looking behind me. [5.38] Only after checking to see what lies before me or behind me will I go forward or return back, respectively. And just as in this example of examining the directions, I will, in all situations of any of the four physical activities,[162] only proceed after ascertaining what is to be done. [5.39] Every physical activity that I set out to do, I prepare with the mental impulse where I consciously decide, "To carry out this activity, this action is suitable, and I should do it in this position." Then, while I am active, I verify whether [the body] has indeed remained like I had initially intended.

Next is examining activities of the mind. [5.40–41] Since this mind behaves like a mad elephant, I tie it to the pillar of reflection on the Dharma, so beneficial for myself and others. I examine the mind with all my effort, so that it does not stray onto erroneous paths. What is the manner of examination? In all situations, I diligently keep one-pointed concentration on virtue as a reference point. Not straying onto erroneous paths for even one instant, I inquire, "Which virtuous or nonvirtuous object is my mind dealing with at present?" In this way, I will inspect every aspect of my mind.

Indicating situations where one could remain at ease is as follows. [5.42–43] We might be involved in circumstances where we cannot maintain this strict restraint, such as when our life may be in danger, during large celebrations such as offering [ceremonies] to the Three Jewels, when engaged in important tasks for the welfare of beings, and so forth. In those situations, we behave in a way appropriate to the situation. For example, that when practicing generosity, one can be more relaxed with respect to certain aspects of moral discipline is stated in the *Teachings of Akṣayamati*:

> At the time of practicing generosity, one relaxes ethical discipline and, with respect to it, remains in equanimity.[163]

One example for such a case is that of telling a lie to prevent a murder, saying, "I haven't seen him," even though one has; so explains the *Exposition*.[164] Our virtue should be matched with strength in the following way. [5.44] After we have planned and started an action, we do not abandon it to get involved with something else. Instead, we carry out that work with a focused mind. Once completed, we may move on to the next. In such a way, both the former and the later activities will be successful. If done otherwise, neither will be completed. If we practice virtue in a progressive manner in such a way, the secondary affliction of a lack of meta-awareness[165] will not remain dominant.

## Having examined them, bringing them under control

This has three parts: stopping inappropriate behavior, engaging in [the appropriate] activities, and cultivating the antidote against not conducting oneself in such a manner. The first is threefold: giving up attachment to distraction, forsaking meaningless activities, and forsaking activities driven by the afflictions.

[Giving up attachment to distraction] is as follows. [5.45] If I find myself engaged in all sorts of nonsensical and irrelevant talk, or in watching fictional or other curious stories, I will give up my attachment for them.

Next is forsaking meaningless activities. [5.46] If I find myself doing things such as stabbing the earth, pulling up grass, or tracing idle patterns on the ground, I remember the Sugata's precepts that forbid such activities. Wary of transgressing them, I immediately exercise restraint.

Forsaking activities driven by afflictions has three parts; [a brief presentation, a detailed explanation, and a summary]. The brief presentation is this. [5.47] When I wish to move my body or wish to speak, I will first examine my mind to determine my motivation. Then, once it is free of the afflictions' influence, I will act judiciously and in a wholesome way.

Second is a detailed explanation. [5.48] When I see that my mind has been affected by attachment or anger, then I should not engage in the nonvirtuous action this might induce—that is, not pursue any action with my body or speech. Understanding all phenomena to be without an agent, I will remain like a block of wood, without any action. [5.49] [I will do the same] when I experience excitation with my mind utterly distracted;

when feeling sarcastic, searching to inflict harm through words; when I am full of myself and proud; when decadent, indulging in my wealth and getting addicted to it; when I am overly critical, seeking to expose someone's faults; or when I am evasive or have the intention to deceive others—Kṣemadeva subsumes these two ["evasive" and "the intention to deceive others"] as "pretense and dissimulation."[166] [5.50] Or when I am desperate for praise while at the same time belittling others; or when I want to abuse another with harsh words; or if I have the thought of instigating an argument and causing a fight—those are times to be like a block of wood. [5.51] When I long for wealth, respect, and reputation; when I want to find followers and people to serve me; and when my mind hankers after special honors, such as having a ceremonial foot bath—those are times when I will be like a block of wood. [5.52] When I forsake the needs of others but do everything to fulfill mine—here the commentaries add "when I wish to have a following," which they explain to mean the wish for disciples—and when, prompted by them, I feel the urge to speak—those are times to be like a block of wood. [5.53] When I lack forbearance and cannot endure much, or when lazy, or when fear arises, or when I am arrogant and bold, or when I am noisily babbling all kind of nonsense, or when I am biased and very attached to my side—when these mental states occur, that is when to be like a block of wood.

The summary is as follows. [5.54] In this way, I examine whether my mind is occupied with matters that are either stained by afflictions or that demand a lot of energy for a meaningless outcome. When such things occur, the brave bodhisattva should apply antidotes to stabilize and control the mind, without succumbing to selfishness.

Next is engaging in the appropriate activities. [5.55] With a firm resolution, committed to always acting virtuously; with deep faith and joy about the qualities thereof; with a stable mind that comes from never avoiding hardship; with respect, expressed in mentally paying homage and expressed physically, which Vairocana explains to refer to bowing down;[167] with a sense of integrity that avoids negative behavior; with the fear of making mistakes; and with calmness due to having the senses under control, I am eager to help other beings. [5.56] The mutually conflicting desires of childish people do not wear me down. Their hurtful actions are born from their afflictions, as they have no control over their destructive thoughts. Thinking that, I shall develop heartfelt compassion for them. This is also stated in *Ornament of Mahāyāna Sūtras*:

> The wise do not regard beings as flawed,
> knowing that they are always acting out of error, with no self-control.
> "Their inappropriate actions happen against their will"—
> thinking thus enhances their compassion for beings.[168]

[5.57] I will only do what is morally irreproachable, after having considered the benefit to myself and others. Alternatively, it could be read, as in the *Exposition*, as "I will abide with a sense of integrity and decency on the basis of considering myself and others."[169] In this way, when I engage, even though I will act in the manner of a magical conjuration, with no delusion of self, I will maintain a constant hold on my mind.

Next, cultivating the antidote against not conducting oneself in such a manner has two parts: (1) reflecting on [the human existence of] leisure and opportunity, so hard to obtain, and (2) making the life obtained meaningful. The first is as follows. [5.58] After an eternity, I have obtained this [human existence of] supreme leisure, which is so hard to gain. Reflecting on this time and time again, I will firmly hold my mind as stable as Mount Meru, following the previous explanations, so that even strong afflictions will not upset it.

Making the life obtained meaningful is twofold: the body in

itself is not worthy to be attached to, and it can be used for a meaningful purpose. The first is as follows. [5.59] Here, Prajñākaramati, Vairocana, and Kṣemadeva[170] relate [the lines to the fact] that one must take hold of the mind, not the body, because the latter does not have the power to bring about even its own well-being. In the *Exposition*, we read, "You might ask why we should protect the body. It is because if we do not protect it, we become unhappy." Once I am dead, vultures will be greedy for my flesh, dragging and pulling it back and forth in all directions. Since you, my mind, will not be unhappy then, why do you care now and hold the body so dear? [5.60] Mind, why are you identifying with this body and guarding it? If you think that you need it, then, my mind, consider that you and the body are distinct. What can this body do for you? Although they are apart, I do need something as my support, and therefore I hold on to it, [the mind] thinks. [5.61] Foolish mind, why don't you identify with a clean wooden statue then? That would make sense, but why guard this rotting machine constructed of unclean parts?

Since there is no essence that could be pure or anything else, in what sense can it be impure? [5.62] First, just in your imagination, peel the layers of skin from the flesh. Then, with the knife of wisdom, remove the flesh from the cage of bones. [5.63] Open the bones, too, look at the marrow within. Examine for yourself what essence is there, be it pure or anything else. [5.64] Searching hard like this, you see no essence here. Now explain why it is that you are still attached to this body and continue to protect it? If you say, "I need it to have enjoyable experiences." [The text says [5.65]:]

> You cannot eat it, unclean as it is,
> nor drink the blood,
> nor suck out the entrails.
> What will you do with your body?

Since it is unfit to serve as enjoyment [5.66ab],

> Of course, it is right to protect it,
> but as a food for foxes and vultures.

Second, it can be used for a meaningful purpose. [5.66cd–5.70] This body's only purpose is to be employed for virtuous activities that benefit all of humankind. Even though you protect your body, the merciless Lord of Death will snatch it away and give it to the vultures. Then what will you do? Consider this analogy: You will not give clothes and other things to a servant who is not fit to be employed. Why then do you exhaust yourself to feed this body, which will definitely leave one day, although you have nourished and cared for it? So, be irreproachable and pay this body its wages in the form of food, clothing, and so on, but then put it to practice the awakening mind for your own sake and make it work for the benefit of others. This is how Kṣemadeva interprets it.[171] Do not give all you have to a cause that brings no benefit to others. Rather, just as a ship is a support for traveling back and forth on the water, the body is a support for myself and others to cross the ocean of cyclic existence. Therefore think of the body as a ship. And so that it may fulfill the welfare of all beings, transform it into a wish-fulfilling body—the body of the conquerors! With that kind of support, [your goal] will be accomplished.

### Having brought them under control, training in the practices that purify the mind

This has three parts: engaging in all activities with awareness, stating the primacy of the purification of mind, and purifying obscurations that hamper the mind from transformation.

## Engaging in all activities with awareness

The first has four parts: the activities to be engaged in all situations in general, specific activities to be engaged in for a virtuous life, abandoning behavior that elicits disrespect from worldly people, and the method to guard [one's mind] in relation to sleep.

The first, in turn, is threefold: being calm in everyday activities, being confident in my interaction with others, and ensuring that my own behavior is virtuous.

The first is as follows. [5.71–73] Master your own mind in this way, and have an ever-smiling countenance. Give up frowning or dark expressions, and be a friend who accomplishes the welfare of beings. Be sincere; speak the truth. Do not throw seats and mats down carelessly, inconsiderately causing a loud noise. Do not open doors aggressively. Appreciate silence,[172] and behave in ways that delight others. Consider the example of cranes, cats, and thieves: they achieve their goals by moving quietly and gently. A sage—that is, a bodhisattva—who correctly applies the discipline should likewise practice a calm behavior with body and speech at all times.

Second is being confident in my interaction with others. [5.74–78] When a good and helpful person, skilled in counseling and admonishing others in such things as how to right a wrong, gives me unsolicited advice, I will receive their words with humble respect. Curbing my pride, I will learn from all others. Subduing my arrogance, I will praise good Dharma teachers, telling them that their instructions were excellent. Whenever I see people acting virtuously, I will praise them openly to make them happy. When I want to avoid flattery, I will speak of others' virtues in their absence. When people express their sincere appreciation of someone else's qualities, I will do likewise. And when, as a bodhisattva, my own qualities are praised, I will not become inflated but will instead appreciate the wisdom that enables others to recognize virtue in me. If I act in such a way, all the virtues and successes of others will become a reason for me to feel joy. Such joy is rare and cannot be bought. I will enjoy happiness by rejoicing in other people's virtues, acquired through their hard work. Acting in such a way will not deprive me of anything in this life and will be sure to grant me great happiness in future lives. Resenting others for their qualities is a mistake that makes me unhappy and miserable in this life and even more unhappy in future lives.

The third is ensuring that my behavior is virtuous. [5.79–80] When speaking, my words shall be trustworthy, inspire confidence, be relevant to the situation and the level [of maturity of the audience], express the meaning in a clear way, and be kind. I will abandon being motivated by attachment and aversion, and I will speak with a soft voice and in moderation. When seeing other people, I will think, "It is through them that I attain buddhahood." Therefore I will seek no fault in them. Without any insincerity, I will look upon them in a frank and loving manner.

Next, specific activities to be engaged in for a virtuous life has two parts: how to cultivate this yourself and how to benefit others. The first is threefold: how the virtue being cultivated is powerful, how to cultivate it, and how to rank the superiority and inferiority with respect to what is to be adopted and rejected.

The first is as follows. [5.81] Actions will result in great virtue when we carry them out in the following ways: we do them all the time, in a continuous manner; we are highly engaged in them, maintaining a strong aspiration; we are energized by the antidotes that have the power to overcome the opposing forces; and we do them for a field of excellences such as the buddhas, for a field of beneficiaries such as our parents, or for a field of sufferers such as the sick. However, the same [factors] also apply to nonvirtue. As *Letter to a Friend* states:

Actions that are done constantly and with intense
engagement,
not attenuated by opposing forces, and carried out toward
special objects—
great are those with five attributes, virtuous or
nonvirtuous.
Therefore exert yourself in virtuous behavior![173]

The second, how to cultivate it, is as follows. [5.82] Having learned how powerful virtuous behavior is, I will engage in it with joy and enthusiasm, in a consistent manner, so as to benefit myself and others. Any and all work I will not leave to another person. I will not have the fault of one who eschews wholesome behavior but portrays themself as an enthusiast of virtue whose duty it is to do good.

Third is how to rank the superiority and inferiority with respect to what is to be adopted and rejected. [5.83] The six perfections, generosity and the others, needed to be taught [in a certain way]. Therefore they are arranged in a sequence, the latter higher than the lower. I should give preference to the practice of the higher [perfection]. Although the sequence of preference [generally] goes from the higher to the lower, as one example given above demonstrated, because the [prātimokṣa] discipline is inferior [to the bodhisattva discipline], one should not abandon great generosity [for it]. How then is the order determined? The key point is to think of the benefit of others. "Whatever is the superior action, that is what you should do," explains the *Exposition*.[174]

How to benefit others consists of a brief presentation and a detailed explanation. Of these, the first is as follows. [5.84] Apply the explanations that have just been given. Understand them and act accordingly, always striving for others' well-being. Here the Buddha, the great compassionate one who is far-sighted and knows all that is to be adopted and to be rejected, has in fact given permission [to the bodhisattva] to engage in deeds that are prohibited for inferior beings who are fixated on their own self-interest. This is, for example, like the statement in the *Skillful Means with the Secrets of All Buddhas* about how the greatly compassionate captain killed the criminal, thereby saving him from being oppressed in cyclic existence for a hundred thousand eons.[175]

The detailed explanation has two parts: benefiting others through material resources and benefiting others through [giving the] Dharma.

The first is threefold. Of these, the first is *giving food*. [5.85abc] From the edible alms I obtain, I should share a part with those fallen into the realms of the animals and hungry ghosts, another part with those who are without protection, such as beggars, and a part with those who have embraced yogic discipline, leading a life of pure conduct (*brahmacaryā*). The fourth part I will eat myself, thinking, as *Letter to a Friend* instructs:

> Knowing food to be akin to medicine,
> eat it free of attachment and anger.[176]

So, as advised, I will eat with the intention that my body becomes neither too weak nor too heavy. Otherwise, if I am driven by attachment and I make no effort in practicing virtue, it is like the *Moon Lamp Sūtra* says:

> When they find food that is delicious and pleasing,
> they do not practice their discipline but eat and drink.
> For them that food becomes poison,
> like an unclean lotus root for an elephant calf.[177]

In this way, [food] can become a source of fault.

The second is *giving clothing and so forth*. [5.85d] Excluding my own three robes—the excellent outer, inner, and lower robes—I will offer all possessions. These three shall not be given away. The *Bodhisattvas' Individual Liberation* says:

> If someone were to come and ask for the alms bowl and the robes, and if, beyond the three robes given by the Buddha, one has one left over, one should give and offer whatever one has. If [the giving] would lead one to possess fewer than the three robes, one should not give away the robes that one needs to live the life of a monastic. Why? Because the Tathāgata stated that one should not give away the three robes.[178]

The third is *giving one's body*. [5.86–87] This body, with which I practice the sacred Dharma, should not be harmed to help others in lesser ways. If I protect this body with which I practice the Dharma, I will progress quickly toward fulfilling all beings' wishes. The *Four Hundred Verses* states:

> Though you may see this body as an enemy,
> you should still protect it.
> A disciplined one with a long life
> can perform great acts of merit through it.[179]

As long as my compassionate aspirations are not pure, as long as I have not entered the state of supreme altruism, this body should not be given away literally, because I risk being of questionable benefit to others, having regrets, changing my mind, or creating obstacles for my practice of virtue. The *Compendium of Training* states:

> For example, the seed of a splendid medicinal tree
> from which everything, its roots and so on, can be used
> [to heal],

even if it were to be given, one should do so guarding
against inappropriate time.
The same is true of the medicinal tree of supreme
enlightenment.[180]

Some versions of the text have the line "Those with the mind of equanimity should give it away";[181] this admonishes us to give the body with an impartial attitude, thinking the same of everyone. However, Vairocana does not offer any further explanation. One might object, "If I do not give away my body, would this contradict my pledge?" [Answer:] It does not, because [the body] unquestionably is the cause of achieving great benefit for others, in this and other lives, too. Thereby, the *Exposition* explains, I am offering it to be the servant of others.[182] Later, when my aspirations are pure, I will give away whatever is suitable.

Next is benefiting others through [giving the] Dharma. [5.88–90] We should not explain the Dharma to people whose attitude is disrespectful. If their behavior includes wrapping cloths around their heads although they are not sick, holding an umbrella, a stick, or a knife, or veiling their head, the Dharma should not be explained.[183] To individuals whose understanding is limited, we should not explain the profound and vast [teachings]. Without other people present, we should not give a Dharma teaching to a woman alone. We should always act with equal respect to the lower teachings of the śrāvakas and the higher teachings of the Great Vehicle. Otherwise, people will reject the Dharma. This is as stated below in the *Gathering All Fragments Sūtra*:

> Mañjuśrī, among those who receive teachings from the tathāgatas, some will see them as good, some as bad. The latter group will reject the Dharma.[184]

We should not lead those who have the potential for the vast Dharma to practice lesser Dharma.[185] The *Heap of Jewels* states:

> Bodhisattvas are mistaken when they teach the vast Dharma to beings who are not [suitable] recipients. Bodhisattvas are mistaken when they teach the Lesser Vehicle to those who have faith in the vast [teachings].[186]

We should not neglect our conduct—that is, the precepts. If we do, [others] will be misled, [thinking] that one can be liberated by merely reading the sūtras and tantras.

Abandoning behavior that elicits disrespect from worldly people is as follows. [5.91] When spitting out a toothpick or saliva, we should cover that with earth or something. Dumping excrement, urine, or other filth into water or onto fields that are destined for public use is despicable. [5.92] When eating, we should avoid stuffing too much food in our mouth, producing noises like "chak chak," or chewing with our mouth open. The legs should not be stretched out while sitting, and we should not rub both arms at the same time. [5.93] Whether monastic or lay, we should not travel, sleep, or stay alone in a house with a woman of another [householder]. For monastics, this applies to any woman whatsoever. In brief, we should notice and consult the wise about what behavior destroys the faith of worldly people and avoid it all. [5.94] When pointing out a direction, we should not indicate it with the left hand or with a finger, because that is dismissive and disrespectful behavior. Instead, we should use the entire right hand to respectfully point out the way. [5.95] We should not make big gestures with the arms to convey a minor thing. Minimize gestures and sounds; use signs such as snapping with fingers. Overreacting verbally or physically to minor issues is [a display of] uncontrolled behavior. If we do not give up behavior that leads worldly people to lose faith, we cannot accomplish their welfare, and we instead create conditions for its opposite. The *Compendium of Training* states:

> Failing to respect what is worthy of that,
> like a fire covered in ash,
> people who despise the Conqueror's offspring
> end up burning in the hells and so on.[187]

Therefore we should strive to abandon such behavior.

Next is the method to guard [one's mind] in relation to sleep. [5.96] After finishing the evening session, we should lie down in the posture the Protector demonstrated when he passed into nirvāṇa: turned onto the right side, one leg placed on top of the other, stretched out with the right hand under the cheek and the left placed on the thigh, one sleeps with the body completely covered by the monastic robe and the head pointing in whichever direction we wish. Maintaining meta-awareness, we think, "For the purpose of practicing virtue, I will quickly rise again." With this thought, we fall asleep. The *Jewel Cloud Sūtra* states, "When they go to sleep, they sleep laying down on their right side, placing one leg on top of the other, the body covered by the monastic robe. They fall asleep with the idea to rise again with mindfulness and meta-awareness and with a bright consciousness."[188]

## Stating the Primacy of the Purification of Mind

[5.97] The deeds of bodhisattvas can be divided into innumerable categories. If we do not have the capacity to practice them all, we should implement the practices aimed at purifying and training the mind, such as have been taught above, until the mind is definitely [purified].

## Purifying obscurations that hamper the mind from transformation

[5.98] We should confess negative actions, rejoice in merit, and dedicate virtue to awakening by reciting the *Three Heaps Sūtra* three times by day and three times by night. We should, after having gone for refuge to the victorious ones and their children and established the awakening mind, apply the four powers of purification to cleanse all the remaining faults, in addition to their root transgressions, just as explained above.

## The elements of a perfect training

This has five parts: engaging in the fields of training with effort, training in many domains, training with the welfare of others as the objective, relying on spiritual mentors as support, and reading the sūtras and so on to understand the ways of training.

The first is as follows. [5.99] In all situations, whatever we do, whether our actions are decided by ourself or subject to another's will, we should implement with diligence the training the victorious ones advised for that situation.

Second is training in many domains. [5.100] There is no topic of knowledge that the children of the victorious ones should not learn, because if there is anything they do not know, they will not be able to fulfill the welfare of others. *Ornament of Mahāyāna Sūtras* states:

> If they do not diligently [study] the five areas of
> knowledge,
> even the supremely noble ones cannot attain omniscience.
> Therefore, to edify others, care for others, and for their
> own sake,
> they diligently strive to master all topics of knowledge.[189]

Therefore, for those who know well all fields of training and are skilled in implementing them in all situations, there will be no action that cannot produce merit.

The third, training with the welfare of others as the objective, is this: [5.101] All our actions should be, either directly or indirectly, for the benefit of beings. We should not engage in any other work. And all virtue should be dedicated solely toward all beings' awakening.

Fourth is relying on spiritual mentors as support. [5.102–3ab] At all times, rely on spiritual mentors who are versed in the essential points of the Great Vehicle. It is called a "vehicle" because it is what conveys us, and it refers to [the union of] method and wisdom. With respect to the "great" in Great Vehicle, *Ornament of Mahāyāna Sūtras* says:

> Its scope is great;
> likewise, its twofold practice,
> wisdom, application of diligence,
> skillfulness in means,
> the perfect attainment, and
> the Buddha's great enlightened activities—
> since it is endowed with such greatness,
> it is definitely called the Great Vehicle.[190]

Thus, since it is endowed with these seven forms of greatness, it is the Great Vehicle. Even at the cost of our lives, we should not abandon a person qualified in this vehicle who practices the supreme discipline of bodhisattvas and abides by the precepts. How to rely on [such a spiritual mentor] is explained in the *Array of Trees Sūtra* in the chapter on the liberation of Śrīsambhava:

> Honor the guru with a mind unwearied like the earth, bearing all burdens without weariness; with a mind

> whose determination is like a diamond, indestructible; with a mind like a rampart, unthreatened by any suffering; with a mind like a servant, carrying out all tasks without resentment; a mind like a street sweeper who has shunned pride and arrogance; with a mind like a vehicle, carrying heavy loads; with a mind like a dog that is never angry; with a mind like a ship, unwearied by going and coming; and with a mind like a wise son, gazing upon the spiritual mentor with joy. Child of good family, think of yourself as a sick person, think of the spiritual mentor as the physician, think of the instructions as medicine, and think of your sincere practice as the cure for the sickness.[191]

The fifth is reading the sūtras and so on to understand the ways of training. [5.103c–5.107] These teachings in their original wording along with other instructions given by the Buddha should be known from reciting the sūtras, because all the training rules derive from the collection of sūtras and are clearly explained there. The first sūtra to consult is the *Ākāśagarbha Sūtra*, since that teaches the transgressions and the ways to repair [the bodhisattva vow].[192] We need to know this from the very beginning. The *Compendium of Training*, composed by the master [Śāntideva] himself, is another indispensable reference that we should consult again and again, because it explains in detail the conduct that bodhisattvas should embrace at all times. In addition, we should regularly consult the master's *Compendium of Sūtras*, which contains condensed explanations of the meaning of the instructions. We should also study with diligence the *Compendium of Training* and the *Compendium of Sūtras* compiled by the master Nāgārjuna.[193] "This is because of the intention that they contain those that are not discussed here [as well]," states the *Extensive Commentary*.[194] Having learned which activities we should do and which we should refrain from, we should perform them according to these works. In all situations, to protect the mind from losing faith, we should look into the *Compendium of Training* and other works and put them into practice in a perfect manner.

### A concise definition of guarding meta-awareness

[5.108] The practice of guarding meta-awareness can be defined in the following concise way: repeatedly examining the state of one's body, speech, and mind, with the mind knowing the norms of what is to be adopted and what is to be rejected. This alone is, in brief, what it means to guard awareness.

### Exhorting oneself to relate these practices to one's own mind

[5.109] If we think that we will properly apply all this with body and mind but then do not put anything into practice but merely repeat the words, how will anything be achieved? This would be like wanting to cure patients by merely reading medical treatises. What would that accomplish? Nothing at all.

> Without the two eyes of mindfulness and meta-awareness,
> even if you have physical strength, education, and the like,
> you will not be able to go beyond this land of saṃsāra, so
> full of defects.
> Therefore, O wise people, treasure mindfulness and
> meta-awareness!

This concludes the explanation of chapter 5.

# 6. Forbearance

THE CHAPTER on forbearance contains two parts: the value of cultivating forbearance and the methods for cultivating it.

## THE VALUE OF CULTIVATING FORBEARANCE

The first point has two parts: the faults of anger, and the benefits of forbearance.

### THE FAULTS OF ANGER

The first is threefold: the consequences not [immediately] observable, the observable consequences, and the summary.

The first is as follows. [6.1] Even if a person accumulates good actions over a thousand eons through making offerings, through worshiping the Three Jewels, the sugatas, and other [objects of veneration], and through morality, all of that will be destroyed by a single moment of anger. All the commentaries agree on this. The *Miraculous Play of Mañjuśrī* states: "Mañjuśrī, anger destroys the roots of virtue collected for a hundred eons."[195] To explain this, there are three points: the object that will be destroyed, the agent that brings about the destruction, and the specific way it destroys.

The first is as follows. Generally speaking, there are three types of virtue: that which is *concordant with merit*, namely virtue not accompanied by skillful means or wisdom; that which is *concordant with liberation*, namely virtue informed by the realization of selflessness; and *virtue of the Great Vehicle*, which is sustained by both skillful means and wisdom. In the present case, it is the first kind of virtue that is being destroyed.

Second is the agent that brings about the destruction. This refers to [a state of mind] whose character is extreme hostility directed against an exceptional object and that is not attenuated, even afterward, by an antidote such as remorse.

As to the third, the specific ways it destroys,[196] some assert the following. It is not that [said virtue] is destroyed from its root; rather, it overwhelms the potency [of the virtuous karma] to bear its result in the immediately subsequent birth and transforms [the karma] into one that will bear its [fruitional effect] in some other subsequent lives. The reason for this is because, as stated in the following by the elder Rahula, the heavier karma's effect will mature first:

> As for karma's fruitions, those heavier,
> those closer in time, those most habitual,
> and those committed earliest—
> among all karma, these are reaped first.[197]

That said, since a change in when [the result] is experienced can occur for virtue concordant with liberation as well, there is no certainty here. Thus it cannot be stated with certainty what exactly is destroyed [by anger] nor the specific way it is destroyed. Therefore a Sarvāstivāda [sūtra] says:

> Upāli, since anger diminishes, removes, and annihilates even great roots of virtue, do not be angry even at a lump of charred wood, let alone an embodied being with consciousness.[198]

[6.2] There is no negativity like anger, and there is no fortitude like its antidote, forbearance. Therefore one should diligently train in forbearance with various methods and great sincerity.

Next is the observable consequences. [6.3–5ab] When the mind is gripped by the agony of hatred, we have no peace of mind and cannot experience equanimity, nor can we experience joy or the sensual pleasures of saṃsāra. Succumbing to insomnia, lacking proper grounding, we are unable to watch our body or mind. If a master overflows with hatred, his servants, though they have received favors of material goods and respect from him, and though they have served him, will oppose and kill the aggressive master. His hatred will cause even friends to grow weary of him. Even if he attracts people by distributing gifts, those people, because of his hatred, will not be loyal or befriend him.

The summary is as follows. [6.5cd–6.6ab] In sum, there is no sense in which someone prone to anger can live at ease and be joyful. Thus anger is an enemy that brings these and other kinds of suffering to ourselves and others.

## THE BENEFITS OF FORBEARANCE

[6.6cd] The benefits of forbearance are that those who control their anger and overcome it will be happy in this and future lives.

## [THE METHODS FOR CULTIVATING FORBEARANCE]

The methods for cultivating forbearance has two parts: a brief presentation and a detailed explanation. The brief explanation is twofold: (1) contemplating the faults of what is to be abandoned, and (2) how it is therefore logical to avert it.

The first is as follows. [6.7] The fuel of discontent arising from [others] doing things I do not want or obstructing what I want enhances the power of anger, which then overwhelms me.

The second, how it is therefore logical to avert it, is this: [6.8–

10] Since the fuel of my enemy anger is this mind of discontent, it is certain that I must overcome it completely. I cannot expect anything but hurt from this enemy. Whatever happens, I will not allow my joyful mind to be disturbed. I will not entertain bitter thoughts. Being irritable is itself sufficient to prevent me from attaining my goals. It will ruin all my virtue. If there is a solution to a problem, what does it help to feel annoyed? It is not helpful. And if there is no solution, what does it help to feel annoyed? That is not helpful either. It does not ever make sense.

The detailed explanation has two parts: presenting the objects of anger in general and controlling our anger about them. The first is as follows. [6.11] Suffering, humiliation, harsh words, and ill repute—we wish these neither for ourselves nor for our loved ones. But for our enemies, it is the reverse—we wish them suffering and do not want to see them happy. When we encounter these twelve unwanted situations, or encounter obstacles that thwart the twelve desirable situations, anger arises.[199]

The second, controlling anger, has two parts: controlling anger against those who create unwanted things for me, and controlling anger against those who obstruct my attainment of what I desire. The first point divides controlling anger into three parts: in relation to the four unwanted things done to myself, in relation to the four misdeeds against my loved ones, and in relation to the four good things done to my enemy.

## Controlling anger in relation to four unwanted things done to myself

The first point is twofold: controlling anger toward those who cause me suffering, and controlling anger toward those who commit humiliation, harsh words, and ill repute against me.

## Controlling anger toward those who cause me suffering

The first point has three parts: forbearance of voluntary acceptance of suffering, forbearance through gaining certainty in the Dharma, and forbearance of being unperturbed by harm.

## Forbearance of voluntary acceptance of suffering

The first has four parts: forbearance through examining the nature of cyclic existence, forbearance through examining it as a cause of renunciation, forbearance through examining how [suffering can be accepted] through habituation, and bringing to mind positive qualities [of suffering].

Forbearance through examining the nature of cyclic existence is as follows. [6.12ab] In cyclic existence, the causes of happiness—virtuous actions—are rare, only appearing occasionally, but the causes of suffering—nonvirtuous actions—are extremely numerous and come about effortlessly. Since this is the nature of cyclic existence, it requires my forbearance.

Next is forbearance through examining [suffering] as a cause of renunciation. [6.12c–6.13] Without suffering, one does not become weary of and develop renunciation for cyclic existence. Therefore, O mind, be steadfast and accept suffering! [There are people like] the devotees of the goddess Uma,[200] who obstructs Śiva's asceticism. Each ninth day of the middle autumn month, they fast for one to three days, throughout which they cut and burn their own bodies. Or there are the inhabitants of Karṇāṭa who, for the purpose of combat, inflict injuries on themselves with their weapons. If they can bear these senseless sufferings, why should I be afraid to endure pain for the goal of liberation?

Forbearance through examining how [suffering can be

accepted] through habituation is threefold: a brief presentation, a detailed explanation, and a summary.

First is the brief presentation. [6.14] There is nothing that does not become easier through habituation. For example, miserly people can perceive pain as happiness through the power of habituation.[201] Likewise, bodhisattvas perceive all suffering as happiness. Finally, as explained in the *Meeting of Father and Son Sūtra*, they will attain the meditative concentration called "traversing all phenomena with ease."[202] This is how the *Extensive Commentary* explains it.[203] Therefore, through practicing forbearance with minor discomforts, we train ourselves to bear major discomforts later on.

Next is the detailed explanation. [6.15–18ab] The commentaries connect the lines "Snake bites, insect bites, hunger, thirst, a painful skin rash, and so forth—do we not see them as unimportant irritations?" with the statement "Now, to present minor sufferings that one could become habituated to . . ." That said, it is better to read these lines in the sense of "on encountering these, it is appropriate to cultivate forbearance." Furthermore, [the text says] we should not be too squeamish about cold and heat, rain and wind, travel, sickness, imprisonment, and beatings. We should not fail in our forbearance. Otherwise, our hurt and suffering worsen. Some people, upon seeing their own blood, become heroic and steadfast, while others fall apart and faint even when they see the blood of others. These two reactions depend on the state of mind, which is either steady or fearful, respectively. Both are results of habituation.

The summary is this: [6.18c–6.19ab] By the power of habituation, we will learn to disregard all harm, and suffering will not perturb us! Wise people remain completely serene, unmoved, and unperturbed in the face of suffering.

Next is bringing to mind the positive qualities of suffering. [6.19c–6.21] We must wage many battles against the afflictions, and when fighting battles, one gets hurt many times. However, those who transcend the pain of these injuries will overcome the enemy—namely, hatred and the other afflictions. Those who win the battle against these enemies are heroes. As for the [conventional warriors], killing other people is like killing what is already dead and is a pointless act. Suffering has another positive aspect: it shakes us and makes us humble. Compassion arises as the wish that those who are burdened by suffering in cyclic existence will be freed from it. We will avoid the cause [of suffering], negative actions, and will joyfully engage in virtue, the antidote.

## [Forbearance through Gaining Certainty in the Dharma]

This has three parts, overcoming anger against those who harm us, abandoning false reasoning, and summarizing the section. The first, in turn, has three parts: (1) Since those who harm us lack autonomous power, it does not make sense to be angry with them, (2) refutation of an autonomous aggressor, and (3) the summary. The first point is threefold: they lack autonomy, they do not have the intention, and the summary.

The first, that [those who harm us] lack autonomy, is as follows. [6.22–23] We might think, "I am angry because my enemy brought suffering upon me." However, bile and phlegm and other [physical conditions] are also major sources of various sufferings, yet we are not angry at them. Why are we angry only with sentient antagonists? We might respond, "Bile and so forth are physical conditions that afflict us without having any autonomy. Therefore I do not get angry." But all those negative people only hurt us because they themselves are being controlled by the afflictions. And those afflictions arise without being wanted; they are the product of circumstances and impose themselves. Like diseases, they come although nobody wants them.

Second, [those who harm us] do not have the intention. [6.24] We might think, "Bile and other physical conditions do not intend to afflict us, but antagonists do. Therefore I am angry." But people do not decide, "Now I will get angry." They become angry simply because of the conditions they are in. Those conditions, likewise, do not decide "Now we will provoke anger"; anger simply arises due to them.

Third is the summary. [6.25–26] Since neither autonomy nor intention is at play, we can conclude that, firstly, all those faults—the afflictions and the whole range of evil actions committed under their influence—are products of conditions, not of some autonomously acting agent. Secondly, the various conditions that bring about all those faults do not have the intention "We will produce this result or this disaster." And the results produced, too, do not think that a [dominant] condition has produced them.

Next is the refutation of an autonomous aggressor. Here, the Sāṃkhya, the Naiyāyika, and others might object, "It is not true that all domination conditions [principal causes] lack autonomous existence. For as will be explained below, autonomous entities such as the primal matter, self, and so forth do produce effects, such as the hostile intent of the enemies and so forth."[204]

Refuting this is twofold: refuting the primal matter and self in general, and refuting a permanent self in particular.

The first is as follows: [6.27–28ab] That which is postulated as "the primal matter" and what they label "self" do not arise from a premeditated thought "I will now come into being in order to hurt someone." Why? Because they are themselves unborn. They are as unborn as the child of a barren woman. As for the logical proof: You have asserted those phenomena to be permanent and independent, for if they have arisen, they would then become impermanent and dependent on the influence of causes and conditions. The logical entailment is if all unborn phenomena are nonexistent, who can then desire to come into existence as an aggressor? There is no one. That is the logical conclusion.

Refuting a permanent self in particular has two parts: the refutation of the [self as] experiencer, and the refutation of the [self as] an agent that produces results. As to the first, [6.28cd] if it were asserted that the self enjoys objects projected by the primal matter, then that [self] that apprehends a single object like an enemy cannot attempt to cease, and thus such an apprehension would never cease to exist. This is because the perceiver who is exclusively engrossed in the object—the enemy, for example—is permanent. This line of reasoning is something accepted [by the Sāṃkhya]. The word "either" indicates that it cannot engage because it is permanent.[205]

Second is refuting the [self as] an agent that produces results. [6.29–30] The *Extensive Commentary* relates this to the refutation of the Nyāya assertion of a permanent self that is devoid of consciousness. Such a self cannot function as an aggressor either, because a permanent entity is inactive like space. To [say that] the permanent self came into contact with impermanent external conditioning factors, and these interacted with [the self] does not make sense, because its nature is unchanging. How will external factors bring about a variation that has not existed before? That is impossible. Similarly, even if the external factors could interact at the moment of acting, since the self cannot change from its previous state, how could it, by means of such factors, produce a variation that has not existed before? It could not, because change would disprove the state of permanence. To that, they say that those are the assisting agents of the self. But what relationship could there be between that which is assisted and the assisting agents, since no assisting agent whatsoever could interact with something permanent?

Third, the summary is as follows. [6.31] In this way, everything arises in dependence upon something else. And each previous condition arises because of another previous condition. None of them is therefore autonomous and independent. Since there is no prior ultimate, it is impossible to have an autonomous entity. Having understood this, we will not be angry with all those objects that appear like illusions but lack true reality.

Next is abandoning false reasoning. [6.32] [The opponent:] If all things are illusions without true reality, then which person or which antidote would fight against which anger? Combating [anger] too would not be tenable. [Response:] On the level of conventional reality, it is not at all unreasonable to speak of controlling anger and the ceasing the continuity of suffering based on anger. This is how Kṣemadeva and the *Exposition* read it.[206] The *Extensive Commentary*, on the other hand, reads this as a response to the objection "If everything depends on their conditions, then it would be inappropriate to control anger."[207]

Summarizing the section is as follows. [6.33–34] Therefore, when seeing someone act badly, be it enemy or friend, recall that the bad action has not been done out of autonomous power but is a product of conditions. In this way, our mind remains at ease and undisturbed. If we all [actually] had the means to fulfill our needs and wishes, then—since no one desires pain—all beings would be free of suffering.

## The forbearance of being unperturbed by harm

This has three parts: why it makes sense to have compassion for the perpetrator of harm, why it makes no sense to be angry with the perpetrator, and why the reasons for being angry are illogical.

The first is as follows. [6.35–38] These perpetrators of harm, due to their heedlessness—that is, because of their afflictions—injure their own bodies with, for example, thorns and other [sharp things]. In their pursuit of women and wealth, they withstand hunger and fasting. Some people hang themselves or jump off cliffs; some ingest poison or toxic substances. Through their unethical conduct, they bring long-term harm onto themselves. Since the power of their afflictions causes them to hurt what they cherish most—themselves—why would they not abuse others? It only makes sense to have compassion for people who are driven by their afflictions in such ways that they commit suicide or other [unwholesome acts]. Even if we cannot arouse compassion [for them], what would it gain us to be angry about them? It would make no sense.

Next, why it makes no sense to be angry with the perpetrator of harm has two parts: examining the nature of the aggressor, and examining the harm in terms of one's own fault. The first is twofold: investigating the character, and investigating how the harm is done.

Of these, the first is as follows. [6.39–40] Now if it is the nature of the childish ordinary people to hurt others, it would be illogical to be angry with them, just as it would be wrong to be angry and enraged with the fire whose nature is to burn! If, however, people's harmful behavior is a passing fault and they are naturally good-natured, then again it would be wrong to be angry. This would be analogous to being angry with the sky, whose nature is absence, for being filled with smoke!

The second is investigating how the harm is done. [6.41] If the enemy harms me by using an object such as a stick or a weapon, it would make sense to be angry with the object, since it is what actually hurts me. Now, say I am angry at the enemy because he wields the weapon, but since the enemy too is driven by anger, I should be angry at both, the enemy and his anger.

Examining the harm in terms of one's own fault has three parts: how one has caused harm to others, how it is the fault of my own body, and how it is the fault of my own karma.

The first is this: [6.42] Previously, I injured living beings in just the same way. Therefore it is just that the one who caused distress to other beings must experience aggression in return.

The second is how it is the fault of my own body. [6.43–44] The enemies' weapons and my [attachment to my] body are both the causes of suffering, which is the karmic [result]. They grasped their weapons; I grasped my body—so when I am wounded, where should I direct my anger? They are equally causes. I have become blind because of attachment to this human body, which is [only a source of] pain, sensitive like an open wound, unable to bear being touched. As my eye of wisdom has been obstructed, I have clung to [this body], and that has brought forth all those hurtful situations. With whom should I be angry when [this body] is hurt? It makes no sense to be angry with others.

The third point, how it is the fault of my own karma, is as follows. [6.45–46] Like a fool, I try to avoid suffering by multiplying its causes—through negative actions and attachment to [my] body. Since it is me who does these two things, and my pain comes from the fault of grasping, why should I resent someone else when harm arises? Consider the analogy of those creatures whose private hells with their hell guards and infernal forests of razor leaves are really the product of their own actions! Likewise, all aggressive events are really produced by my own karma. With whom should I become angry? It makes no sense to be angry with anyone.

Why the reasons for being angry are illogical is as follows. [6.47–51] My own actions whose karmic result is to experience aggression are the reason that I encounter aggressive situations. My assailants will end up in hell for it. Is it not I who is actually harming them? It is indeed. In fact, aggressive people give me the opportunity to cultivate forbearance, yet through me they incur a lot of negative karma.[208] They will proceed to the hell of interminable agony because they assaulted me. Really, it is I who am harmful to these enemies, and they who bring me benefit! Then, evil mind, why are you distorting the facts and becoming angry at them? You get angry for no reason.

"In that case," you might ask, "since I have been the condition for others to commit negative karma, wouldn't I too go to hell?"

[Answer:] "If you have a positive quality of mind—namely, forbearance—you will not go to the hells."

If you think, "So the aggressors and I are fundamentally equal. What makes the difference that they will go to hell and I would not?" There is indeed this difference: your positive state of mind is what protects you from the hells.

Now if the thought occurs, "Since the two cases are alike in causing harm, this differentiation of one leading to hell and the other not is untenable." [Answer:] This is tenable, because it is the quality of my mind that has protected me from hells, while in their case such a protection did not come about.

"In that case," one might think, "my forbearance protected me from the hells but not the enemy, who brought benefit. This would mean that I either have no gratitude or lack compassion." [Answer:] It is true that my forbearance could not protect them [from the hells], but even without my forbearance, what could protect them? Now, if I were to harm them in retaliation, my negative karma would greatly increase, and I would never be able to protect them. I would fail in the fourfold conduct of a paragon of virtue.[209] In this way, therefore, the supreme fortitude, forbearance, would be undone.

## Controlling anger toward those who commit humiliation, harsh words, and ill repute against me

This is threefold: (1) humiliation and so forth cannot harm me, (2) it is illogical to be angry because that will obstruct my material gains, and (3) it is illogical to be angry because people will lose respect for me.

The first is as follows. [6.52–54] Getting angry at my adversary for hurting me mentally or physically is, first of all, meaningless, because the mind lacks a physical form and therefore cannot be destroyed by any weapon or any person. However, because the mind clings to the body, taking it to be real, the body's pain has the power to cause hurt. When [the body] is hurt, I feel hurt, both physically and mentally, and I cling to that. As for disrespect, abusive language, or unpleasant comments—they do not even hurt me physically. How then could they harm the mind? Why then, mind, do you get angry? I might think that, by disrespecting me, others have the power to make me unhappy. But since it cannot devour or harm me in this or future lives, why is it that I shun this disrespect?

The second, it is illogical to be angry because that will obstruct my material gains, is threefold: the negative karma of anger weighs heavily, material possessions have no intrinsic value, and refuting the notion that they possess intrinsic value.[210]

The first is as follows. [6.55–56] "I do not want disrespect and so forth directed against me, because when others disrespect and mistrust me, it gets in the way of my material success." Whoever thinks like that should consider this: Even if I am successful in acquiring material wealth in this life, it will be lost, because I cannot take it into future lives. Yet being angry for its sake, I have created a great deal of negative karma, and that will persist until I experience the result. Therefore it would be better to die right now with no material gain than to have a long life lived improperly by harming others. Even if I live here for a long time, I will never transcend the suffering of dying; and after death, I will suffer the full karmic result of my improper livelihood.

The second is that material possessions have no intrinsic value. [6.57–59] We might live a hundred years of happiness in a dream, but then we wake up. Another person may have just an instant of joy in their dream before waking up. The dream happiness is equally lost for both once they are awake, and it will never return. Likewise, whether we die after a long life or a short one, the happiness we have experienced in the past will never come back. It is finished as well. Of the material possessions that we have heaped up and enjoyed for these many years, we cannot carry the smallest thing into our future life when we die. Instead, we will be like a person stripped naked by robbers. Powerless, destitute, and empty-handed we must go. For all these reasons, material possessions have no true value.

Third is refuting the notion that they possess intrinsic value. [6.60–61] "By means of my material possessions, I will live a long life complete with all opportunities, according to the idea:

> As long as I live a long life of Dharma practice,
> I will increase the stream of my virtue.[211]

I will then exhaust my negative karma and increase my merit. Thus acquiring material possessions does have a purpose, and whoever interferes with that deserves my anger." [Answer:] If gaining wealth entails aggression against those who cause problems, is it not rather that [your] merit will be exhausted and your negative karma increase? Therefore, if you think that your aim in life is to gain merit, why lead a life wherein you do nothing but evil? It makes no sense.

The third point, it is illogical to be angry because people will lose respect for me, is as follows. [6.62–63] "I become angry at people who, with their offensive words, destroy the trust that others have in me." If you say that, then why do you not become angry in the same way when they speak ill of others? For, from this, people's respect for others will be damaged as well. Think, "It is the case indeed that people's respect for others or lack of it depends on whether others possess positive qualities [to merit such respect]. Since I am able to tolerate others' lack of respect for other people, why can I not tolerate when others speak ill of me? After all, this too depends on the arising of afflictions [in those who speak ill of me]."

## Controlling anger in relation to the four misdeeds against my loved ones

This has two parts: how there can be no harm with respect to [certain] objects, and controlling anger toward those who harm the vulnerable.

The first is as follows. [6.64] Even if Buddha statues, objects of worship [such as stupas], or the sacred Dharma are being desecrated, even if they are being ill treated or spoken about in inappropriate ways, it is not right to hate the aggressors or shun them from our compassion. After all, buddhas cannot be damaged in any way, whereas aggressors need our compassion.

Second, controlling anger toward those who harm the vulnerable is threefold: being certain of the Dharma, being fearless toward aggressors, and cultivating the forbearance of accepting suffering.

The first is as follows. [6.65] Even those aggressive toward my teachers, relatives, friends, or others act in dependence on factors, just as it was explained above [in verse 6.31]: "Everything arises in dependence upon something else." Understanding this, I should curb my wrath.

Being fearless toward aggressors is threefold: (1) being angry toward an antagonist is not right; (2) therefore, giving up anger against them; and to that end, (3) giving up attachment. The first, in turn, has three parts: (1) it is comparable to being injured through inanimate objects, (2) it is just as wrong as the faults of the aggressors, and (3) since it arises from having done harm, it is not right to be angry with antagonists.

The first point is as follows. [6.66] Having a body entails getting injured by both living beings [who possess consciousness] and inanimate objects [which do not possess consciousness]. Why single out living beings and resent them? Instead I should simply bear the injury.

The second, it is just as wrong as the faults of the aggressors, is as follows. [6.67] Antagonists do wrong out of delusion. Others, just like myself, react with anger out of delusion. Who among them is blameless? Whose actions are wrong? They are both equally at fault.

Third, since it arises from having done harm, it is not right to be angry with antagonists. [6.68] Why did I do those actions in the past, which are now the cause of those injuries I receive from others? Since all painful experiences depend on my own actions, why should I direct my anger at the antagonists?

Next is therefore giving up our anger against them. [6.69]. Having seen that all harm is produced by [one's own previous] actions, I will do everything so that people renounce their mutual anger and develop a loving mind. To that end, I will observe a virtuous path and invest all my effort into it.

As to giving up attachment, [6.70–71] consider this analogy: When a house has caught fire and the flames threaten to spread to the next house, the reasonable action is to remove the hay and other [flammable material] that would spread the fire and put it far away. Similarly, when I desire things, my mind fills with attachment. Any circumstance that interferes with that fuels my anger, which is like the fire that, once ignited, completely burns down the house of our merit. Fearing this might happen, I should immediately reject any kind of attachment the moment [it arises].

Cultivating the forbearance of accepting suffering is as follows. [6.72–75] "If a hostile person hurts me badly, I will not be able to practice forbearance," I might think. But consider this: If a man condemned to death instead has his hand cut off and his life is spared, is he not lucky? He is indeed! Likewise, am I not lucky to be spared from hell by accepting this much human suffering and by cultivating forbearance? And if I cannot tolerate even this small measure of suffering now, why do I persist in my anger, which is the cause of [future] infernal torment? Stopping it would be the right thing to do. For each thing that

I crave, each desire that I gratify, I have experienced hell a thousand times—because of my anger. Here, the *Extensive Commentary* reads [the line in terms of] "because of my anger."[212] And despite enduring such suffering, I have benefited neither myself nor others. However, the suffering when accepting this harm will clear away the hurt of all beings. Joy is the only appropriate response to it.

### Controlling anger in relation to the four good things done to my enemy

This has three parts: controlling my anger about the praises they receive, controlling my anger when they are happy, and controlling my anger about their success. The first is threefold: (1) they [praises for my enemy] should be embraced because they could be causes of my own happiness, (2) they should not be rejected since they are causes of others' happiness, and (3) they show how I am confused about what to adopt and what to reject.

The first is as follows. [6.76–77] If it is unbearable for you, O mind, that other people praise my opponents, saying that they have many talents, and that others then rejoice in these talents, then you are simply mistaken and should practice forbearance. Why should I not also praise my opponents and feel joy like those others who praise them? The happiness that I experience when I delight in others' qualities and praise them is, in fact, an impeccable source of happiness. It is the virtuous way that all the buddhas and [bodhisattvas] practice. It is also the best way to attract people, since they recognize that I am free from envy and jealousy, and they therefore develop confidence.

The second point is that they should not be rejected since they are causes of others' happiness. [6.78] I might think that praising others only brings happiness to *them* and I don't want them to experience the joy of being complimented. But if that is so, then I should also stop paying wages to my employees, because that also brings them joy. But if I behave like this, it will only cause loss: in this life I lose my employees, and in the next life I will not experience the [karmic] result of generosity.

Third is they show how I am confused about what to adopt and what to reject. [6.79] When my qualities are being praised, I relish that praise, but when the compliment is paid to others, I resist rejoicing. This reveals, therefore, how I am confused.

Next is controlling my anger when they are happy. [6.80] I have cultivated the mind of awakening with the aspiration to make all beings happy. Why would I be angry at them when they do not need my help but find happiness on their own? That would not make sense.

Controlling my anger about their success has two parts: it is inappropriate to become angry at others for having achieved success, and it is inappropriate to be angry at others for my not having achieved such success. The first, in turn, is twofold: (1) anger is inappropriate because my own wishes are being fulfilled, and (2) anger is inappropriate because I am not getting hurt.

The first is as follows. [6.81–83] If I made the pledge "May all beings become buddhas, honored by all beings in the three realms," why then am I in agony when I see them receive some slight honor? Consider this analogy: Imagine that you have relatives who rely on you and to whom you are obliged to give food and material support. Then those relatives release you from that obligation because they acquire the means of livelihood themselves. It would be like being unhappy about this and becoming angry at them. If I cannot rejoice when others receive even small temporary honors, how can I possibly wish them to attain awakening? Kṣemadeva explains the line as "If you do wish these [honor and so forth] for *your adversaries . . .*"[213] How could someone become angry about the good fortune of another person while [simultaneously] cultivating the awakening mind? They do not go together.

Second, anger is inappropriate because I am not getting hurt.

[6.84] Whether an adversary receives a donation from a sponsor or the sponsor keeps it for himself, in neither case will it be mine. It is the same to me, given or withheld. Therefore whether that grant is blocked or awarded is not my concern, and it is meaningless [to think about it].

Next, it is inappropriate to be angry at others for my not having achieved such success. [6.85–86] I might be angry that my adversaries receive donations when I very much want donations for myself. But consider this: the causes for receiving such gifts are my previously [accumulated] merit, the faith of the sponsors, and any qualities I possess at present. Why would I destroy all these through hostile behavior? Since it is I myself who is not securing the causes for my success, shouldn't I be angry with myself? Not only that, but in addition, I might think, "If I do not manage to get that [donation], no one else should receive it either." But consider this: The reason that I do not succeed is my own past negative behavior. And yet, not only do I not feel regret for that, but I even wish to compete with those who have behaved in meritorious ways in the past and have thereby earned the causes for receiving donations. Such an attitude is totally inappropriate.

## Controlling anger against those who obstruct my attainment of what I desire

Controlling my anger against those who obstruct my attainment of what I desire has two parts: causing misfortune to my adversaries, and controlling anger against those who obstruct my own success and that of my loved ones. The first is twofold: the misfortune of my adversaries does not benefit me, and wishing misfortune on them only harms me.

Of these, the first is as follows. [6.87] Suppose an adversary is unhappy and experiences suffering. Why would I delight in it? Even if it gave me satisfaction, my mind's mere wish to subdue my enemy does not actually harm him. Therefore gloating is meaningless.

Second, wishing misfortune on them only harms me. [6.88–89] Even if my rivals were indeed harmed through my wishes, how would that bring me joy? "When I see them [suffer], I feel satisfaction!" one might say. But is anything more ruinous than that? Seized definitely by the relentless hook that is the wish for others to suffer cast by the fisherman—the afflictive motivation behind my karmic act—I will be flung by the wardens of hell into copper cauldrons, where I am certain to be boiled to death.

Controlling anger against those who obstruct my own success and that of my loved ones has two parts: controlling anger against those who obstruct my worldly concerns, and controlling anger against those who obstruct my merit.

## Controlling anger against those who obstruct my worldly concerns

The first, in turn, is twofold: (1) those who prevent my gaining praise and who ruin my reputation are not evil, and (2) I should see them as helpers. The first has two parts: praise and reputation bring neither spiritual nor temporal well-being, and it is pointless to be overjoyed by [praise].

The first is as follows. [6.90–93] Praise, good reputation, and fame do not bring about the merit that would be so helpful in the future. These things do not cause greater happiness in this life either. They do not strengthen my body, protect me from sickness, or bring about relaxation and well-being. If I examine their advantages and disadvantages, I conclude that they do not bring about any real benefit for myself. "Well, they produce a little bit of satisfaction in the mind," one might say. But whoever wants this kind of superficial pleasure can just as well gamble, drink, or enjoy the other sex. All of it is simply pointless. For the sake of gaining a reputation as a magnanimous benefactor, people squander their wealth, and for the sake of becoming a hero, they join the army and get themselves killed in war. I might do all manner of wrong actions [to elicit praise], but what use are words in the end? Whom will that fame please when I am dead? Nevertheless, my mind becomes unhappy when I do not get praised or when my reputation is damaged. It is like children who cannot help crying when their sandcastles come crumbling down. It does not make sense.

Second, it is pointless to be overjoyed by praise. [6.94–97] Since a brief sound of praise does not have consciousness, I cannot assume that it is that [sound] that praises me. It makes no sense to feel joy about [a sound]. [One might protest,] "No, [I am happy] because there is another person who is happy about me and praises me. That person's joy is what causes me joy." But even if it is my rival who compliments me, how can the joy of the one who expresses the compliment benefit me in any way? That joy is theirs alone. I cannot obtain even the tiniest part of it. I might say, "Since I am a bodhisattva, I rejoice when the person who praises another is happy." But if that were the case, then I should rejoice in the happiness of all beings in the same way. When others, my rivals included, are made happy through the joy [of receiving praise], why am I not happy then, too? It would be right to feel happy. Therefore to become overjoyed about being praised by others does not make sense. It is pointless. It is nothing but a child's folly.

Next, I should see them as helpers. [6.98–101] Praise, fame and the like distract the mind from focusing on virtue. They sabotage my revulsion with saṃsāra and my fears. They cause me to envy other people's qualities and to get angry about their success. This is how the *Extensive Commentary* and the *Exposition* explain it.[214] Vairocana, on the other hand, reads the line as "My anger will destroy the prosperity of others as well."[215] Therefore people who conspire to destroy my good reputation are in truth working to save me from falling into hell, where I would surely go because of my negative actions. Therefore I should not be angry with them. In addition, material gain and honors are obstacles that keep me trapped while I am striving to be free from saṃsāra. I do not need them. If someone undermines them, and thereby helps free me from saṃsāra, why would I be angry with them? While my negative actions [for the sake of gain and honors] want to take me straight to hell, obstacles act like a blessing of the buddhas, for they bar the door and prevent me from going there. How could I be angry with them? Getting angry does not make sense.

## Controlling anger against those who obstruct my merit

This is threefold: anger is the obstacle to merit, perpetrators of harm are conducive factors, and I should therefore control my anger and be respectful.

The first is as follows. [6.102–3] "This rival makes it impossible for me to do good deeds," I might think, but it does not make sense to get angry at those who create problems when I want to do good. No spiritual practice generates good as much as forbearance. Shouldn't I just remain patient then? That would be the right thing to do. And it is thanks to my rival that I can practice it. If I cannot be patient with my rival, it is my own fault, since I alone created that problem when the opportunity for doing good through the practice of forbearance was offered.

Second, perpetrators of harm are conducive factors. [6.104–5] When a result does not occur if a certain factor is absent but does occur when that factor is present, then that factor is indeed its cause. Therefore, when I am engaged in the practice of forbearance, how could an adversary be a hindrance to the [generation of] good? An adversary is in fact its cause! Consider this analogy: At a charity event, beggars are the cause for giving; one would not see them as an obstacle [to your generosity], just as it would be inappropriate to describe a preceptor who confers the vows of renunciation as a hindrance to renunciation. That would not make sense.

The third point, I should therefore control anger and be respectful, has three parts: I should be respectful on account of sentient beings' own qualities, I should be respectful out of faith in the buddhas, and I should be respectful based on examining the effects.

### I should be respectful on account of sentient beings' own qualities

The first, in turn, is twofold: honoring them because they help me attain buddhahood, and honoring them through establishing them as being equal to the buddhas. The first has two parts: the reasoning why they should be respected, and refuting any potential confusion about it.

The first is as follows. [6.106–8] Beggars and adversaries are similar in that they serve as causes for generating positive karma. However, while beggars are numerous in the world, people trying to hurt me are rare. That is because nobody would want to harm me if I had not harmed them in the first place. But the kindness of adversaries is actually the greater kindness because the positive karma generated through forbearance is greater [than through generosity]. Therefore it is as if a treasure had arrived in my home without any effort from my side. My rivals are my helpers for training as a bodhisattva and, thereby, for attaining buddhahood. Consequently, I should be happy about them. In addition, since my rivals contributed to my accomplishment of forbearance just as much as I did, they are equally its cause. They therefore deserve that the reward, the nectar of sacred Dharma, is conferred on them first, because it was they who elicited my forbearance.

Second is refuting any potential confusion about it. [6.109–

11] "This rival did not intend for me to achieve forbearance," one might think. "He might well be its cause, but he deserves no honor." If so, the sacred Dharma, which is the cause for accomplishing virtue, should not be honored either. "That is not comparable. The Dharma is without harmful intentions, while my rival did want to hurt me. There is no reason to honor him." How could I achieve forbearance if I dealt only with people who strive for my well-being, like a doctor, and give me no reason to be patient? Since forbearance arises as a response to hostile intentions, the cause of forbearance really is my rivals. Like the true Dharma, they are worthy of veneration.

Honoring them through establishing them as being equal to the buddhas has two parts: citing scripture and establishing its meaning. The first is as follows. [6.112ab] Our virtue grows because of beings. That is, buddha qualities arise from both the field of beings and the field of the conquerors. The Sage stated in the *Perfectly Gathering the Teachings Sūtra*:

> The field of beings is the field of the buddhas. From this field of the buddhas, one obtains all the attributes of the buddha. So one should not engage wrongly with such [a field].[216]

The second, establishing its meaning, has two parts: the main argument, and refuting others' objections. The first is as follows. [6.112cd–6.113] I might want to argue that the truth of the quoted statement cannot be established through reason and that I do not believe it. However, there is supporting evidence: Numerous [practitioners] have reached excellence by way of serving beings, thereby attaining perfect buddhahood. This shows that one obtains the final result, the buddha qualities, just as much through ordinary beings as through the victorious ones. Yet I insist on honoring the victorious ones but not beings. Why is that so? It does not make sense.

Second, refuting others' objections: [6.114–18] One might object, "The two do not have the same qualities, and therefore it is not appropriate to pay them respect in the same way." The two are not being cast as equal in their states of mind or qualities; they are posited as equal in that they both produce the result, buddhahood. Therefore, since ordinary beings, just like the buddhas, possess the virtue of giving rise to buddhahood, the two are equal. Likewise, with respect to the manifest merits of honoring those in whom the meditative concentration of lovingkindness has arisen, such merits cannot manifest without their object, which is sentient beings. Having faith in the buddhas generates merit, too, and that exemplifies the greatness of the buddhas.

In sum, because of this one equal aspect—namely, the ability to bring out buddhahood—ordinary beings are equal to the buddhas. However, the buddhas possess infinite oceans of qualities, whereas ordinary beings only possess few. In this respect, they are not equal. But if we make offerings to one single ordinary individual who, without possessing an entire range of supreme qualities, engenders [in us] a mere glimpse of a buddha quality, then even the three realms would be an inadequate [offering for that person]. Thus, even if the qualities are not the same, it is right to honor living beings because they have a share in bringing out the very best buddha qualities [in us].

## I should be respectful out of faith in the buddhas

This has two parts: the Teacher embraces sentient beings as his own, and the Teacher identifies them as himself. The first, in turn, is twofold: why it is appropriate to be respectful, and rectifying the error of being disrespectful.

The first is as follows. [6.119–23] There is yet another reason for being respectful toward living beings. The buddhas and bodhisattvas give immeasurable help to all beings and act without deceit. What better way to repay them could there be than working toward beings' contentment? In fact, there is no better way. Some [bodhisattvas] sacrifice their bodies or enter the hell of Avīci for the sake of others. To repay the kindness of their helping behavior, I will treat beings only in beneficial ways and do them nothing but good with my body, speech, and mind. I will do so even if they are hostile toward me. Moreover, now that sentient beings are my lords, for the sake of whom [bodhisattvas] pay no heed to their own body, even giving it away, how can I ignore this and treat beings with arrogance rather than goodwill? When someone is happy, the sages are pleased, since it fulfills their wishes. When someone is harmed, they are displeased. By bringing joy to beings, I will please all the sages, and by offending them, I am obstructing the sages' wishes, thereby offending them, too.

To explain this by means of an analogy, a person whose body is completely on fire will find no satisfaction in any of the sensual pleasures he normally desires. Likewise, if I harm sentient beings, there is no way to please the great compassionate ones.

Second is rectifying the error of being disrespectful. [6.124–25] I have caused suffering to beings and, thereby, sorrow for all those who have great compassion. Therefore I confess this negative behavior today, and I pray to all those sages that I have disappointed and beg their forbearance. From now on, to honor the tathāgatas, I am determined to never again harm beings but to become a servant to the world. May I delight the protectors of the world by not harming others, even if streams of people place their foot upon my head or strike me down.

Next, the Teacher identifies with them as himself. [6.126] Since all those whose very nature is compassion have realized the equality of the dharmadhātu [of all beings] and have practiced the exchange of self and other, they consider all beings to be themselves and have no doubt about it. And who are those who realize the very essence of beings? It is the protectors, the buddhas. Why would I not have respect for them? Respecting them is appropriate.

## I should be respectful based on examining the effects

This is threefold: (1) demonstrating that making beings happy is the cause of all good things, (2) pledging to put all my effort into [making others happy], and (3) the summary.

The first is as follows. [6.127] Making beings happy is what pleases the tathāgatas. It is the very thing that fulfills my own goal. It is what dispels suffering in all the worlds. Therefore I will devote myself to it forever.

The second is pledging to put all my effort into [making others happy]. [6.128–32] Consider the analogy of a king's official who tyrannizes a lot of people. Understanding future negative and positive consequences, farsighted individuals will not respond with aggression, even if they have the power to do so. Remember, that official is not acting on his own accord, without any support; he acts on behalf of the king's power. Similarly, I will not treat even a minor aggressor scornfully, because they are merely acting on behalf of the hell guardians and of the compassionate ones. By retaliating with harm, I will displease these. Just like subjects honor their king even if he punishes severely their smallest crimes, I will honor all beings. Can that king, even in his greatest wrath, inflict the kind of hellish suffering that we experience from not making beings happy? No, he cannot. On the other hand, even if I venerate him, he cannot grant me buddhahood, but that is, however, achieved by making beings happy. This analogy demonstrates that with respect to both benefit and harm, there is no comparison [between displeasing or pleasing a king and sentient beings].

The third is the summary: [6.133–34] Bringing happiness to

beings will accomplish future buddhahood. Not only that, even in this life, good fortune, fame, and well-being will come. How can I not see this? In addition, for as long as I remain in saṃsāra, by practicing forbearance with other beings, I will enjoy beauty, health, a good reputation, and much more. I will then enjoy a very long life and the exalted happiness of a universal monarch.

> Embracing suffering thanks to the hidden kindness
> of perpetrators of harm—this is a cause of great joy.
> When examined, there is no object of anger or one who is angry.
> O intelligent ones, let not anger burn your mind.

This concludes the explanation of chapter 6.

# 7. Diligence

THE CHAPTER on diligence has two parts: first, an exhortation to cultivate diligence linked to the foregoing passage and, second, the actual explanation of diligence, the object of cultivation.

The first is as follows. [7.1] Thus those who have developed forbearance in the [aforementioned] way should then cultivate diligence. Awakening will dawn in the diligent and remain in them. However, for those who lack diligence, the causes of awakening—merit and wisdom—will not manifest, just like there would be no propulsion [via a sail] when there is no wind.

Second, the actual explanation of diligence, the object of cultivation, has three parts: defining diligence, countering the opposing factors, and fortifying the antidotes.

The first is as follows. [7.2a] What is diligence? It is enthusiasm for virtue and the actions that it brings forth.

The second, countering the opposing factors, has two parts: (1) explaining laziness, what is being countered, [and (2) countering laziness]. Of these, the first is as follows. [7.2bcd] To explain laziness, the antithesis of diligence, there are three types: *indolence* opposes virtue through lack of engagement, *indulgence in unhelpful behaviors* pursues those that are either negative or merely not virtuous—just neutral—and the *despondency* of self-contempt thinks "I cannot cultivate virtue."[217]

The second, countering laziness, is threefold: countering indolence, countering indulgence in unhelpful behaviors, and countering despondency.

## Countering indolence

This has two parts: identifying the causes, and relinquishing these causes. The first is as follows. [7.3] Our idleness leads us to a mental state where we have no wish to put effort into good actions. We experience pleasure in doing nothing and get attached to that. Sleeping many hours, we crave even more sleep. Preoccupied with our cravings, we become inured to the sufferings in cyclic existence. This is how laziness arises. Alternatively, we could read this, as in the *Extensive Commentary*, as "Inured to the sufferings of saṃsāra, we experience the comfort of idleness, and that leads to craving for sleep."[218]

Relinquishing these causes has two parts: setting the intention to be diligent, and applying it in practice. The first is twofold: contemplating this life to be transient, and contemplating the suffering of future lives. The first, in turn, has two parts: contemplating the certainty of death, and urging oneself through contemplating that one will die soon.

The first is as follows. [7.4–6] [As if addressing yourself, contemplate:] "Snared by the trappers, the afflictions, you have been caught. Under their influence, you have walked into the trap of birth, landing in the jaws of the Lord of Death. Why have you still not understood? Have you not witnessed that death is killing all your kin, one by one? You are seeing it again and again. And yet you keep sleeping, and you do not cultivate any wholesome behavior. Such a person is stupid like a buffalo slumbering beside its butcher, only to find itself next in line to be slaughtered. Having blocked all the paths of escape, the Lord of Death now has his eyes on you. How can you enjoy food, sleep, or entertainment?" The [*Garland of*] *Birth Stories* says:

> All paths are sealed by the Lord of Death.
> Yet there are people who, unsuspecting,

indulge in all kinds of entertaining diversions.
How strange that they are not afraid![219]

The second, urging oneself through contemplating that one will die soon, consists of a brief presentation and its elaboration. Of these, the first is as follows. You might think, yes, death is indeed certain, but I will think about cultivating virtue when death is near. Here, *Letter to a Friend* says:

If life has many adversities and is more transient
than even water bubbles blown by the wind,
amazing indeed it is that we inhale after exhaling
and awake after falling asleep![220]

[7.7] In light of this, death's swift approach, gather the accumulations [of merit and wisdom] until the very moment when death arrives. When you actually encounter death, you might then wish to give up your apathy, but you will no longer be capable of practicing virtue. Overcoming your indolence at that time will be pointless.

Second is its elaboration. [7.8–10] You say, "I have not yet finished this task, that one I just started, and this one I have only half finished," but suddenly the Lord of Death has arrived. "Oh no, I will be taken away by death!" And you think, "My relatives, shocked by the realization that we will be separated, have swollen red eyes and tears running down their faces. All hopes that I may stay alive are crushed. Meanwhile, I see before me the messengers of the Lord of Death, who will take me to the hell realms. I am in agony thinking of my negative actions. Hearing the sounds of screaming from the hells [tells me] that this is where I am headed." Out of terror, you soil yourself. Unable to control yourself, excrement covers your body, and you are deranged by pain. Which good deed can you do then? None at all!

Next is contemplating the suffering of future lives. [7.11] You are afraid of the moment of death at the end of this life, twisting in agony like a live fish dropped on hot sand. What need speak of the unbearable sufferings of hell that you are bound to experience later on, as a result of your negative deeds? You are right to be afraid of that, for it is appropriate, as stated in the following:

> If simply seeing a painting or hearing about the hells,
> thinking or reading about them, and depicting them in art
> induces terror, what need is there to speak of
> actually experiencing them as the fruition [of one's
> karma]?[221]

[7.12] There [in the hells] you will experience the intense pain of having molten metal poured over your soft-skinned body. You have committed actions that will arise as such hells—how then can you remain so relaxed? [7.13] You have no diligence for virtue, the cause, yet you expect to reap the result of happiness? And though you are sensitive and easily overwhelmed, a lot of misery is bound to fall upon you. All those people wishing to live long as gods, although death already reaches out for them, will have to face their unwanted ends. Overcome with suffering, they cry out in self-pity.

As to applying [the intention to be diligent] in practice, it is as follows. [7.14] This human life is the boat you should use to cross the mighty river of suffering! It will be hard to catch another boat. Hey, fool, this is the time for training in diligence—do not spend it sleeping! Ponder this image and overcome all aspects of laziness!

## Countering indulgence in unhelpful behaviors

[7.15] The infinite joy of the sacred Dharma is supreme, yet you neglect [accumulating] the causes of this joy. Instead, you get distracted in mental and physical stimulation, which are the causes of suffering, or in cracking jokes, singing, and other distracting verbal behavior. How do you find these enjoyable when their enjoyment is so pointless?

## Countering despondency

This has two parts: a brief presentation and its elaboration. Of these, the first is as follows. [7.16] Just as kings are victorious when they possess four attributes,[222] bodhisattvas who seek to gain victory over the objects of elimination, too, first need the armor-like diligence free of defeatism. Then they need gather the four arrays of power, which will be explained below, and after that they need dedication to actually engage in the acts of rejection and adoption through mindfulness and meta-awareness. Next they need to master their three doors through the power of the antidotes, and then they should practice the equality of self and other and the exchanging of self and other.

The second, its elaboration, has two parts: (1) applying the antidote against the cause of despondency, the thought that I have no capacity, and (2) applying the antidote against the condition of despondency, [the thought] that it is difficult to cultivate diligence. The first is as follows. [7.17–18] "How could I possibly achieve buddhahood?" Do not think in such defeatist ways! The Tathāgata, who declared only the truth, spoke these true words: "By rousing the power of their diligence, even those who were flies, mosquitoes, bees, or worms have attained the unsurpassed enlightenment so hard to reach." The *Questions of Subāhu Sūtra* states:

> Furthermore, bodhisattvas train themselves perfectly in the following manner: "If even lions, tigers, dogs, jackals, vultures, cranes, crows, owls, worms, insects, flies, and mosquitos can awaken into the state of unexcelled buddhahood, how could I, a human being, fail to apply the diligence needed to attain awakening, even if it costs me my life?"[223]

The *Teaching on Dreams Sūtra* says:

> No matter how small one's qualities may be,
> if protected by altruistic resolve, one will attain
> enlightenment."[224]

The rationale for this statement is the fact that all beings possess the spiritual potential of buddhahood. In general, of the two types of spiritual potential, the *naturally abiding* potential consists of the mind's ultimate nature, while the *transformational* potential refers to the virtuous propensity imprinted upon the mind due to the purification of any kinds of stains. The *Sublime Continuum* states:

> Since the perfect body of awakening radiates,
> since suchness is indifferentiable,
> and since they possess the lineage, all beings
> are always endowed with buddha essence.[225]

[7.19] I have been born believing in a self, yet I belong to a spiritual lineage, and I am able to recognize positive and negative actions. If I do not abandon the bodhisattva's way of life, how could I not obtain awakening?

The second, applying the antidote against the condition of despondency, [the thought] that it is difficult to cultivate diligence, has two parts: there is no cause for discouragement, and there is actually cause for enthusiasm. The first point has two parts: abandoning the fear that the practice is difficult, and preventing weariness because of the length of time involved. The first is twofold. Of these, the first, *stating the false notion*, is this: "One might think, 'Since I must sacrifice my feet, hands, or other [limbs] for the sake of [bodhisattva practice], I am indeed frightened.'"

The second, *countering this [false notion]*, is twofold: countering this through appreciating its relative context, and countering it through familiarization. The first is as follows. [7.20c–7.21] "Not having examined the difference between what is significant and what is insignificant, you are confused about what to adopt and what to reject. You should extinguish your fear. Even without your practicing austerities for the sake of awakening, you have endured countless times the suffering of having your body cut up, pierced, burned, split open, and much more over the countless eons of your wandering in saṃsāra. And yet, none of it has brought you awakening. [7.22] The hardships you suffer for the sake of accomplishing awakening are few in comparison, and therefore you will be able to endure them. For example, you are able to bear the pain of an incision made for the sake of getting rid of a splinter."

[7.23] All doctors use treatments that entail discomfort to heal diseases. Likewise, we need to endure strenuous austerities. To conquer the many sufferings of the lower realms, we should endure the small discomforts associated with practicing the austerities. [7.24] And yet the Buddha, the best of doctors, does not [even] use such ordinary painful healing methods. His treatments are gentle: through easy practices, all the major diseases—that is, the defilements—will be thoroughly eradicated. Both Prajñākaramati and Vairocana[226] read these [verses] as saying that those on the beginner's stage should not engage in the austerity of giving away one's body.

Second is countering [this false notion] through

familiarization. [7.25–26] "If I have to give away my own flesh and [bones], how could that be called a gentle treatment?" [Answer:] The *Guide* gives instructions for people who lack previous familiarization. At first, give only small objects of little value, such as vegetables and the like. Through familiarization, later on, you progressively acquire the capacity to give even your own flesh. Once thoroughly habituated, when you understand your own flesh to be just like a vegetable or any other object, an attitude devoid of attachment dawns. What hardship can there be, at that point, in donating your own flesh and [bones]?

Preventing weariness because of the length of time involved is as follows. [7.27–28] You might think, "I will have to practice austerities for the sake of others for as long as cyclic existence lasts, and I feel miserable at the prospect of that suffering." This is not correct. We will have no physical pain since we will have abandoned negativity, and the mind will never be joyless, because we understand the natural state of all knowable things. In fact, it is wrong conceptualizations, such as the understanding that the self truly exists and the attachment that results from that, as well as negativity that produces suffering and harms our body. Not only will we remain unharmed by suffering, we will feel physically at ease because of our merit and mentally happy because of our wisdom. How then could compassionate people such as these feel miserable about remaining in cyclic existence for the sake of others?

Next, there is actually cause for enthusiasm. [7.29–30] Through the power of their awakened mind, these bodhisattvas exhaust the causes of suffering—that is, their previous negativity—and collect an ocean of merit, which acts as the cause of their happiness. For these reasons, they are said to be superior to all the śrāvakas. As Prajñākaramati and Kṣemadeva[227] explain this point, they will attain enlightenment quicker than śrāvakas. "Therefore, rousing the horse of bodhicitta that clears away all forms of weariness and conveys us from happiness to happiness, what intelligent person who knows the difference between faults and virtues could feel despondent?"

## Fortifying the antidotes

This is twofold: a brief presentation and its elaboration. Of these, the first is as follows.[228] [7.31–32] To accomplish the welfare of beings, we need forces to overcome the enemies, the target of our elimination. Here, although the text has the word *determination* (*mos pa*), the *Extensive Commentary* glosses "*aspiration* refers here to the wish for virtue,"[229] and the lama Pang Lotsāwa says that the Indian text, in fact, has the word *aspiration* (*'dun pa*) here.[230] Therefore we should understand that in this present context, wherever the word *determination* (*mos pa*) is found, this should be understood as referring to *aspiration* (*'dun pa*). Furthermore, [the "forces" include] having the *aspiration* to do good; doing it with *self-confidence* without regressing; deriving great *joy* from that; and [practicing] *letting go*, which means giving up anything when there is a great need. As for the *dedication*, it is generated through fear: the fear of having to experience the pain resulting from our negative actions. It also comes from reflecting on the benefits of dedication. Having overcome its opposite, apathy, in the way described, we should invest all our energy into increasing our diligence. By which means should we do so? By gathering the previously explained "forces": *aspiration*, *self-confidence*—that is, steadfastness—*joy*, and *letting go*, and through the powers of *dedication* to the norm of adopting and rejecting and *self-mastery* over the body and mind.

The second, its elaboration, is threefold: building up the forces, bringing dedication, and gaining self-mastery. The first [building up the forces] is fourfold: [the forces of] aspiration, self-confidence, joy, and letting go.

## The force of aspiration

The first, in turn, has three parts, the faults of lacking aspiration, the benefits of aspiration, and engendering it through showing its causes. The first is threefold: (1) we fail to engage in the activities we aspire for, (2) the reasons why this is the case, and (3) the faults of lacking aspiration for the Dharma and how it should not be given up.

The first is as follows. [7.33–36] "Because I have generated bodhicitta, the mind of awakening, I must overcome my faults and those of others, countless though they might be. Destroying each individual [fault] will take an ocean of eons, and I should maintain my endeavor just as long. Yet I have not even begun putting the smallest effort into overcoming those faults. Since I am to experience this immeasurable suffering, why does my heart not burst? Similarly, I must acquire many good qualities, both for my own sake and for the sake of others. Each of those qualities requires long training over an ocean of eons, and yet I have not trained even a fraction of any quality. It is shocking indeed that I am leading this hard-won life so meaninglessly."

The second is the reasons why this is the case. [7.37–38] The phrase "I have . . ." Vairocana says answers the question "In what way am I rendering this life meaningless?"[231] The *Extensive Commentary* interprets this [phrase] in a different way, with the following. "I have failed to worship the buddhas, failed to delight people by hosting a great feast, failed in my duties toward the doctrine, failed to fulfill the wants of the destitute, and failed to give fearlessness to the fearful. In sum, I have failed to enact the three kinds of generosity, which are giving the Dharma, material goods, and fearlessness."[232] Prajñākaramati and Vairocana[233] state that "duties toward the doctrine"[234] refers to offering temples. "Not only did I neglect to offer happiness to those struck by misfortune and misery, all I achieved was causing suffering and pain to my mother while in her womb. I have not lived up to the purpose of [my life with its] leisure and opportunities."

The third is the faults of lacking aspiration for the Dharma and how it should not be given up. [7.39] "Lacking aspiration to practice the Dharma, now and in past lives, I have brought this unhappy situation upon myself." This is how the *Extensive Commentary* reads. What intelligent person would neglect the Dharma?

Next, the benefits of aspiration are as follows. [7.40ab] That the root of all virtuous deeds is aspiration is stated in the *Questions of Sāgaramati*: "All virtuous deeds have their root in aspiration."[235] And in *Display of the Qualities of Mañjuśrī's Buddha Realm*, the Sage states:

> It is the condition of all teachings,
> for they abide with the root of aspiration.[236]

Engendering it through showing its causes has three parts: a brief presentation, the elaboration, and the summary. The first is as follows. [7.40cd] "How do we generate such an aspiration?" [Answer:] At the root of aspiration is the continuous contemplation of the fact that we will experience the full result of each and every good and evil action.

The elaboration is twofold: a general presentation of positive and negative karma and their effects, and an explanation of effects of specific forms. The first is as follows. [7.41–43] Karmic results include physical pain related to the five senses, mental unhappiness, various fears, and the inability to fulfill our wishes. The cause that brings about all these is our negative behavior. On the other hand, if our thoughts and intentions motivate us to act in wholesome ways, then no matter where and how we are reborn, that merit will reward us with its results. If we wish for happiness while acting in unwholesome ways, then the weapons of suffering will attack us wherever we go as a consequence of that negative behavior. The *Advice to a King* explains:

> When the time comes for you, O King, to pass away,
> none of your property, loved ones, relatives, or friends can follow.
> Wherever individuals might depart to,
> their karma follows like a shadow.[237]

The second, an explanation of effects of specific forms, is twofold. Of these, the first is *the effect of a specific form of virtuous karma.* [7.44] Instead of being born from a confined, smelly, and hot womb, we will rest within the heart of a spacious, fragrant, and cool lotus. Instead of feeding on phlegm and blood, we will receive the extraordinary food of Dharma teachings, eloquently presented by a victorious one, through which great dignity develops. Instead of being born through a painful narrow passage, the light of that extraordinary buddha will open the lotus, from which we step out in an exquisite body. Instead of being nursed by ordinary beings, we will live in the presence of the extraordinary Vairocana and other victorious ones, protected by their Dharma. In sum, being born as the Buddha's children[238] endowed with such extraordinary qualities is the fruit of ordinary and extraordinary good deeds.

The second is *the effects of a specific form of negative karma.* [7.45] Our own deeds will produce the Lord of Death's minions, who will torture us by flaying our skin and pouring searing-hot molten copper over our bodies. Then they pierce us with blazing swords and pikes, chopping off hundreds of bits of flesh, which drop onto the red-hot iron ground. This is the result of having repeatedly committed grave negative deeds, such as the crimes of [the five acts of] immediate retribution.

The summary is as follows. [7.46ab] Therefore we will nurture our resolution to be virtuous and aspire to virtue. We will respect the principle of adopting virtue and discarding evil. With confidence, we will cultivate the practices of adopting and rejecting.

## The force of self-confidence

This has two parts: initiating engagement, and stabilizing what has been initiated. The first is as follows. [7.46cd] In the sixth dedication of Vajradvaja in the *Flower Ornament* collection, it says:

> O scion of the gods, the sun, for example, is not prevented from shining by external hindrances such as a person's blindness or the obstruction of a mountain, but it shines on all kinds of objects. In the same way, bodhisattvas appear for the sake of others. They are not turned away by anybody's faults but will bring others to maturity and liberate all receptive trainees.[239]

So, through the rite taught therein, we should cultivate self-confidence, thinking, "I am capable of accomplishing the roots of virtue I have initiated." [7.47] At first, before engaging in an activity, we should assess whether we have the capacity to bring it to a successful end. If we do, we begin it; if we do not, we should not start it. If we do not have the capacity, not beginning is better than turning back once we have begun. [7.48] If we back out, it will lead us to develop the habit of not honoring our promises in future lives, too, as the karmic result in accordance with the action's cause. Such behavior leads to negativity and to the fully ripened result of increasing suffering. Having given up once, future opportunities of beginning wholesome activities and of experiencing their result are lost as well. In the end, [opportunities] will not arise and thus cannot be accomplished.

The second, stabilizing what has been initiated, is twofold:

a brief presentation and its elaboration. The first is as follows. [7.49ab] We must build self-confidence in three areas: those of wholesome actions, the overcoming of afflictions, and our abilities in these [two tasks].[240]

Its elaboration is threefold. Of these, the first point is *self-confidence in action*. [7.49cd] Self-confidence with regard to wholesome actions manifests by thinking "I will take it upon myself to carry out all wholesome actions [necessary to] benefit self and others." This is self-confidence regarding wholesome actions. [7.50] Such an attitude is grounded in the insight that people are overpowered by their afflictions and therefore lack the ability to benefit themselves or others in this world. These beings lack the force to do all those beneficial actions for the sake of self or others. It will therefore be my task to do everything [possible] to benefit self and all others. [7.51] This attitude might, however, lead us to think "I will not do ordinary work." We might want others to do menial tasks such as carrying heavy loads and refuse to associate ourselves with such ordinary work. That would be a mistake. If we think "This work is beneath me. I am an important person," and we arrogantly refuse to do it, this only reveals our arrogance,[241] which we are better off without. It needs to be given up.

The next point, *self-confidence regarding our abilities*, is fourfold: the appropriateness of developing such self-confidence, the nature of this curative form of pride, criticism of the pride that is to be relinquished, and praise for this curative form of pride.

The first is as follows. [7.52] To illustrate, when met with a dead snake, even a crow might carry on contemptuously, as if it were a garuḍa! Similarly, when we lack self-confidence in our own abilities, even a small degree of infraction can undermine us. We will thus be discouraged with respect to eliminating the afflictions. [7.53] With despondency, giving up making active effort, how can liberation ever come from such impoverishment? However, if we practice an attitude of self-confidence and build up our diligence, it will be difficult for even major adversities to overpower us. [7.54] Therefore, with a firm mind, we will eliminate all faults. If we let our own faults defeat us, our wish to be victorious over the triple world would be laughable.

The second point is the nature of this curative form of pride. [7.55] We will maintain the form of pride where we think, "We, the bodhisattvas, the children of the Victorious One, lion among men, will triumph over all adversities. No adverse situation whatsoever will defeat us."

Third is criticism of the pride that is to be relinquished. [7.56] Based on their education and other qualities, some people are filled with an arrogant self-confidence that overpowers them. They are actually afflicted, not self-confident. Self-confident people are not defeated by enemies, whereas those afflicted are under the sway of the enemy arrogance. You might wonder, where does this mistake lead? [7.57] Inflated by the afflicted form, pride will lead you to the lower realms. Even if you are born human, your joy will be ruined because the mind will never be happy. You will become a slave of others just to get food. You will be feeble-minded, you will have an ugly appearance and a weak body, [7.58] and others will constantly despise you. Ascetics puffed up with arrogance are full of afflictions, so they too are included among the arrogant ones. What need is there to say that they are objects deserving of compassion?

The fourth point is praise for this curative form of pride. [7.59] Those who wish to defeat the enemy of arrogance need to take hold of the curative type of self-confidence. Such people will be truly self-confident, successful, and brave. They will fully overcome the rising enemy of arrogance so as to perfectly accomplish beings' short-term wishes as well as their ultimate aim—the final state of the victorious ones.

Next, *self-confidence in overcoming the afflictions* is this. [7.60] When we find ourselves on the side of the afflictions—that is to say, amid a mass of afflictions—we should withstand [the afflictions] in a thousand ways by applying the antidotes. Like a lion stands unharmed in a crowd of foxes and other animals, we will not be affected by a mass of afflictions. [7.61] Even when we are in danger, overflowing with great fear and other intense afflictions, just like a person takes care of their eyes, squinting to protect them, we will take care of ourselves. That means, we do not become overwhelmed by those afflictions. This is clearly how it reads in the translation of the root text. However, Prajñākaramati and Kṣemadeva[242] read the [first two] lines as "Even amid great suffering, just as the eyes do not perceive taste," interpreting the lines to state that "likewise, in situations of danger, we should not be overwhelmed by afflictions." [7.61(a)][243] It would be better for us to be burned to death or to have our head cut off than to ever bow down to the enemy, those ever-present afflictions, and get overwhelmed by them. In some texts, there is the statement that these two lines—"Similarly, in all situations,/ I will do nothing but what is appropriate"—to be also by the master. This is a difficult matter to analyze, so I feel it is better left as it is.[244]

## The force of joy

The force of joy consists of a brief presentation and its elaboration. First [the brief presentation]. [7.62] People who enjoy games wish to find happiness through playing. With that same kind of longing, we should take up the virtuous activity of bodhisattvas, whose every deed is wholesome. Without ever feeling satisfied, we will joyfully engage in this work.

The second, the elaboration, has three parts: (1) it is right to behave virtuously because its essence is happiness, (2) the fruit of happiness is what one should not be content with, and (3) therefore we should engage [in the bodhisattva conduct] with joy.

The first is as follows. [7.63] Worldly people work hard for their own happiness, even though there is no guarantee they will succeed in finding it. Moreover, if their actions are not the kind that results in happiness or are happiness in themselves, how could they become happy? The *Extensive Commentary* explains these lines in these terms: "How could we become happy if we are not doing the very actions that lead to future happiness and are instead chasing other forms of pleasure?"[245]

Second, the fruit of happiness is what one should not be content with. [7.64] If we can never get enough of sense pleasures, which are like honey on the edge of a razor blade—providing little benefit but bringing great disadvantages—then how could we ever feel that we have had enough of the merit that ripens into the result of happiness—namely, higher rebirths in the short term and ultimately peace, nirvāṇa?

Third, therefore we should engage [in the bodhisattva conduct] with joy. [7.65] So that the tasks we have initiated are brought to successful completion, we should engage in our virtuous activities with joy, like elephants plagued by the heat of the summer's noonday sun who dive into a lake.

## The force of letting go

The force of letting go is twofold. Of these, the first is *letting go temporarily when one does not have the ability*. [7.66] When our strength weakens, we should put our task aside, since in that moment, we do not have the energy to finish our work. To build up some energy once again, we should put the work aside temporarily.

The second is *letting go permanently when tasks have been completed*. [7.67] This means that if, after properly completing the first task, we wish to accomplish the next task and the one after that, one more excellent than the other, then we must leave that first task behind us.[246]

## Bringing dedication

Bringing dedication through the forces[247] has three parts: bringing dedication to [applying] the antidotes, relinquishing the faults, and engaging in the activities that accord with this [twin task of applying the antidotes and relinquishing the faults].

The first is twofold. Of these, the first is *embracing conscientiousness with dedication*. [7.68] Just like when old, experienced fighters meet the enemy on the battlefield, they skillfully avoid the enemy's swords but strike out against them, similarly, we should guard against the weapons of our afflictions while resolutely attacking them so that they cannot harm us ever again.

The second is *applying mindfulness with dedication*. [7.69] When a fighter drops his sword in the middle of a battle, in fear he will pick it up immediately. Similarly, when we drop our weapon of recollection—which means, when we forget to apply the antidotes—then we should recollect our fear of the hell realms. In this way, we immediately retrieve the weapon of recollection.

Relinquishing the faults is twofold. Of these, the first is *ensuring that no faults arise* [*in the first place*]. [7.70–71] When a poisoned arrow pierces our body, the poison spreads, transported by the blood, throughout the whole body. Likewise, a small evil that finds an opening will progressively spread and permeate our entire mind. If we were forced to walk a slippery path carrying a jar filled to the brim with mustard oil while a sword-brandishing man stood before us threatening, "Spill one drop and I will kill you," we in our fear would concentrate hard. Ascetics keep their vows similarly, and we must control our mind in just the same way.

The second is *counteracting it when faults do arise*. [7.72] Even tiny mistakes can cause serious harm. Therefore, as quickly as we would leap up if a venomous snake were to glide into our lap, we should fight back when sleepiness, idleness, and the like arise. Therefore if, despite our efforts, we commit a small fault, at each such occurrence, we will reflect extensively that such failure will not occur again, no matter the circumstance.

Next is engaging in the activities that accord with this [twin task of applying the antidotes and relinquishing the faults]. [7.73] We should think about how to prevent wrong actions from happening and how to counteract those that have already happened. In such situations, we resolve to make it our habit to remember the antidotes. Such thinking will lead us to meeting spiritual teachers. "Appropriate tasks," according to the *Extensive Commentary*, means implementing the instructions of such [a teacher], rising up from infractions, and to that end, having the willingness to undertake the necessary restorative tasks.[248]

## Gaining self-mastery

Gaining self-mastery is as follows. [7.74–75] Even before we engage in any kind of virtuous activity, we ensure we have all the resources to act with joyful energy. To do so, we need to recall the instructions on how to practice conscientiousness. Then we will "rise lightly," which means we apply ourselves with great enthusiasm. What do we need to do for this? Just like the to and fro of the wind has the power to move the cottonwoods, the joyful energy of our wholesome intentions will give us the power over body and speech. We will engage in wholesome actions, and all will be accomplished.

This completes the explanation of chapter 7.

# 8. Meditation

THE CHAPTER on meditation has three parts: (1) an exhortation to cultivate meditative absorption linked [to the foregoing passage], (2) renouncing unconducive factors, and (3) cultivating discipline, the antidote. The first is as follows. [8.1ab] Once we have developed diligence through the methods for settling in equanimity, such as listening, reflecting, and so on, we should stabilize the mind in meditation with single-pointed focus. This is as stated in the following in the *Compendium of Training*:

> Cultivate endurance and seek learning;
> then go and live in the woods.[249]

## RENOUNCING UNCONDUCIVE FACTORS

The second is twofold. Of these, the first is *a brief presentation*. [8.1c–8.2] What will happen if we do not rest in absorption? People with distracted minds are held between the fangs of the afflictions and will be quickly overwhelmed by them. How then do we get rid of distraction? When body and mind are in seclusion, distraction does not arise. So we should abandon this worldly life's hustle and bustle; that is physical seclusion. Ridding ourselves of thoughts of desire and so on leads to mental seclusion.

The second, *its elaboration*, has two parts: renouncing the mundane world, and discarding [extraneous] thinking.

### Renouncing the mundane world

This has two parts: renouncing distracting activities because of their shortcomings, and seeking a place of solitude because of its qualities.

### Renouncing distractive activities because of their shortcomings

The first is twofold: developing the attitude of renunciation, and applying the methods that help renounce.

The first is as follows. [8.3] Because we are attached to people and because we crave material possessions and other things, we do not abandon worldly life. However, wise persons, desiring to give up the afflictions, thoroughly abandon these attachments and cravings. We should act like them. *Ornament of Mahāyāna Sūtras* says:

> Based on abiding in a perfect way,
> the mind is placed on the mind
> and thoroughly discerns phenomena—
> this is tranquil abiding and insight.[250]

Accordingly, we should gain full mastery of tranquil abiding by resting one-pointedly in the nature of the mind. [8.4] Being perfectly endowed with tranquil abiding, we should unite it with insight, which is the direct realization of the ultimate nature of phenomena. Thereby the afflictions will be completely uprooted. We should understand this and first cultivate tranquil abiding, which cannot be achieved except through feeling deep joy about being free from attachment to the mundane world.

Applying the methods that help renounce has three parts: giving up "inner" attachment to people, giving up attachment to external material possessions, and giving up attachment to unachievable work for others.

## Giving up "inner" attachment to people

This has two parts. The first is *the faults of attachment.* [8.5] We are impermanent, and we get deeply attached to equally ephemeral family and friends. However, this attachment will prevent us from seeing those we love for a thousand lifetimes, because our bad actions will only lead us to undesirable destinies. [8.6] When we cannot see them, we lose all joy, and with an unhappy state of mind, we are unable to rest in a balanced, concentrated state. But even when we are able to see them, we never feel it is enough. Just like before, our longing for them torments us terribly. [8.7] Our attachment to beings veils our mind, preventing any insight into the truth of reality. Our sense of renunciation fades away. [8.8ab] We end up being tormented by the pain of separation, doing nothing but thinking about them. Meanwhile time goes by without us practicing any wholesome action. Our lives are spent meaninglessly.

The second, *the faults of the objects of our attachment,* is twofold: the childish are not to be attached to and relied upon, and how to interact with them when the context is right. The first has three parts: a brief presentation, the elaboration, and the summary.

The first is as follows. [8.8cd] Because of impermanent objects such as friends and relatives, we lose that which is permanent—liberation—and the Dharma that is its cause. This is how Kṣemadeva reads [the lines].[251] [8.9] "The childish" can refer to the opposites of these three—the elderly, ārya beings, and learned ones. In this context, the reference is to the opposite of the latter two, and primarily the last one. If we resemble them [the childish] and behave like them, we will certainly go to the lower realms. What is the use of relying on childish people who have nothing in common with spiritually noble ones, who do not follow them and instead lead us in other directions?

The elaboration is twofold: we cannot benefit them, and they cannot benefit us. The first is as follows. [8.10–11] People are our friends in one moment but turn into enemies in the next. Even when we act in wholesome ways, which should bring joy, it only provokes their anger. It is very difficult to please ordinary people. When we tell them how helpful the Dharma is, they become angry and refuse to accept it. They even want to dissuade us, and if we do not accept what they say, they become aggressive, which only pulls them down to the lower realms.

Second, they cannot benefit us. [8.12–13] They feel envy toward their superiors, competitive with equals, and haughty toward inferiors. When we praise them, they become arrogant; when we criticize them, they become upset. When could there be any benefit from keeping company with childish fools? Not only is there no benefit, but surely all kinds of negative actions will follow. When befriending childish people, we will adopt from these childish fools self-aggrandizement, criticizing others, indulging in saṃsāra, talking about our attachment to it, and so forth.

The summary is as follows. [8.14–15a] Should we rely on such people as companions, it will only cause our ruin. They will not do us any good, nor will we benefit them. Therefore let us flee far from childish people. This is as stated in the *Garland of Birth Stories*:

> With respect to childish people, not hearing from them,
> not seeing them, and never speaking with them, and
> not experiencing the pain of disappointment from
> associating
> with them—such an excellent state is what I seek from
> you![252]

Next is how to interact with them when the context is right. [8.15b–8.16] If it happens that we meet people, we should show friendly behavior and respect. Without being overly affectionate, we should simply act normally. We should act without attachment or aversion. Just like bees take nectar from flowers without getting attached to them, we should take only what serves the Dharma—that is, what is conducive to meaningful conduct according to the well-spoken Dharma. We should treat everyone like first-time acquaintances, without encouraging familiarity.

### Giving up attachment to external material possessions

This has two parts: attachment gives rise to suffering, and the objects of attachment are meaningless. The first is as follows. [8.17] We may think, "I have obtained a lot and am well respected. Many people appreciate me." However, being conceited and proud like this will cause us to experience much fear after death. In the *Great Lion's Roar of Maitreya*, to be arrogant because of four things—one's material possessions, one's friends, one's houses for charitable giving to the poor, and one's learning and practice—is a cause for being born in the hells.[253] [8.18] Every little thing and every worldly gain that this obsessed mind craves and in which we get tied up will together rise up as suffering multiplied a thousand times. By "a thousandfold of this [object] and that [attachment]" means that "the material possessions and so forth become suffering as well as the causes of suffering"; so it is stated.[254] [8.19ab] Intelligent people therefore do not crave or get attached to anything, because it is from attachment that fear arises.

The second, the objects of attachment are meaningless, is twofold. First, *material possessions and so forth are transient.* [8.19c–8.20] This is the indisputable nature of attainments.

We need the firm determination to reject them, and we need to understand this from deep within. Many people have acquired a lot of property and have achieved renown and fame. In spite of that, nobody knows where they will go with their great gain and fame. In fact, as Śāntideva says, at the moment of death, it will be left behind.

Second, *it is inappropriate to be happy and unhappy for praise and criticism.* [8.21] Why should we feel flattered when some people praise us, given that others criticize us, which disturbs our joy? And why be unhappy about being criticized, since there are others who praise us, which counteracts [the criticism]?

## Giving up attachment to unachievable work for others

[8.22] People have various interests. Even the Buddha was not able to satisfy them all, as seen with the monk Sunakṣatra[255] and others. What to say then of a lowly person like myself? We should simply abandon the wish for relationships with worldly people. [8.23] "Why is it difficult to satisfy beings?" you might ask. It is because people look down on those who have no achievements but are unwilling to praise those who do. No matter what, they are not content. It is this nature that makes it difficult to relate to them. How, then, could they be content by relying on me? This is how the *Extensive Commentary* explains these [lines].[256] [8.24] Why should we avoid the company of childish people? Because childish people are discontented in all situations unless their own purposes are served by others. Since that is the case, the tathāgatas all teach that we should not befriend the childish. *Entering the Domain of the All the Tathāgatas* says:

> Just as one can never remain with joy
> if one is amid wild beasts,

likewise, one can never remain with joy
through befriending the childish.[257]

If you think that this contradicts the previous teaching on working exclusively for the benefit of beings based on the mind of awakening, that is not so. Previously, [Śāntideva] was teaching in the context of not hurting others but benefiting them. Here he is [teaching] from the opposite perspective. Those who are not [yet] capable of actually benefiting others but who practice virtue with the intention of benefiting others are not abandoning the benefit of others. Although we are not yet truly able to benefit others, if we practice virtue with that intention, we have not abandoned the *intention* of benefiting others. For it is stated:

Even if you lack power to engage in altruistic deeds,
you should always cultivate the intention to do so.
For in whom there is the intention,
such a person will engage in the deeds.[258]

## Seeking a place of solitude because of its qualities

This has three parts: developing enthusiasm for the place of solitude, renouncing the causes that make us lack enthusiasm for solitude, and the advice to seek such a place. The first is in relation to four things: companions [appropriate] in solitude, the site, the resources, and the state of mind to aspire for.

The first is as follows. [8.25] In a remote wood, the special companions—deer, birds, and trees—never speak in unpleasant ways. When may I live together with those in whose company I will be happy? In this way we should wish and pray.

The second is the site. [8.26–27] Residing in such places as caves, empty shrines, or beneath trees, free from the wish to return to my previous home and so on, when will I live without looking back, and without attachment to any [place at all]? Living in areas unclaimed by anyone, wide and naturally unconfined, a place where I will not rely on any other person but act on my own free will and without attachment—when will I live like that?

Third is the resources. [8.28] Living with just a begging bowl made from clay and few possessions for my daily needs, dressed in clothes no one else wants, taken from a rubbish heap, without regard for the body and without the need to hide possessions and body, when will I live without any fear?

Fourth is the state of mind to aspire for. [8.29] Occasionally roaming through the charnel grounds and observing the bare bones of others and this, my own body, which is ultimately subject to decay, when will I see them as equal?

Next is renouncing the causes that make us lack enthusiasm for solitude. [8.30] This body of mine, too, will rot. Its foul smell will be such that even jackals in search of flesh will not come near, even less so other [people]. This is how it is bound to happen. Therefore the body is not an object to which we should be attached. [8.31] This body appears to be a single entity. It is, however, pieces of flesh and bone that grew together and in the end will disintegrate. It is even more obvious that close friends and others will separate. Therefore we have to be free from [attachment] both [to self and to others]. [8.32] At birth, we are born alone; at death, we die alone. Our share of sorrow will not be carried by anyone else. What use have we of "friends" who hinder our virtuous deeds? Such friends and companions are of no benefit. [8.33] Like visitors who travel the roads, abandoning one place and reaching another, so are those who have entered the road of existence, abandoning one place of birth and reaching another. Since it is unpredictable how long this body and these companions will be with us, we should therefore discard all attachment to them.

The advice to seek such a place is as follows. [8.34] "Until the time when four men will carry my body from house to cemetery amid the grief-stricken laments of worldly folks, companions, and so on, I will remain in the forest, [the text] advises. [8.35–36] Why go to the forest? It is there I find nobody to befriend or resent. Therefore this body will remain alone in solitude. From the outset, my relatives will consider me dead. So when I actually die, I will cause pain to no one, and nobody will stay around to trouble me with their grief about my dying. Therefore I also cannot become unhappy by seeing the grief that I would cause. Nobody will distract me from recollecting the Buddha and from other virtuous activities."

Having explained these positive aspects, the advice is to dwell like this in a place of solitude. [8.37] Because of that, in these lush, beautiful, and pleasant forests, I will encounter few difficulties. Having pacified all the distractions related to the three doors, I will happily reside in solitude.

## Discarding extraneous thinking

Discarding extraneous thinking has two parts: a brief presentation, and the elaboration. The first is as follows. [8.38] Banish everything from your mind apart from virtuous intentions. As it says:

> Do not dwell on thoughts about one's own and others'
> faults,
> or what others have done or not done,
> but examine carefully whether or not
> you are in meditative equanimity.[259]

As a means to strengthen bodhicitta, place the mind in isolation. Set it in equanimity through tranquil abiding and train it through insight. Toward this goal exert effort.

The elaboration has two parts: developing disenchantment with [the objects of] desire, and generating a delight in solitude.

### Developing disenchantment with the objects of desire

The first is threefold: examining the effects [of lust] as terrifying, examining how the nature [of the desired one] is unclean, and examining how its causes bring harm.

The first is as follows. [8.39] In this world and in the next, lust leads to disaster. Here it is the cause for killing, bondage, and harm, and beyond, it brings hell and so on upon us. The *Prophecy of the Girl Candrottarā* says:

> The slaves of lust will be cut and chopped up;
> their head, eyes, legs, and arms will be cut and thrown away;
> through attachment sentient beings plunge into the hells;
> through attachment they go to the hungry ghost and animal realms.[260]

And the *Play in Full Sūtra* says:

> The faults of desire—I know them all without exception.
> Along with fighting and malice, it is the root of sorrow and pain.
> It is like the poisonous leaf of the Lord of Death.
> It is like fire, and like the blade of a sword.[261]

Examining how the nature [of the desired one] is unclean has two parts: examining it to be similar to a lifeless corpse, and examining how the living body itself is unclean. The first is sixfold. First, *it is not worth fretting about.* [8.40–42] When you want to meet a woman, you request many times, sending ahead messengers both male and female. To pursue your goal, you shun neither negative actions nor ill reputation. Throwing yourself into danger, even risking your life, and exhausting your material resources, the perfect embrace with her becomes supreme bliss. Those women are nothing to you but a pile of bones. They possess neither autonomous existence nor self. Why then crave them so ardently and be obsessed with them? This [obsession] will keep you from reaching nirvāṇa. The *Application of Mindfulness Sūtra* says:

> Women bring me to ruin,
> ruin in this world and in the next.
> If I want to help myself,
> I should totally abandon women.[262]

The *Extensive Commentary* states that this part pertains to others' women while the subsequent lines pertain to attachment to one's own wife.[263]

Second, *it is not worth viewing with attachment.* [8.43–44] A man goes to great pains to take a clear look at the woman's face for the first time, lifting and drawing it close—however, she gazes down in modesty. This refers to "before going to the charnel ground," according to the *Extensive Commentary*,[264] when others might not see the bride, since a veil or other covering conceals the bride's face. This is the tradition adopted by the dominant patriarchal system in the Central Land [in India]. The face that you fervently desired to see is now openly visible at the cemetery, revealed by the vultures. Seeing it now, why are you terrified and fleeing?

Third, *it is not worth jealously protecting.* [8.45] When other men laid eyes on her, you carefully guarded [her]. Why don't you protect that body [now], O miser, while the vultures tear at it?

Fourth, *it is not worthy of great devotion.* [8.46] If vultures and other beasts—jackals, wolves, and so on—devour this heap of flesh as soon as they see it, why would you offer flower garlands, sandal, ornaments, and such to their meal?

Fifth, *it is not worth touching with delight.* [8.47] If you are terrified when seeing her in the charnel ground as bare bones that do not even move, why were you not frightened when, in life, when she was like an animated corpse stirred into action?

Sixth, *it is not worth embracing with attachment.* [8.48] You wanted her when she was covered with skin. Why do you not desire her when not covered with skin? If you say, "Uncovered it is useless," what use did it really have when covered?

Examining how the living body itself is unclean has three parts: making its foulness evident, ascertaining through reasoning, and refuting the characteristics of purity. The first is twofold: attachment to what is characterized by impurity is illogical, and a critique of the deluded.[265] The first is threefold: refuting attachment to saliva, to touch, and to the flesh.

The first is as follows. [8.49] One might say, "I like a woman's saliva." But the same cause, food, generates both excrement and saliva as results. Why then, between these two, do you dislike excrement but you like a woman's saliva?

Second, refuting attachment to touch. [8.50] One might say, "I like the soft touch." But you take no special delight in touching cotton or a soft pillow, even though it does not stink. Why then do you become a fool of desire so deluded by filth? [8.51] Fools of desire, deluded and evil, would get mad at cotton, though soft to the touch, since they cannot sleep with it. Therefore do not crave touch, and cut your attachment to what is unclean. [8.52] If you have no attachment to unclean things, why do you coddle on your lap a cage of bones lashed together with sinew and plastered with the mud of flesh? [8.53] Your own body has plenty of filth. Enjoying it constantly, you also hanker after other bags of filth, [i.e.,] women. You crave filth. Why do you desire it so?

The third is refuting attachment to the flesh. [8.54–55] You might say, "I do not like [touching] cotton and such, but I do like the flesh." If you desire touching and gazing upon flesh, why do you not desire her inanimate flesh upon death? Now, if you say, "I do not desire it because it does not have a mind," that mind that you desire is without texture and form, and therefore it cannot be touched or seen. The body that you can touch and see is not the mind. Why do you want to embrace that meaningless body?

Next, a critique of the deluded. [8.56–57] It is not at all strange that you do not understand [how] filthy the natural impurity of another's body is. However, being filthy yourself and not understanding that is very strange. You may say, "Although some parts of the body are filthy, it has a very good color, shape, taste, and texture, and therefore I am attached to it." If you see it like this, why do you neglect the fresh lotus blossoms that open in the sunlight of a cloudless sky, no matter how pure they may be, while your filth-addicted mind enjoys a sack of crap?

Ascertaining through reasoning has three parts: ascertaining [the body's foulness] in terms of cause and effect, through its function, and through an analogy. The first is twofold: the actual point and a critique of attachment to it.

With respect to the first, that [the body] is the *cause* of impurity is as follows. [8.58] If you have no wish to touch a place smeared with filth such as excrement, why do you wish to touch the body from which it came?

It is also an impure *result*: [8.59–60] If you do not desire what is impure, why do you want to embrace in your lap that body that grew out of a filthy place? It was the seed in the mother's womb [conceived by] the semen and blood of father and mother and nourished by the mother's food. If you do not wish to touch a tiny filthy maggot that emerges from filth and excrement, why do you desire that body which was also born from, and is naturally full of, filth?

Next is a critique of attachment to it. You might think, "It may be like this, but I myself am also like this. Therefore why should I not desire it? It is like harmful spirits and the *torma*."[266] [8.61] It would make sense to dislike your own filth, but not only do you not despise it—you dirtbag who thirsts for foulness—you desire even the filth of others. That makes no sense at all.

As to ascertaining [the body's foulness] through its function, it is this: [8.62] Exquisite spices, substances such as camphor and the like, cooked rice, and vegetables are all pure. If, however, you put them into your mouth and spit them out again, even the ground becomes unclean and dirty. Since this is so, what can we say about the body?

Next, ascertaining [the body's foulness] through an analogy is as follows. [8.63–64] Although the filthiness of the body has been clearly demonstrated, if you still have doubts, observe the bodies flung into charnel grounds. When these are observed and analyzed being flayed, they cause a great fright to anyone who sees them. Even though you know that, why do you like it so damn much?

Refuting the characteristics of purity has three parts: (1) it is illogical to be attached to the body because of some extrinsic qualities, (2) its very nature is not something to become attached to, and (3) it makes no sense to enjoy it.

The first is as follows. One might say, "I am attached to the body because it has a good scent thanks to the sandalwood or other [perfumes] that have been applied," [8.65] The scent with which you anoint the body belongs to the sandalwood or other [perfumes], not to the body. Why is it, then, that through the scent of one thing you crave another? [8.66] If you are attached to a [good] scent, would it not be better to be detached from the body, whose natural smell is repulsive? You crave a meaningless worldly thing, and that is why you [must] smear ointments on it. [8.67] "Even if it does not naturally have a nice smell, with a perfume it acquires an attractive smell, and I am attached to that." That delicious perfume belongs to the sandalwood alone. From the body itself, what delicious perfume can arise? None! So why are you attached to something because of something else's perfume?

Second, its nature is something to become attached to. [8.68–69b] If you do not tend to the body, its hair and nails will become excessively long; the teeth will take on a yellowish color and a bad smell. It will be covered with smelly grime, its nakedness terrifying. Why exert yourself to clean this body when it is like polishing a weapon that will injure you?

Third, it makes no sense to enjoy it. [8.69c–8.70] Alas, due to bewilderment regarding the impurity of your own body, endeavors to clean and decorate it are meaningless. People who are maddened by afflictions pervade and convulse the world. If all of these people feel revulsion when they see bare skeletons in the charnel grounds, how could they be attracted to the charnel ground-like cities filled with animated skeletons roaming around? They should not.

Next, examining how its causes bring harm is twofold: a brief presentation and its elaboration. Of these, the brief presentation is as follows. [8.71] That unclean woman does not come without a price, either. For her, you have to make money. That will exhaust you in this life. And in future lives, you will suffer the pains of the hells and other realms.

The elaboration is twofold: there is no time to enjoy the [objects of] desire, and it entails other faults.

The first is as follows. [8.72] When you are a child, you are not able to earn the wealth that is needed for winning a woman. When you are in the prime of your life, since you have not yet found her, what will you enjoy? Then, while you accumulate wealth, life is drawing to its end. When you are old, what will you do with your desire? You are not able to satisfy it. [8.73] Some people, wretched in their desire, are worn out by working all day long. When they come home at night with broken bodies, they sleep like corpses. Thus they are not able to satisfy their desire. [8.74] Some people are forced to travel. Going to places far from home, they suffer. Although they desire it, they are not embraced by their families or even seen by them. How can their desire be satisfied?

Second, that it entails other faults, is sixfold. Of these, first, *one suffers physically.* [8.75] Wishing to fulfill their ambitions but ignorant about how to go about it, some, in order to support their wife and children, sell their bodies, losing all control over it themselves, and are exploited by others. [8.76] When their wives give birth, since they are without a home of their own, they [must] temporarily take shelter under trees and such, enduring [much] suffering. [8.77] Looking for a livelihood, some foolish people, misled by desire, think, "I will make a living by joining the army." Though fearing for their lives, they go to war, and for the sake of profit, they make themselves the slaves of others. [8.78] Thus one can see that, because of desire, covetous people have their bodies slashed, impaled on stakes, pierced by short spears, or burned to death.

Second, *it obstructs the opportunity for liberation.* [8.79] Since they hurt from the pain of gaining, losing, and protecting, they should know that possessions are the cause of limitless ruin. Those distracted by their attraction to possessions lose the opportunity for liberation from cyclic existence.

Third, *illustrating the disadvantages through analogy.* [8.80] Desirous people have lots of disadvantages, such as those explained above, and gain very little. This is like the oxen who snatch mouthfuls of grass while dragging wooden carts.

Fourth, *it wastes away a life of leisure and opportunity.* [8.81] For the sake of small ordinary things that are easy to accomplish, things that even oxen can obtain, they destroy their life of leisure and opportunity. The *Letter to a Student* says:

> By relying on the path of the Sugata, the guide of beings,
> humans can attain the powerful [awakening] mind,
> which is not achievable by gods, nāgas, or demigods,
> nor by garuḍas, vidyādharas, kinnaras, or mahoragas.[267]

As stated above, the qualities that enable you to attain awakening are excellent and difficult to gain. They are destroyed by those who, because of previous karma, suffer and are ignorant about what to adopt and what to reject, thus rendering [their life of leisure and opportunity] meaningless.

Fifth, *the suffering [through desire] would be meaningless.* [8.82–83] Desires by their very nature inevitably come to an end, yet their consequences plunge beings into the hells and the other lower realms. They are devoid of deep meaning, yet for their sake beings endure constant suffering, which causes great exhaustion and requires great exertion. Even a ten millionth part of that exertion would accomplish buddhahood itself. People with desire strain under greater suffering than those practicing the awakened conduct, yet the result is not awakening.

Sixth, *how the suffering entailed transcends analogy.* [8.84] When you reflect on the suffering of the hells and other [realms], which are the result of desire, then none of the analogies, be it poison, fire, abyss, or enemy, suffice to exemplify [the pitfalls of] desire.

## Generating a delight in solitude

Generating a delight in solitude has two parts. First, the brief presentation linked to the preceding section is this: [8.85ab] Feeling disgust for desire, we should generate joy for solitude.

The second, the explanation, has two parts. Of these, the first is *[identifying] the perfect factors [of solitude]*. [8.85c–8.86] In the middle of the forest, free of outer conflicts and inner afflictions, it is peaceful; we need not fear robbers or [other criminals]. Fortunate ones who possess the mind of awakening are like this example: A king walks about in a mansion perfumed with sandalwood, a serene palace with high stone walls, cool beneath the moonlight and the sandalwood trees. Cooling canopies [studded] with turquoise sway back and forth without making loud sounds; it is a peaceful place. Just like that [king] who, while residing [in his palace] with canopies swaying in the gentle breeze, contemplates the welfare of his subjects, the bodhisattva of good fortune walks about with the altruistic intent to bring about others' welfare.

The second, *the characteristic of joy*, is as follows. [8.87–88] Dwelling as long as we wish in empty houses, at the feet of trees, and in solitary places, we relinquish the suffering of hoarding and protecting our possessions. Not oppressed by hope and fear, we live with an open and free mind. To live autonomously, only according to our wishes, without attachment to any possession, not bonded to any being, and thereby enjoying the happiness of contentment—such a life even Indra is hard pressed to find. This is as described in the *Letter to a Student*:

> Adorned beautifully by [resplendent] full moon
> and its neck wrapped by great rain-bearing clouds,
> at the peak of such a forest mountain with no attachment
> at all,
> where one can move about with abandon like the wind,
> I seek the company of animals roaming free in the forest,
> where one is happy and one's experience filled with joy.
> Does such a joyful forest exist even in [the heavens] filled
> with goddesses and streams flowing gently over perfectly
> shaped stones?[268]

Since what was discussed earlier pertains to [the isolation of] the body and what is stated here pertains to the isolation of the mind, this is not a repetition.[269]

## Cultivating the antidote[270]

This has three parts: a general presentation linked to the preceding section, cultivating conventional awakening mind, and cultivating ultimate awakening mind. The first is as follows. [8.89] Having reflected on the qualities of solitude in this and other ways, and having completely pacified thoughts of desire and so on, we should cultivate awakening mind.

## Cultivating conventional awakening mind

This has three sections: equalizing self and others, exchanging self and others, and practices common to both.

## Equalizing self and others

Equalizing self and others has three parts: the advice to equalize self and others, the extensive explanation of what is to be practiced, and the summation.

## The advice to equalize self and others

The first is as follows. [8.90ab] Of the two awakening minds, the conventional and the ultimate, we should first cultivate [the conventional], making effort to equalize self and others. Without it, the genuine resolve to benefit others will not arise.

### The extensive explanation of what is to be practiced

This has two parts: the actual point, and the benefits [of the practice]. The first is threefold: a brief description, the explanation, and the summary. The first is as follows. [8.90cd] The subject being discussed is "all sentient beings." It is right to protect them the same way we do ourselves, because we are equal in desiring happiness and not wanting to suffer.

The explanation has two parts: we can generate the attitude of equality, and it is logical to generate such an attitude. The first is as follows. [8.91] Although [the body] has many parts—arms and legs and so forth—we consider it all to be a single body. They are one in that they must be protected. Likewise, although there are many different beings, they and I must be considered as one because we are one and the same in wanting to be happy and avoid suffering. [8.92] You may ask how we can reach such a conclusion, since I and others do not experience one another's pain. Although this pain of mine does not afflict another's body, we could say that the reason this pain is mine is because I cling and take it for my own, making it hard for me to bear. [8.93] Thus, even though the pain of others does not befall me, if I identify with it, their suffering becomes mine. By identifying with it, it becomes difficult to bear. This is how it is explained in the *Extensive Commentary*.[271] So the meaning is this: If I identify with others, the understanding that there is no difference between their suffering and my own suffering would emerge.

That it is logical to generate such an attitude is twofold: presenting the reasoning, and establishing the entailment. The first is twofold: (1) the equality of the objective, happiness and suffering [of self and others], and (2) the equality of the subject, the desire [to be happy and avoid suffering]. The first is as follows. [8.94] Take "the suffering of others" as the subject. "It deserves to be removed by me because it is suffering" [the reasoning], like, for example, my own suffering. "Other sentient beings," the subject, "are worthy of my help because they are sentient beings," like, for example, my own body.

The equality of the subject, the desire [to be happy and avoid suffering], is as follows. [8.95–96] In that both I and others are alike in wanting to be happy, what difference is there between myself and others? Why should I strive for my happiness alone and not for others'? Likewise, since both I and others are equal and alike in not wanting to suffer, what is special about me that I should protect myself and not others? The meaning is this: Since we are equal in our desire, we should not discriminate here with respect to what is enhanced and what is relieved. The *Extensive Commentary*, on the other hand, interprets this [verse] as part of the establishment of the entailment of [the reasoning in] the previous verse.[272]

Establishing the entailment has two parts: the actual point and the rebuttal of the responses. The first is twofold: (1) the consequence that one should not protect the other since distinct entities lack truly existing oneness, and (2) it is therefore logical to relinquish grasping at self. The first, in turn, has two parts.

Of these, the first is *the consequence that one should not protect oneself from suffering separated by time*. [8.97–98] One might say, "My own suffering affects me, and therefore I need to protect myself, whereas others' suffering does not affect me, and therefore I need not shield myself from such suffering." In that case, why do you shield yourself against the future suffering of the lower realms by eliminating its causes in this life? The logical consequence would be to not protect yourself from it, since it does not harm you in this [life]. If you think, "That [future] suffering will not affect me in this [life], but in the next life I will have to experience it, and therefore I am protecting myself," then you are taking the body aggregates of this life and of the next life as one and the same. That is wrong! Why? Because just like [the difference between others and myself], that which has died, [the body of] this life, is one entity, and that which is born, the next life's [body], is another entity. We also [become another person when we go] from the one moment to the next.

The second is *the consequence that one should not protect oneself from suffering separated by space*. [8.99] You may object that, when there is pain in one place, you protect exactly that place and not another. But in that case, if you have pain in the foot, why should the hand be concerned with it? Logically it would not need to, since [the pain] is not in the hand.

Next, it is therefore logical to relinquish grasping at self. [8.100] One might say, "Although illogical, I have gotten accustomed to clinging to a self here in this life. For that reason, I believe that in this life I have to protect future lives, that foot and hand mutually protect each other, and so on." [Answer:] Whether it concerns me or others, [suffering] is inappropriate and therefore needs to be abandoned by every means. So interpret the commentaries.[273]

The rebuttal of the responses is as follows. One might say, "Even though they appear to be separate, my present life and my future life are one continuum, and my foot and hand are one conglomeration. However, individual beings who [should] mutually protect one another are not one [continuum], and therefore they do not protect [one another]." [8.101] [Answer:] "What is called a *continuum* is [really] a series of many elements that form one thing; and what is called a *conglomeration* is many individuals forming one troop. These and other similar [constructs] are conceptual errors and cannot be ascertained to be truly existent as one [entity]." Again, one might say, "Or else, even though those objects and times are distinct [entities], there is only one central person that experiences it, and that should be protected." [Answer:] That pain-experiencing entity, whatever it may be, is nonexistent. Who then owns that suffering? [8.102ab] Suffering has no possessor who experiences it. No distinction of self and all others can be made with respect to it [suffering]. Therefore it does not make sense to discriminate about protecting from it based on whether the owner [of suffering] is the same.

The summary has two parts: the actual point and the rebuttal of the objections. The first is as follows. [8.102cd–8.103] Since it is suffering, others' suffering must also be cleared away. As they are similar, what is there to determine that I should clear away mine but not that of others? Those who wish to end [their] own suffering say, "Since suffering and sufferer do not exist, why should the suffering of all be averted?" You cannot argue in this way. Although it is right [that they do not exist], if my suffering is to be removed, it is right to remove all suffering. And for the same reason, if theirs is not removed, then it would be congruent that, like that of other beings, mine should also not be removed.

Next, the rebuttal of the objections. [8.104] "If, out of compassion, we identify with the pain of all others, we will suffer very much. Why then should we strive to generate compassion?" If we compare it to the suffering of beings in the hells and so on, how would our compassion be too painful? It is not much at all. [8.105] And even if there is a little bit of pain, if through such a single pain arising from compassion, the great amount of suffering of others can be cured, people with lovingkindness must engender such pain in themselves and others. [8.106] Thus Supuṣpacandra, knowing that the king would cause him harm, did nothing to evade his own suffering but went to the source of harm because, based on that, the pains of many would be ended. The *King of Meditations* says:

> At the time of the precious tathāgata Padmacandra, at a time when the teachings of the Conqueror were manifestly in decline, a monk called Supuṣpacandra lived together with seven thousand bodhisattvas in a forest called Samantabhadra. With his supernatural

> capacities, he saw that if he went to King Śūradatta's jeweled palace to teach the Dharma, many beings would reach higher realms and liberation, and if he failed to teach them, they would not reach them. He also knew that the king would kill him. Nevertheless he went there and fasted seven days, and then at night, he circumambulated the stupa that held the tathāgata's fingernails. The [next] day, he went to the palace, taught the Dharma, established a few trillion beings in awakening, and was then killed by the king. But the king, having regretted [his deed], built a stupa for his bone [relics] and venerated them.[274]

The benefits of the practice are as follows. [8.107] Those whose minds are trained in such a way in the equalization of self and other, whose happiness it is to soothe the suffering of others, will, when they see the opportunity, venture into Avīci hell as joyfully as geese dive into a lotus pond. You might say, "If liberation is great happiness, I should make liberation the object of my desire. The joy about others' welfare, however, is not great happiness, so why should I be invested in such joy?" [8.108] When beings are liberated from suffering, the ocean of joy will be limitless. Is that not enough? Seen from that angle, liberating myself alone will produce a kind of happiness that is insipid and without flavor. The commentaries explicitly contain the line "What would be the point of happiness without sweetness?"[275] It says:

> The state of tathāgata itself emerges incidentally
> for you who have actualized the nature of all beings.
> You who are beholden to others, your qualities
> I, a poet, have expressed here in a few words.[276]

[8.109] For all these reasons, although I work for the welfare of others, I will not be proud and indulge in self-admiration.

The welfare of others is my only joy. I am not even hoping for a resulting reward.

## The summation

The summation is this.[277] [8.110] If self and others are equal, it follows that I would develop a compassionate and protective mind for others just as I would protect myself from the slightest criticism. [8.111] "I do not have the strength to do that," we might think. However, we already manage to identify through strong habituation with something external to ourselves—namely, the drops of the father's seed and the mother's blood. Even though there is no entity of self in such substances, we relate to them as "I." If we extend this understanding, [8.112] why could we not identify with another's body and perceive it as our own through the power of habituation in just the same way? We are able to do so, affirms the *Extensive Commentary*.[278]

## Exchanging self and others

Exchanging self and others has a brief presentation and an extensive explanation.

The first is as follows. The *Extensive Commentary* reads [lines 8.112cd] as part of the section on *equalizing* self and others, in terms of "Just as one is able to perceive self and others, similarly, there would be no difficulty in considering my own as that of others."[279] But here, we explain these lines as part of *exchanging* self and others, which is the tradition of Kṣemadeva.[280] [8.113] In any case, once we perceive the "I," or that which we hold so dear, as being full of faults and see an ocean of good qualities in others, holding them dear, then we will lay aside all infatuation with ourselves and gain the habit of adopting other beings.

The second, the extensive explanation, has two parts: the defining characteristics, and the act of exchanging.

### The defining characteristics

The first has five subsections: (1) embracing others, (2) discarding one's own self, (3) the benefit and faults of taking either self or others to be the most important, (4) the disadvantages of not exchanging, and (5) the summation.

### Embracing others

The first is threefold: it is appropriate to engage in embracing others, it is inappropriate to turn away from embracing others, and the summary. The first is fourfold: the logic of embracing [others], one's capacity for embracing others, the positive qualities of doing so, and the instruction on how to do this.

The first point is [the logic of embracing others]. One might think, "Taking the numerous beings, who are all separate from one another, as one single self [as 'I'] does not make sense." And that seems logical. [8.114] However, just as you accept that the hands and the many other body parts belong to one single body, then since all beings are like the limbs of a living being, why would you not call it a being and love it as a single entity, relating to it in the same way with accepting and rejecting. That would be equally reasonable.

Second is one's capacity for [embracing others]. [8.115] You might think that the line of reasoning is comparable, but such a way of thinking is unlikely to develop. However, just as in connection with our own body we developed a sense of "I," although there is no self, through mere habituation to self-grasping, why should habituation not bring us to have the same attitude toward another person's body, since the causes are the same?

Third, the positive qualities of doing so. [8.116] Having developed a sense of "I" in relation to others, then, when we work for others' sake, there will be no sense of boasting or self-congratulation. To take an analogy, when we feed ourselves, we do not expect anything in return; we do not expect a reward. It will be like that [when we serve others].

Fourth is the instruction on how to do this. [8.117] [Practicing to adopt others] is reasonable, powerful, and beneficial. Therefore, just as we protect ourselves against even a slight disparagement, likewise, we will grow used to having a mind protective and compassionate toward others. The *Exposition* says here that "since [to read it as] 'compassion' would involve redundancy with the word 'attitude of protection,' this is to be understood as 'lovingkindness.'"[281] [8.118] We have to get thoroughly habituated to that attitude. To this end, as stated in the *Array of Trees Sūtra*, the protector Avalokita blessed his name out of great compassion, saying, "By recalling my name three times, may there be even in the cyclic existence no fear and terror."[282]

Next, it is inappropriate to turn away from embracing others. One might think, "Even though there is great benefit and it is possible, it would be extremely difficult." [8.119] We should not turn away from difficulty because, through habituation, it can get easier. For instance, through the power of habituation, even in relation to someone whose name was once a source of terror, if you become habituated to being together, a time could come when that person's absence would make you unhappy.

The summary is this: [8.120] Those who wish to protect themselves and others from all suffering quickly should practice exchanging self and others, which is a great mystery to be kept secret from those who are not appropriate vessels.

## Discarding one's own self

This has two parts. First, *it is appropriate to discard because it engenders fear within this life.* [8.121] If attachment to my own body induces fear at even a small danger, why would any intelligent person not abhor that body of one's self, on the basis of which all sorts of fears arise like a terrifying enemy?

Second, *it is appropriate to discard because it engenders suffering in the future.* [8.122–24] Some [people], wanting to quell physical pains such as hunger and thirst, kill birds, fish, and deer and lie in ambush at a crossroads to rob others of their possessions. Some embodied [beings], for the sake of some gain and material benefit, kill their parents and steal the property of the Three Jewels. They will burn in the hell of Avīci. So what wise person would happily desire such a body and protect and venerate it?[283] Who would not see it as an enemy and scorn it? One should.

## The benefits and faults of taking either self or others to be the most important

This has two parts. Of these, the first is *the characteristic of the state of mind.* [8.125] "If I give it away, what will I enjoy?" Thinking in this way out of concern only for oneself is the attitude of a demon—that of a hungry ghost. "If I enjoy it, what will I give away?" Thinking in this way out of concern for others is the way of the gods; it is an excellent Dharma.

The second, *the characteristic of its effects*, is threefold. Of these, the first is explaining them individually. [8.126] If, for the sake of oneself, one harms others, one will be burnt in hells and the like; but if, on the other hand, one induces harm upon oneself for the sake of others, one will achieve all the excellences. [8.127] The desire for self-aggrandizement would lead one to the lower realms, inferior caste and appearance, and stupidity. If one switches this desire and transfers it to someone else, one will obtain higher rebirth, and that too with respect and honor. [8.128] If, for my own sake, I order others around, I will experience the position of a servant and the like; but if I order myself around for the sake of others, I will experience the position of a master with attending servants and the like.

The second is summarizing them. [8.129] In brief, all those who are happy in the world are so because they desire happiness for others, and all those who are unhappy in the world are so because they desire their own happiness.

The third is illustrating the point by analogy. [8.130] What need is there to say more, such as citing reasons? Look at the difference between the two: the childish person who seeks his own benefit and the Sage, who works only to benefit others.

## The disadvantages of not exchanging

The disadvantages of not exchanging [self and others] has two parts: the actual point, and the advice to renounce the causes [that makes one not engage in such exchanging]. The first is threefold. Of these, the first is *the faults that are not visible.* [8.131] One who does not exchange his own happiness for the suffering of others surely does not achieve buddhahood, and even in the cycle of existence, how could they obtain the happiness of rebirth in higher realms?

Second is *the faults that are visible.* [8.132] Not to mention not obtaining happiness in the next life, even with respect to this life they will not achieve their desired goals: [they will not acquire] food, clothing, and so on; their servants will not do their duties, and their master will not pay their wages.

The third is *the summary.* [8.133] Those ignorant of the causes of happiness and suffering, by forsaking this exchange of self and others, which is the cause of all such visible and invisible happiness, thoroughly relinquish all perfect happiness. And due to causing harms that bring pain on others, they embrace relentless suffering both visible and invisible.

The advice to renounce the causes [that make one not engage in such exchanging] is as follows. [8.134] Whatever myriad adversities exist in the world, and whatever dangers and sufferings exist, since they all arise from grasping the self, what use is this great demon that brings every harm? You should shun it. [8.135] If you do not forsake this grasping at self, you will not be able to eliminate suffering, just as if you do not avoid fire, you cannot avoid being burned.

### The summation

This is twofold: with respect to attitude, and with respect to action. The first is as follows. [8.136] Given that cherishing oneself is a source of many harms and suffering of self and others, so that I may alleviate my own suffering and alleviate all the suffering of others, I will give myself up to others and hold others and cherish them as my own self. [8.137] This being so, O mind, know this with certainty: "I am bound to others." From now on, I must not be concerned with anything but the welfare of all sentient beings.

Second, with respect to action: [8.138] For a person with such an attitude, it is inappropriate to seek one's own welfare with the actions of the sense faculties, such as the eyes and so on, which have been dedicated to others. For they belong now to others. For that matter, it is inappropriate for the eyes and so on to be used wrongly against others, because they have been dedicated to the welfare of others. In place of "the eyes," the commentaries read "the hands."[284] [8.139] Therefore, regarding others as most important, whatever desirable things you see on your own body—clothes and so forth—snatch them all away and use them to benefit others.

### The act of exchanging

The act of exchanging has two parts: exchanging through thought, and exchanging through action.

## Exchanging through thought

The first, in turn, has three parts—a brief presentation, an explanation, and the summation. Of these, the first is as follows. [8.140] To relinquish the faults stated above—namely, envy toward the superior, competitiveness toward the equal, and arrogance toward the inferior—view your own self as the inferior, the equal, and the superior and identify others as yourself. Then, with the mind free of false notions such as doubt, cultivate the attitudes, such as of envy from the perspective of the inferior, competitiveness from the perspective of an equal, and pride from the perspective of a superior.[285]

The explanation consists of two parts: the actual meditations, and its rationale. The first, in turn, has three parts: cultivating envy, cultivating competitiveness, and cultivating pride.

## Cultivating envy

This is twofold. Of these, the first is *being envious of worldly success*. [8.141] "He, this bodhisattva, is respected by the world, not I, a [mere] sentient being. I am not wealthy as he is. He is praised, while I am despised. I am unhappy, while he is happy. [8.142ab] I do all chores while he lives at ease." In these ways, the other whom you have identified as the "self" cultivates envy toward your [old superior] self, which is turned into the "other." All uses of the [two] terms of "self" and "other" in the context here [of this particular meditation] should be understood in this manner.[286]

Next is *being envious of his qualities*. [8.142cd] It is well known that this one is great in the world, while I am debased and lacking good qualities. [8.143] What can I do without good qualities? That is to say, I do not desire to be without qualities, so I too will seek to become endowed with good qualities. In fact, since I am endowed with the natural quality, the tathāgata essence, it is not the case that I am entirely bereft of good qualities! Furthermore, qualities are defined in relative terms, what is superior and what is less so, and since the [world is] filled with those with great qualities, there are those in relation to whom this bodhisattva could be inferior. Likewise, since the [world is] filled with those who are inferior, there are those in relation to whom I am superior. It is along these lines that the *Extensive Commentary* explains [this verse].

One might ask, "Since in the present context one is identifying oneself as the inferior other, to whom should one posit oneself as superior?" [Answer:] One cannot speak of someone being inferior in relation to everything, so one should bring to mind some specific ways of being inferior and engage in the meditation on that basis. Given [these designations are] relative to a given context, doing this would be no problem.

One might say, "Now, from the point of view of your degeneration of moral discipline, view, and so forth, you are indeed inferior to the bodhisattva." [Response:] [8.144] The degeneration of my moral discipline, view, and so on—which includes [right] livelihood—is due to the power of my afflictions and not my own free will. Since you [bodhisattva] accept yourself as an embodiment of compassion, you must heal me as well as you can. For if I am healed, I will accept the pain entailed in the hardship of practice. [8.145] Now if I am not worthy of being healed by the bodhisattva—that is, if you cannot cure me—in that case, why do you, taking yourself to be better, disdain me? And if, despite all your qualities, you cannot heal me, what use are your good qualities to me? They have no benefit for me. [8.146] Furthermore, as for the flawed one who has no compassion for beings—we who, due to the force of our negative karma, stand at the door of the lower realms of existence, as if in the jaws of beasts of prey like snakes and wild beasts—not only do you admit this flaw, in fact, out of pride in your qualities, you desire to surpass the wise! This is most inappropriate.

In this way, saying that not only does [the superior bodhisattva] lack qualities, they in fact possess many flaws, we cultivate envy.

## Cultivating competitiveness

Cultivating competitiveness is as follows. [8.147] Seeing myself as equal to the other, I must enhance my superiority. Through possessions, I will seek superior wealth and prestige for myself, even taking them away from him through fighting and discord. [8.148] If my good qualities become apparent to everyone in the world, then I will ensure that no one even hears of his good qualities. [8.149] My own faults I will conceal, and if I expose his faults, the masses will honor me and not him. I will acquire possessions excellently, he will not; I will be celebrated, while he will not. [8.150] Insomuch as he is subjected to such ill treatment, being made to suffer, I will look on this with delight for a long time; I will see him ridiculed and reviled by all beings.

## Cultivating pride

Next is cultivating pride. [8.151] Identifying with one who is superior [in relation to your old self], contemplate, "It is said that this miserable being is jealous of me, but are his learning, wisdom, beauty, lineage, and wealth equal to mine? [8.152] Thus, everyone hearing of my good qualities renowned throughout the world, I experience a joy that makes my hair bristle with delight." [8.153] If, despite my efforts to obstruct, this one happens to acquire possessions, if he would work for me without arrogance, I will give him just enough to survive and forcibly snatch the rest away from him. This is how the commentaries interpret it. [8.154ab] We should deprive him of happiness and, not only that, always yoke him to harm and suffering.

Presenting its rationale is as follows. [8.154cd] One might ask, "Why be so harsh toward him?"[287] [Answer:] He has inflicted harm on me in cyclic existence in hundreds of places hundreds of times.

The summation of the points is threefold. First, *the fault of not cultivating the exchange*: [8.155] O mind, countless eons have passed during which you have yearned to accomplish only your own self-interest, and yet through such great toil in pursuing your own interest, you have gained only suffering! So it deserves to be abandoned. From this point on [in the text], the words "self" and "other" should be understood in the sense of their normal usage.[288]

*The benefits of such meditations*: [8.156] Thus, on the basis of exchanging self with others, definitely apply yourself to the interests of others. Then, since the words of the Sage are never fallible, the benefits of exchanging self and others of which the Sage has spoken will become manifest later when you attain the [bodhisattva] grounds. [8.157] Had you done this exchange of self and others earlier, a situation such as this—which is not the excellence and bliss of someone bearing the label *buddha* but instead your current situation of suffering—would never have occurred.

*The advice therefore to exchange*: [8.158] Therefore, just as you have identified with the drops of blood and semen of others as "my body," likewise you should accustom yourself to [identifying with] others—namely, other sentient beings.

## Exchanging through action

Exchanging through action has two parts: cultivating the practices, and gaining mastery over the mind through the practices. The first consists of three parts: bringing benefit to others, renouncing the cherishing of self, and summarizing the points.

The first is as follows. [8.159] Having become a scout for

others, I will watch what this self does and act as punisher, snatching away whatever appears desirable on this self's body and using it to benefit others.

Next, [renouncing the cherishing of self] is threefold: being envious in thought, in action connecting [the self] to suffering, and positing both [one's thought and action] as inferior. The first is as follows. [8.160] Why do you not arouse the envy that thinks [in relation to your self], "He is happy while others are not. He is high while others are low. And he does what is beneficial, such as engaging in virtuous deeds, while others do not"?

Second, in action connecting [the self] to suffering is as follows. [8.161ab] Deprive this self of happiness, and bring all the suffering of others upon this self.

The third, positing both [one's thought and action] as inferior, is as follows. [8.161cd] In all situations, examine your own culpability with the consideration "What have I done at what time?" [8.162] Even for mistakes made by others, take the blame on yourself, and if you commit even a small misdeed, confess it to many people, saying, "I have this fault." [8.163] Let your own reputation become invisible through being outshone by exalting the reputation of others, and like the least of servants and without conceit, commit yourself to everyone's welfare. [8.164] This one—namely, "self"—has the nature of having numerous defects; even if it were to possess minor adventitious good qualities, it should not be praised on the basis of those qualities. Instead, act so that no one may know of this one's good qualities.

Summarizing the points is as follows. [8.165] In brief, let whatever harm you have inflicted on others for your own benefit descend on you in the future for the sake of sentient beings. [8.166] This one, the self, should not be encouraged to be an aggressive upstart.[289] Instead, be left mortified by your self-cherishing and so forth, as shy, meek, and restrained, in the manner of a new bride.

The next topic, gaining mastery over the mind through the

practices, has three parts: (1) mastering the antidotes, (2) viewing what is to be abandoned as unconducive, and (3) being skilled in the methods of applying the antidotes. The first is twofold: a brief presentation, and the elaboration.

The first is as follows. [8.167] Cultivate this thought focused on others' welfare, and live that through your deeds. If your self-centered thought and action[290] prevent you from acting like that, then subjugate your mind by the power of the antidote; and if you transgress that norm of what is to be adopted and what is to be rejected, subdue yourself with the antidotes.

The second is the elaboration. [8.168] Now, even after being advised in this way, O mind, if you do not do this, then since you would be indulging in all the faults, there is nothing for you but to be subjugated. If the thought occurs "I am not capable of such a task," [8.169] then, O mind, the time when you could ruin me through your pursuit of [only] self-interest was a time when I could not see the faults. Now that I can see your true nature and your faults, where would you go?[291] You cannot go anywhere! I will destroy your arrogance. [8.170] Now cast off the thought "Still I must protect my own self-interest!" I have sold you to others, so offer your strength tirelessly to the welfare of others!

Next, viewing what is to be abandoned as unconducive. [8.171] If, due to your self-centeredness, O mind, you do not offer yourself willingly to sentient beings, you will undoubtedly deliver me to the guardians of hell. [8.172] In the past too, you have handed me over in that way to the guardians of hell and have inflicted harm on me for ages upon ages. Now, remembering those grudges, I will destroy your attitude of self-centeredness.

Being skilled in the methods of applying the antidotes is twofold: a brief explanation and the elaboration. Of these, the first is as follows. [8.173] If you wish for your own lasting happiness and well-being, do not take pleasure in yourself and be attached to it. If you wish to protect yourself from suffering, always protect others.

The elaboration has two parts: renouncing attachment to the body and upholding it for others' welfare. The first is twofold: the faults of having such attachment and the inappropriateness of such attachment. Of these, the first consists of (1) the actual point and (2) presenting, as an aside, the benefits of contentment.

The first is as follows. [8.174] The more this body is pampered and protected, the more exceedingly fragile it becomes, such that one plunges into immense suffering when one fails in satisfying even a minor desire. The thought may occur, "Still, if all of its desires were met, then there would be no suffering," [8.175] but given that it has been sunk in this way, not even this earth could completely fulfill its desire. Who could ever satisfy all it desires? It is stated:

> All the grains on this earth,
> all the gold, cattle, and freedom from illness—
> none of these can satisfy this one thing!
> Know this and abide in tranquility.[292]

[8.176ab] So, despite there being no such ability [to satisfy], the desire to fulfill it nonetheless afflicts us with fatigue, anger, and so forth and undermines the mind. And through this failure to satisfy its desires and through this lack of fulfillment, it gives rise to unhappiness.

The second, presenting, as an aside, the benefits of contentment, is as follows. [8.176cd] Given that the perfect happiness of the one who abides with no regard for body, material resources, and so forth is inexhaustible, [8.177] you should not give free rein to your body's desires. As for the riches of the person who does not grasp [the object of desire] as something excellent, first of all, it is easy to access; and [such a resource] does not give rise to the pain of clinging in the middle and that of separation at the end. So it is most wonderful. This is as stated in *Letter to a Friend*:

> "Contentment is the most excellent of all wealth":
> this the teacher of the gods and humans said.
> So maintain contentment; one who knows contentment
> is rich indeed, even if he lacks material wealth.[293]

The inappropriateness of such attachment [to the body] has two parts: it is lowly, and it is inappropriate to be attached to it for it does not know what is beneficial and what is harmful. The first is as follows. [8.178] One might think, "Even though I must not be attached to material resources, it is indeed appropriate to be attached to my body." [Response:] This body, which in the end culminates in ashes—that is to say, it turns into ashes—cannot move on its own but is moved by something other, the mind. So why do I grasp onto this awful, impure body and identify with it? [8.179] Be it dead or alive, what use is this machine to me? What difference is there at all between this and a clump of soil and so forth? Alas, why is it that I do not dispel the pride rooted in identifying in terms of "I" and "mine"? [8.180] By favoring the body of mine, I uselessly accumulate suffering. Of what use is anger or love to something equal to a piece of wood? It should not be an object of either of these two [anger or love].

Second, it is inappropriate to be attached to it for it does not know what is beneficial and what is harmful. [8.181] Whether it is nurtured by me with cherishing or is to be eaten by vultures, it feels neither affection nor aversion in relation to the two. So why am I attached to it? [8.182] If this body, which has no anger due to abuse nor happiness due to praise—that is, it has no consciousness—then for whose sake am I exerting myself by adopting [certain things] and shunning [certain things], such as through praise and disparagement? [8.183] One might say,

"Even though the body does not know such things, I feel close to the one who is attached to this body and finds it attractive; so I am fond of it." [Response:] Since everyone is attached to their own bodies, why am I not fond of everyone [as well]? The same logic should apply.

Next is upholding it for others' welfare. [8.184] Since attachment to my self has so many faults, therefore, with no attachment, I will give away this body of mine for the benefit of beings, as their servants or as something to be used. In that it has the capacity to benefit others, even though it has many faults, I will keep it as an instrument for that task.

## The practices common to both equalizing and exchanging self and others

The practices common to both[294] has two parts: dispelling the obscurations, and striving in the antidotes. The first is as follows. [8.185] Thus—that is, since it is necessary to practice equalizing and exchanging self and others—enough now of this foolish behavior attached to meaningless things! It is pointless. [Instead] I will follow the wise—the buddhas and the bodhisattvas—and cultivate the awakening mind. To do this, I will recall the discourse on conscientiousness explained in chapter 4 of this text as well as in the *Compendium of Training*, and I will avert the five hindrances, such as lethargy and sleep, as mentioned in *Letter to a Friend*:

> Excitation and regret, ill will, lethargy and
> sleep, sense desire, and doubt—
> these five obscurations are the thieves that steal
> the wealth of virtuous karma; so do know of this.[295]

Second is striving in the antidotes. [8.186][296] Like the compassionate children of the conquerors, to relinquish the faults already arisen and prevent their arising in the future, I will establish the strength of the antidote—namely, virtue. And in this way, I will constantly strive day and night; for if I do not strive, when could my suffering ever come to an end? Never!

### Cultivating the ultimate awakening mind

This is as follows. [8.187] For the reasons stated above, therefore, to dispel the afflictions of attachment and so forth, as well as the nonafflictive conceptualizations—namely, the obscuration to knowledge—I will withdraw the mind from false ways, such as thoughts of desire, and place it constantly upon a perfect or a virtuous meditative object.

This completes the explanation of chapter 8.

# 9. Wisdom

THE CHAPTER on wisdom has three parts: linking [to the preceding section] and advising to cultivate wisdom, the method to cultivate it, and the activity of one who has attained wisdom.

## LINKING [TO THE PRECEDING SECTION] AND ADVISING TO CULTIVATE WISDOM

[9.1] All these branches, from generating the awakening mind up to meditative absorption—namely, the collection of the causes of wisdom—the Sage stated are for the sake of cultivating wisdom. The *Perfectly Gathering the Teachings Sūtra* states, "By resting the mind in equipoise, one will see the perfect truth as it is," and so on.[297] This same point is found in the *Compendium of Training*:

> "In equipoise in meditation, one will know
> the perfect truth as it is," said the Sage.[298]

Therefore those who wish to pacify their own suffering and that of others should cultivate wisdom. All the sufferings of cyclic existence come from contaminated action and afflictions, and they in turn come from grasping at true existence. The *Sixty Stanzas of Reasoning* says:

> If one has the thesis of real entities,
> relentless attachment and aversion will arise.[299]

Through eliminating that [grasping at true existence] with wisdom realizing emptiness, all sufferings will be pacified. The *Condensed Perfection of Wisdom in Verse* says:

> Through knowing the nature of phenomena with
> wisdom,
> one will go perfectly beyond the entire world of three
> realms.[300]

And when you realize emptiness, then as the *Commentary on the Awakening Mind* states, you will teach emptiness to others and help them dispel their suffering:

> Thus, when the yogis become
> accustomed to emptiness,
> then with no difficulty at all,
> their minds will delight in others' welfare.[301]

### The method to cultivate wisdom

This has three parts: (1) how to identify the nature of wisdom, (2) how to engage with selflessness, the object of wisdom, and (3) how to eliminate grasping at true existence, the object of elimination.

### How to identify the nature of wisdom

The first is twofold: (1) establishing the two truths, the objects, and (2) establishing the subject as the path.

### Establishing the two truths, the objects

This has two parts: setting forth the nature of the two truths, and rebutting the objections. The first is threefold: the division, their natures, and the characteristics of the mind cognizing them.

The first is as follows. [9.2] *Conventional* [in the context of conventional truth] refers to the deluded cognition that obscures perfect truth, while *truth* refers to that which is real from such a perspective. *Entering the Middle Way* states:

> Because delusion obscures the true nature, it is a *concealer*;
> that which is contrived by it and appears to be real
> the Buddha spoke of as *true for a concealer*;
> and fabricated entities are merely *conventional*.[302]

*Ultimate* [in the context of ultimate truth] refers to an ārya's appearance-free gnosis,[303] and given that [emptiness] is the object to be realized by [such cognition], it is referred to as the ultimate truth. This is similar to the line "For it is the sphere of experience of the āryas" in *Differentiation of the Middle and Extremes*.[304] These two [conventional and the ultimate], then, are accepted to constitute the two truths.

Second is their natures. On the [nature of] ultimate truth, the *Teaching on the Conventional and the Ultimate Truth Sūtra* says:

> O celestial child, if the ultimate truth were to be the object of body, speech, and mind, then it would not count as an ultimate truth. It would become a conventional truth . . . Indeed the ultimate truth lies beyond the sphere of omniscient gnosis as well.[305]

As stated here, it is not something that exists as an object of positive determination by the intellect in terms of "it's this." For the intellect is accepted to be a concealer that obscures the vision of ultimate truth. This is how Kṣemadeva interprets it.[306] Prajñākaramati and Vairocana, on the other hand, take "the intellect" to refer to conceptualization, which in turn constitutes ignorance, and hence [the ultimate truth] is not its object.[307] Here, "the intellect" refers to the mind and mental factors of the three realms, as stated in *Differentiation of the Middle and Extremes*:

> The incorrect conceptualizations
> consist of the mind and mental factors of the three
> realms.[308]

So it is not inconsistent [for the ultimate truth] to be an object of the tathāgatas and an object of realization by the ārya's gnosis. As for the statement in the sūtra about it being not even the object of the buddhas, this is to be understood as meaning that it does not exist in terms of "this or that." Given that it does not exist in any such terms as "this" or "that," it is also not realized as "this" or "that." That the [ārya's] appearance-free gnosis does not apprehend it in any such terms is itself to be posited as its realization. The *Ajātaśatru Sūtra* says,

> O Great King, not seeing all phenomena is itself perfect seeing. For, O King, perfect seeing is devoid of seeing.[309]

As this states, there is no contradiction between these two [not seeing and perfect seeing].[310]

The third, characteristics of the mind that cognizes them, has three parts: types of persons, the stages of impairment, and the reasoning that undermines.

The first is as follows. [9.3ab] As for the world or the person that engages with the two truths, one sees two types: the yogis who possess the concentration uniting tranquil abiding and insight, and ordinary persons who do not possess such concentration. This is how the commentaries explain it.[311] However, it would be more appropriate to differentiate based on who possesses or lacks any of the three forms of wisdom pertaining to selflessness.[312]

Second is the stages of impairment. [9.3c–9.4b] Within this world of two types of persons, the ordinary persons of the world view their body as a unitary entity and their mind as permanent. Such perspectives would be undermined by the world's yogis when they reason that "The body is not unitary because it is composed of multiple parts," "The mind is impermanent because it can change its character," and so on. Among the three types of yogis—those who propound external reality, the Cittamātra, and the Mādhyamika—based on how well their perspectives reflect the nature of reality, the perspective of the higher would undermine the perspective of the lower. For example, the two realist schools, since they propound external reality,[313] view the objective [material] world as composed of real indivisible particles and the subjective world of consciousness as composed of real indivisible momentary instances. This is undermined by the following Cittamātra reasoning:

> If six converge at the same time,
> an atom would have six parts.
> If these six occupied the same spatial location,
> a composite mass would be merely the size of a particle.[314]

Since the constitutive elements, atoms, lack existence, there cannot be macroscopic objects composed through their aggregation. And if they lack existence, then the two [indivisible atoms and moments of consciousness] can have no true existence. Now the Cittamātra's view is that the nondual consciousness, free of subject-object duality, is self-revealing and possesses true existence. Against this, the Mādhyamika's reasoning refuting reflexive awareness, such as those presented in this text,[315] would cause damage.

Third is the reasoning that undermines. [9.4cd] Kṣemadeva

explains [the lines][316] as, "Thanks to analogies accepted and known to both parties, there is no need to analyze [further] for the sake of establishing a thesis." Vairocana's position is the following. If asked, "Since things do appear to the cognitions of the worldly, it is not the case that these objects have no true existence. So how can their perspectives be erroneous?" [Answer:] It's through analogies accepted as delusory by both ordinary people and the yogis, such as a magical illusion. What appear as real from the perspective of the realists are negated as possessing real existence. So if their perspectives are established as deluded, what need is there to speak of the perspectives of ordinary people?[317] Explaining in this manner, he interprets the line (9.4d) in the sense of a response to an objection.

## Rebutting the objections

Rebutting the objections has two parts: rebutting objections pertaining to conventional truth, and rebutting objections pertaining to ultimate truth.

### Rebutting objections pertaining to conventional truth

The first is fivefold: rebutting the objection that no one will enter the path, [rebutting the objection] that the dispute is not about the objects [themselves], [the perception of objects as real] is negated by valid cognition, [rebutting the objection] that it contradicts the scriptures, and rebutting the charge of an absurd consequence.

The first is as follows. [9.4d][318] [Objection:] "If all phenomena lack true existence, there could be no attainment of enlightenment through [the perfection of] generosity and so on, so no one would engage in these practices." [Response:] Although they do not exist on the ultimate level, they do exist on the unanalyzed level of conventional truth, so there is no inconsistency in engaging in generosity and so on for the sake of their results.

Second, [rebutting the objection] that the dispute is not about the objects themselves. [9.5–6] [Objection:] "Since things appear to both yogis and ordinary people, why would there be a dispute about distinguishing them?" [Answer:] Although things appear to them equally, when ordinary worldly people perceive form and so forth, they conceive them to be real and do not understand them to be illusion-like. Yogis, on the other hand, understand things in such a manner. Hence the dispute between yogis and the worldly.

Third, [the perception of objects as real] is negated by valid cognition. [9.7ab] [Objection:] "Since form and so forth are established by direct perception, it is inconsistent to assert them to be unreal." [Response:] There is no such inconsistency. They are merely known to the world but not established as real by the criteria of validity. Just as the body that is impure, impermanent, and so on, is known [to the world] as pure and so forth, so too are things unreal. This is as stated in the *King of Meditations Sūtra*:

> The eyes, ears, and nose are not valid cognitions;
> the tongue and the body, as well as the mind, are not valid
> cognitions.
> For if these organs meet the criteria of valid cognition,
> what use is the ārya's path for anyone?[319]

Fourth, [rebutting the objection] that it contradicts the scriptures. [9.7c–9.8] [Objection:] "If all phenomena lack intrinsic existence, why did the Sage teach that things are by nature momentary?" [Answer:] This is a statement with a special intent. Taking, as the basis of his intention, the simple fact that things do appear, the Lord stated that things are impermanent [in this way] to guide the worldly, who grasp at things as real, in a gradual manner. This is as stated in the following:

Just as the conquerors speak of
"I" and "mine" for a practical purpose,
they also speak of the "aggregates,"
"elements," and "sense fields" for pragmatic reasons.[320]

In reality, the statement that things are momentary is untrue, for it is undermined by the reasoning that negates momentariness. One may say, "Momentariness does not appear to the worldly cognition either, so it would be contradictory to assert that it is real on the conventional level." [Response:] Although it does not appear to [the worldly cognition of] ordinary people, it does appear to the worldly cognition of yogis—namely, those who perceive only the selflessness of persons.[321] Hence there is no fault in holding [momentariness] to be a conventional truth. One may object, "In that case, you would contradict the [sūtra] statement that to see momentariness is to see reality." [Response:] This is stated because momentariness is a similitude of ultimate truth. Were it otherwise—if, as opposed to yogis, ordinary people did perceive reality—then the yogis' ascertainment of the woman's body[322] as impure would be invalidated by the worldly perception of it as pure. This is the explanation that Kṣemadeva gives.[323]

The fifth, rebutting the charge of an absurd consequence, has four parts: rejecting that there would be no obtaining of merit, rejecting that there would no connecting to a new birth, rejecting there would be no positive or negative karma, and rejecting that engaging in the deeds would be pointless.

The first is as follows. [9.9ab] [Objection:] "If all phenomena lacked true existence, then the buddhas would be unreal, and this would mean that no merit could come from honoring them." [Response:] Just as you accept that from honoring truly existing conquerors, truly existing merit comes about, likewise, honoring illusion-like conquerors generates illusion-like merit; so there is no problem.

Second, rejecting that there would be no connecting to a new birth. [9.9c–9.10] [Objection:] "If sentient beings resemble illusions, how can they take birth after their death?" [Answer:] Birth will come about through conditions coming together, for when conditions come together, even illusions appear. Perhaps you maintain that, compared to an illusion [which is ephemeral], sentient beings are more enduring, so they must possess true existence. In that case, there would be the consequence that even among illusions, [one would have to differentiate between some being more real and some less so] based on their duration.

Third, rejecting that there would be no positive or negative karma. [9.11–13b] [Objection:] "In that case, between a sentient being killing another sentient being and an illusory being killing another illusory being, there would be total equality with respect to whether any positive or negative karma were accrued." [Response:] In the case of an *illusory* being killing another illusory being, there is no mind in the agent of the act, so there would be no positive or negative karma. In contrast, when an *illusion-like* person—who is endowed with mind—commits such an act, that act would be committed by someone with states of mind like love and hatred, and so there would be merit or negative karma. This difference of the presence or absence of mind comes about because the conditions that create an illusion—the incantatory spell and so forth—have no power to produce a mind, and thus no mind could emerge in the illusory being. In contrast, [this power to produce a mind] is found in the conditions that create [an illusion-like] sentient being. Though equal in being unreal, this difference in their causes leads to a difference in their effects. In relation to illusions, from varied and different conditions arise different kinds of illusions. Nowhere is there a single condition that has the power to produce all effects.

Fourth, rejecting that engaging in the deeds would be point less. [9.13c–9.15b] [Objection:] "If, from the perspective of ultimate truth, all sentient beings are naturally liberated and yet, conventionally, they revolve in cyclic existence, then by the same logic, from the point of view of appearances, the buddhas [too] would be in cyclic existence. In that case, what is the point of engaging in the bodhisattva deeds?" [Answer:] Just as an illusion cannot be averted for as long as its conditions do not cease, likewise, because the conditions for revolving in cyclic existence have not come to an end, sentient beings continue to revolve in cyclic existence. For the buddhas, on the other hand, the conditions for revolving in cyclic existence have ceased, and so even on the conventional level, cyclic existence cannot come about.

The word "even"[324] implies "let alone on the ultimate level." Alternatively, it [the word "even"] is to indicate that the buddhas' appearance in the world is due to the power of their aspiration and not because they have not abandoned the conditions for taking birth in cyclic existence, so there is no problem here. This is how Kṣemadeva explains [the verse].[325] Prajñākaramati, on the other hand, reads it like this: If the conditions do not cease, then let alone cyclic existence, even illusions cannot be averted. In contrast, when the continuity of the conditions for cyclic existence have ceased, even on the conventional level, there would be no possibility of cyclic existence. Through cultivating familiarity with suchness, the buddhas have brought the twelve links of dependent origination such as ignorance to an end and will not revolve in cyclic existence.[326] As for Vairocana, he interprets that even with respect to illusory buddhas, when sentient beings have the merit, the buddhas will appear, and when there is no such merit, the buddhas won't appear even on the conventional level.[327]

## Rebutting objections pertaining to ultimate truth

Rebutting objections pertaining to ultimate truth is twofold: (1) rejecting the objection that if there is no delusory cognition, there would be no apprehension, and (2) rejecting the objection that if no basis of delusion exists, there could be no cyclic existence.

## Rejecting the objection that if there is no delusory cognition, there would be no apprehension

This twofold [the objection and the response]. [9.15cd] First is the objection. A Cittamātra asks, "When not even delusory cognition exists, what is it that ascertains the illusion-like appearance?" The response has three parts: the same objection applies equally to both parties, refuting the opponent's rejoinder, and relating the point to its actual context.

The first is as follows. [9.16ab] When, according to you, Cittamātra, the illusion-like object does not exist, what is it that is perceived then? The two cases are equal.[328]

Refuting the opponent's rejoinder has two parts: asserting the appearance to be the mind, and refuting an entity that is neither matter nor consciousness. The first is twofold. The first is *stating the opponent's view*. [9.16cd] "Even though what is apprehended as an object is false, what apprehends—namely, the cognition that is different from the object—does exist as a real entity. And it is this appearance aspect of mind itself that can be perceived."

The second, *refuting this view*, has three parts: presenting objections to ultimately real reflexive awareness, presenting that there is no proof [for such an awareness], and rejecting objections to our refutation. The first, in turn, is twofold: the actual point, and dispelling confusion. [9.17–18b] The first is as follows. If the mind itself is the same entity as that of the illusion-like object part,[329] there would be no two things—that which is seen and that which sees—so what is seen by what? The Lord of the World also states in the *Descent into Laṅkā Sūtra*:

> The blade of a sword
> does not cut itself, and
> the tip of a nail does not touch itself—
> the self-cognition of mind is the same.[330]

In the *Questions of Ratnacūḍa*, too, it says that just as the blade of a sword cannot cut itself and the tip of a nail cannot touch itself, the mind cannot see itself.[331] Thus, just as the blade of a sword cannot cut itself, a mind cannot see the [same] mind.

Dispelling confusion has two parts: the analogy is not established, and the analogy does not apply to the referent. The first is twofold, the first of which is *refuting the analogy of an oil lamp*. [9.18c–9.19b] One may assert that just as an oil lamp thoroughly illuminates itself, the mind itself cognizes the mind. [Response:] The lamp does not illuminate itself, for that which it illuminates was necessarily obscured by darkness previously. In the case of the light itself, the instant it arises, nothing remains that is obscured by darkness and not luminous. This is as stated in the following in the *Fundamental Verses on the Middle Way*:

> Either in the lamp or where it is present,
> there would be no darkness.
> What does the lamp illuminate?
> Illumination is the dispelling of darkness.[332]

Second is *refuting the analogy of blue color*. [9.19c–9.20] The opponent might assert, "Blue color has two types: the blue of a crystal that is contingent on something other and the blue of a lapis lazuli; the clear crystal becoming blue is a function of some other thing, while the blueness of lapis lazuli is not contingent upon something other than itself. Likewise, things such as vases and so forth depend on something other to illuminate them or to perceive them, whereas things like lamps and sensations of pleasure and pain [illuminate and] perceive without dependence on something other than themselves." [Response:] This is incorrect. The blue of lapis lazuli came into being as blue the instant the gem came into being. So this is not a case of something previously not blue somehow assuming the character of blueness by itself. Thus it cannot serve as an analogy for self-illumination and self-cognition. This is how some learned Tibetans interpret [the text here].[333] Prajñākaramati, on the other hand, interprets it as follows. It is not the case that the blue object becoming blue is not dependent on some other factors; it is dependent upon its causes. For if it came into being from its causes as something that is not blue, then one would have to admit that it came into being as a blue object without dependence on other factors, meaning that it made itself blue. This is logically impossible, for it is logically contradictory for something to act upon itself.[334]

That the analogy does not apply to the referent is as follows. [9.21] When you assert that on the conventional level, lamps illuminate themselves, this is something you know based on your cognition. So on the basis of what kind of cognition do you make the assertion that, on the ultimate level, cognitions are self-illuminating? These two instances, the analogy and its referent, are dissimilar.

Next, that there is no proof [of such an awareness] is twofold. First, *there is no proof of direct perception.* [9.22] Since, on the ultimate level, neither self-cognition nor other-cognition is established, no one has seen cognition that is other-perceiving. So to speak of its being either luminous or non-luminous is pointless. This would be like speaking of the physique of a childless woman's daughter as beautiful or not beautiful.

Second, *there is no proof in the form of inference.* [9.23] One may assert, "If there were no reflexive awareness, how would consciousness be recalled? It would be impossible. It is through the reasoning of recollection that we establish self-cognition." [Response:] There is no logical entailment. Even though cognition does not experience itself, recollection takes place through connection with experiencing some other object—form and so on. For example, [a hibernating animal] does not register being infected by a rodent's poison, but when it experiences pain upon being roused by a clap of thunder, it recalls [being infected by poison] on the basis of the pain being experienced.[335]

[9.24] One may assert, "Owing to the power of some other factor, such as meditative concentration, one can perceive what is distant—namely, others' consciousness. Thus it is logical to state that consciousness can illuminate what is near—itself." [Response:] There is no logical entailment here. For example, through the power of an [eye] salve concocted through a ritual, one might see a distant object, like a vase buried underground, but one cannot see what is near, the salve itself. This interpretation [I have offered] may not conform with some [Indian] commentaries, but I feel that it represents the master's intent.[336]

Next, rejecting objections to our refutation. [9.25] One may object, "If there is no self-cognition, there would be no other-cognition either. In that case there would be nothing—no seeing, no hearing, and so on." [Response:] What is being negated here is not simply what appears to sight, hearing, and knowing; rather, what is being negated here is the conception of these as having true existence. For that is a cause of suffering. This is as stated in *Entering Suchness*:

> Faults are due to grasping at true existence;
> from this comes naturally the enemies—
> attachment, anger, and so on. So when it's removed,
> how can these things emerge?[337]

Next is refuting an entity that is neither matter nor consciousness. [9.26] An opponent might assert, "The object aspect that is illusion-like is not an external reality, something separate from the mind, and neither do we postulate it to be the mind itself. It is something inexpressible as either identical with or different from the mind." [Response:] If it is an entity, how is it neither identical with nor different from the mind? It has to be either identical or different. For if it is neither identical with the mind nor different from it, then it cannot exist as an entity. No such entity is possible.

Relating the point to its actual context is as follows. [9.27ab] Just as, according to the Cittamātra system, the illusion-like object part, though unreal, is still what is seen, likewise, although the mind has no true existence, it appears, on the conventional level, as that which sees.

### Rejecting the objection that if no basis of delusion exists, there could be no cyclic existence

This has two parts. The first is *stating the objection.* [9.27cd] [The objection:] If you claim that the dualistic world of cyclic existence has nondual consciousness as the basis of delusion, then this duality has a basis with true existence. Otherwise, just like space, what is perceived as subject and object would also have no existence. So they assert.

The second is *its refutation.* [9.28–29] If this dualistic appearance, the subject, were dependent upon real existence, how could it possess the activity of appearing as subject and object? It cannot [be dependent upon real existence], for it has no real existence. Therefore what is mind according to your system would be nothing but a solitary nondual cognition with no objective counterpart. Now if the mind were devoid of subject-object duality, then all sentient beings would already be tathāgatas. In that case, why postulate that the basis of dualistic cyclic existence is that only the mind possesses true existence? For according to you, there would be no cyclic existence at all![338]

## Establishing the subject as the path

Establishing the subject as the path has two parts: establishing as path the understanding of conventional truth as illusion, and establishing as path the understanding of ultimate truth as emptiness.

## Establishing as path the understanding of conventional truth as illusion

This has three parts: the actual point, the nature of the path of cultivation, and the fruits of cultivating the path.

Within the first, here is the objection: [9.30] "Even if one were to understand all phenomena as illusion-like, how is it that all the afflictions will come to cease? For instance, even the person who has magically conjured a woman may experience lust toward her." The answer to this is as follows. [9.31–32] The person who magically conjured the woman is incidentally someone who has not destroyed the latent potencies of the affliction of attachment to phenomena such as women. Thus, when he sees the apparition of a woman, the magician's habituation to emptiness remains extremely weak. This is to say, even though he realizes the apparition is unreal, since he has not realized all phenomena are empty, his latent propensity for lust can be activated. Now once one has cultivated propensities for understanding emptiness, one will come to eliminate the latent propensities for clinging to things as having true existence. Then, by realizing that neither empty nor nonempty exists and cultivating familiarity with this, one's grasping at emptiness or unreality would also be later abandoned. And someone who does not grasp in any manner is not subject at all to the arising of afflictions. So these two cases are different.[339]

The nature of the path of cultivation is twofold. Of these, the first is that *the objects do not exist in any terms.* [9.33][340] When an entity that is being examined and negated in terms of "it does not exist" cannot be perceived, then being devoid of a basis it is dependent on, how does a nonentity remain before the mind as a nonentity? This is analogous to how, since there is no son of a childless woman, there can be no death of such a son.

The second is that *the mind does not perceive in any terms.* [9.34] When entity and nonentity do not remain before the mind, some third mode of existence—namely, something neither dual nor nondual—also cannot exist. Through cultivating familiarity with this [fact] and reaching its optimal level, the mind that perceives objects will become no more and will become thoroughly tranquil. This is as stated in *Entering the Middle Way*:

> Burning away the tinder of all objects of knowledge,
> there is the state of peace, the buddhas' perfect
> dharmakāya.
> In such a state there is neither arising nor cessation,
> and with mind ceased, it is actualized by the body.[341]

It does seem that passages such as these could be explained as meaning that buddhas are devoid of gnosis. The *Extensive Commentary*, however, has the following passage: "It is thoroughly tranquil in that all conceptualizations have been thoroughly calmed; it is not like the case of something becoming past and no more."[342] Thus he explains the meaning in the sense of there being no mind that perceives the object in terms of the four possibilities [of entity, nonentity, both, or neither]—namely, the conceptualization that grasps in such terms. Therefore I feel that in the later part of the text as well, when the phrase "no mind" appears, the sense is not the absence of gnosis but of there being no conceptualization in terms of subject and object.

Next, the fruits of cultivating the path has three parts: (1) how aims are realized in the absence of a conscious intention, (2) how even though the agent has ceased, action ensues, and (3) how even though there is no mind, merit arises.

The first is as follows. [9.35] Say one objects, "In that case, the buddhas would not be able to work for the welfare of other beings because they would lack the intention to do so." [Response:] Even though a wish-granting gem and a magical tree are devoid of conscious intention, when their powers and the merit of sentient beings come together, they do fulfill the desires of beings. Likewise, owing to the force of the purity of the trainees and the aspirations made by the bodhisattvas to work for their welfare, conquerors' form bodies will appear, leading to the fulfillment of beings' aims. So there is no problem. This fact of how, with no conscious thought, [buddhas] engage in bringing about others' welfare is explained extensively in *Adornment of the Illumination of Gnosis Sūtra*.[343]

Second, how even though the agent has ceased, action ensues. [9.36] Say one objects, "Given that the bodhisattva's aspiration ceases when he attains buddhahood, at that point, it would be untenable for him to serve the welfare of others." [Response:] Rishi Sangku cultivated a charged pillar with mantras, and even long after his death, that pillar continued to neutralize venom and other poisons. [9.37] Likewise, the bodhisattvas' cultivation of the pillar of a conqueror, due to their collection of deeds concordant with enlightenment, their aspirations, and so forth, brings about the aims of other sentient beings, even though the agent bodhisattvas have transcended to nonabiding nirvāṇa, where the conscious intention to work for other sentient beings has ceased. There is no contradiction.

Third, how even though there is no mind, merit arises. [9.38–39] Those of the śrāvaka schools might assert, "If the buddhas have no thought, how can merit ensue as the fruit of honoring them?" [Response:] There is no logical entailment here. For it has been taught that the merit accrued from worshiping a living tathāgata is equal to the merit from worshiping the reliquary of a tathāgata that has passed into nirvāṇa. This is as stated in the *Benefits of Circumambulating Stupas*:

> Honoring living [tathāgatas]
> and honoring reliquaries of those in nirvāṇa,
> with mind clear and equipoised—
> there is no difference in their merit.[344]

Whether buddhas are [understood to be] with no thought and conventionally true or with thought and ultimately true, scripture establishes that worshiping them results in merit. Just as you [the opponent] assert that truly existing merit ensues from worshiping a buddha that has true existence, in the same manner, we accept that unreal merit ensues from worshiping a buddha that is unreal. So there is no problem. Here, too, the phrase "no mind" should be taken to mean no conceptualizing thought in terms of subject and object. The *Extensive Commentary* reads, "the Blessed One, who is devoid of concealer mind."[345]

### Establishing as path the understanding of ultimate truth as emptiness

This is twofold: [the objection and the response]. First is the objection. [9.40ab] The śrāvaka school Vaibhāṣika asserts, "Through directly seeing the four noble truths in terms of sixteen aspects such as impermanence and meditating on them, one is freed from karma and the afflictions. What is the point of seeing emptiness in terms of not existing in any terms? There is no point at all."

The response to this is threefold: a summary presentation

through scripture, the extensive explanation by way of objections and responses, and a conclusion by way of a general summation. The first is as follows. [9.40cd] Emptiness must be seen because the Perfection of Wisdom scriptures state that without this path of wisdom that realizes emptiness, there would be no fruit of awakening. They state, "One who has notions of real entities is devoid of meditation on the perfection of wisdom ... he does not destroy the afflictions that reinforce the latent propensities."[346] It also says:

> Those who wish to become a śrāvaka of the sugatas
> or to become a pratyekabuddha or likewise a Dharma king
> will not attain these states without this forbearance.[347]

The extensive explanation by way of objections and responses has three parts: stating the objection that the scripture is not established, establishing Mahāyāna scriptures as sacred words of the Buddha, and establishing ultimate truth as the path.

## Stating the Objection That the Scripture Is Not Established

The first is as follows. [9.41a] [Objection:] Among the śrāvakas, of the four that exist—emanation śrāvakas, those who will attain great awakening, those who will proceed solely to nirvāṇa's peace, and those with manifest pride[348]—the last are those who, not seeing the truth, display manifest pride in their own tenets. It is these who assert that "Since Mahāyāna scriptures are not sacred words of the Buddha, they are not authentic scripture."

## Establishing Mahāyāna scriptures as sacred words of the Buddha

This has two parts: posing a specific counter question, and refuting their answers. The first is as follows. [9.41b] "In what way is your scripture, such as the collection of four Nikāyas, established as trustworthy?"

The second, refuting their answers, has two parts: rejecting the opponent's reason for what constitutes scripture, and rejecting the opponent's reason for what constitutes a sacred word of the Buddha. The first, in turn, is twofold: rejecting the opponent's reason that theirs is true scripture, and rejecting the opponent's reason that ours is not true scripture.

The first is as follows. [9.41cd] Suppose they assert, "The collection of four Nikāyas and so forth are trustworthy because they are established for both of us, the two parties." [Response:] By "both parties," do you mean both you and us? Or do you mean either of us [Hīnayāna or Mahāyāna]? If it is the former, then, at first, before you entered your system, the collection of four Nikāyas would not have been scripture for you, for you would not have established them to be so. [9.42] If you respond by saying they are trustworthy because they were transmitted through an uninterrupted lineage of sublime beings, then we would say that the very criterion by which you have confidence in your scriptures applies equally to the Mahāyāna scriptures, for those too have been transmitted through an uninterrupted lineage of sublime beings. Now if it is the latter—that is, if acceptance by any party makes a scripture true—then non-Buddhist scriptures like the Vedas would also become true trustworthy scriptures.

Second, rejecting the opponent's reason that ours is not true scripture. [9.43] You may object, "Because the Mahāyāna is controversial, it cannot be trustworthy scripture." [Response:] In that case, your own scripture would have to be rejected, since it is, in general, contested by non-Buddhists, and specific parts in the scripture are contested by various groups among your fellow Buddhists.

Next is rejecting the opponent's reason for what constitutes a sacred word of the Buddha. [9.49–51][349] This is presented in the three stanzas beginning with the line "If you accept utterances that accord with the sūtras." Prajñākaramati says they represent a later addition by someone else and are thus not part of the master's treatise,[350] while some say they are [part of the treatise]. In some versions of the treatise, these verses appear at this point, while in most versions they appear in a later part. In any case, if they were to be explained [as part of the root text], they should be brought up and explained here.

Here is how they are to be explained. Some schools assert that utterances are to be accepted as having been taught by the Buddha if that they present the training of the mind[351] in accord with the discourses (Sūtra), if they present the training in morality as found in the discipline (Vinaya), and if they present the training in wisdom that does not contradict higher knowledge (Abhidharma). Since Mahāyāna scriptures lack these, they object, they are not sacred words of the Buddha.

[Response:] In that case, since most Mahāyāna scriptures, such as the *Unraveling the Intent Sūtra*, present the threefold training, they are equal to your sūtras. So why do you not accept them as scripture? You should do so.

Now you may say, "Even though some Mahāyāna sūtras might be scripture, those that present all phenomena as devoid of intrinsic existence, such as the *Mother* [*Perfection of Wisdom*], lack the attributes of being sacred words of the Buddha. Hence they are not sacred words of the Buddha."

[Response:] *Ornament of Mahāyāna Sūtras* says:

> It applies to our own sūtras;
> it appears in our discipline texts;

and as it is profound and vast,
it does not contradict the nature of reality.[352]

As stated here, they [Mahāyāna sūtras] are endowed with the three characteristics [of being sacred words of the Buddha]. You simply do not perceive this. If for you, because of a single scripture like the *Mother* [*Perfection of Wisdom*], all Mahāyāna scriptures suffer from the fault of not qualifying as sacred words of the Buddha, then why would you not, based on a single sūtra like *Unraveling the Intent*, accept all Mahāyāna sūtras as being sacred words of the Buddha? The logic is the same.

Now you may say, "If Mahāyāna scriptures and sūtras such as the *Mother* [*Perfection of Wisdom*] are indeed sacred words of the Buddha, then those like the great Kāśyapa should have known about them. Since they did not know them, they cannot be sacred words of the Buddha." [Response:] How can anyone like you determine that the Mahāyāna scriptures, which are so profound that even those like the great Kāśyapa failed to penetrate their subject matter, are not sacred words of the Buddha? For example, *Ornament of Mahāyāna Sūtras* states:

With respect to a body of scripture so inconceivably
varied,
on what grounds can the ignorant make a
determination?[353]

Alternatively, since you have not actually established that those like the great Kāśyapa have not penetrated the subject matter of the Mahāyāna sūtras, how can you, citing this as a reason, assert that the Mahāyāna sūtras are not sacred words of the Buddha? The point here is this: Since your reason is unestablished, your thesis is not proven.[354]

## Establishing ultimate truth as the path

This has three parts: the fault of not meditating on the ultimate truth, the benefits of meditating on it, and a concluding summary. The first, in turn, is threefold: (1) nirvāṇa is not possible without destroying the afflictions, (2) even if destroyed, nirvāṇa would not be attained, and (3) even if the mind were to cease, it could resurface.

The first is as follows. [9.44][355] The root for the perpetuation of the teaching is monasticism, especially arhatship, but monkhood itself remains difficult for those whose minds still grasp at objects—namely, those who have not realized emptiness. For they have not destroyed the afflictions from their root. Not having destroyed the afflictions, nirvāṇa would also be difficult for such people—indeed, they would not attain it.

Second, even if [the afflictions were] destroyed, nirvāṇa would not be attained. [9.45] You may say, "Even without realizing such emptiness, if one meditates on the impermanence of the aggregates and the selflessness of persons, one would still destroy the afflictions and attain freedom from suffering." [Response:] In such an event, the arhat would, in the immediate aftermath of attaining nirvāṇa with residue, become someone who is free of suffering, having destroyed the afflictions. But if you accept this, it would be refuted by the passages [in the sūtras] where some arhats, such as Maudgalyāyana, though free of afflictions, manifest suffering due to the power of their past karma.[356]

[9.46ab] Now you might assert, "Even though the arhats may not become free of suffering the instant they have destroyed the afflictions, they will do so when their life comes to an end. For it is definite that they no longer have craving for the aggregates, the condition that leads to appropriating a new existence." [Response:] [9.46c–9.47b] Just as nonafflictive ignorance of the knowledge of all phenomena exists in them, couldn't they also have aggregates that are not [the results of] karma and afflictions? The fact is, craving will certainly arise when feelings are accompanied by grasping at real entities, and feeling is present in the arhats.

Third, even if the mind were to cease, it could resurface. [9.47c–9.48] Now a mind divorced from the realization of emptiness is necessarily a mind that has objects, and so it would get stuck on some objects and grasp at them. Even if such a mind were to cease temporarily, it would resurface, just as in the case of meditative attainment of nonperception,[357] where even though the mind ceases for a while, it resurfaces. Therefore those who wish to cease suffering should meditate on emptiness.

The benefits of meditating on emptiness are twofold. Of these, the first is *it leads to the fulfillment of two aims*. [9.52] When you realize emptiness, compassion will arise in you for those who are afflicted with the suffering engendered by ignorance of emptiness. Because of this, you will remain in cyclic existence but without either of the two extremes—attachment to existence and fear of suffering—and you will engage in immeasurable acts of helping others. This [fulfilling the aims of self and others] then is the fruit of meditating on emptiness.

The second is that *one destroys the two obscurations*. [9.54][358] In that the meditation on emptiness is the counterforce against the obstacles to omniscience, the darkness of afflictive obscuration and knowledge obscuration—why would those aspiring to omniscience not meditate on emptiness? They should.

The concluding summary is as follows. [9.53] Given the benefits and faults, respectively, of realizing and not realizing emptiness, objecting to the emptiness position is misguided. One should meditate on emptiness without any uncertainty about it being the path of the Buddha.

Next, the conclusion by way of a general summation. [9.55] The thought may arise "I am afraid of emptiness, so I will not meditate on it." [Response:] It is, in fact, appropriate to engender fear at the grasping at real entities, for it gives rise to all the suffering, and yet one is not afraid of it. Emptiness, on the other hand, allays suffering, so why would one engender fear of it? This is inappropriate.[359]

## How to engage with selflessness, the object of wisdom

This has two parts: the selflessness of persons, and the selflessness of phenomena.

## The selflessness of persons

The selflessness of persons, in turn, has two parts. Of these the first is *a summary linked to the preceding section.* [9.56] If there were to be something called self that experiences the fear, then fear would indeed arise from any kind of object. However, since there is no such self, who is it that experiences the fear?

The second, *the extensive explanation*, has three parts: general refutation of self based on deconstructing the aggregates,[360] refuting specific postulations of self, and rejecting objections against the refutation of self.

## General refutation of self based on deconstructing the aggregates

The first is as follows. [9.57–59]

> The teeth, hair, or nails are not self;
> self is not the bone, nor is it the blood;
> neither is it mucus or the phlegm,
> not the synovial fluid or the pus.
>
> Self is neither the bodily oil nor the sweat,
> self is neither lymph nor the intestines,

self is not the other entrails,
and self is not the excrement or the urine.

Neither the flesh nor the sinews are self.
Neither heat nor wind is self.
The orifices are not self. In no way either
are the six consciousnesses self.

As for the six elements, they are [likewise] multiple and devoid of independence.

### Refuting specific postulations of self

This has two parts: refuting the self postulated by Sāṃkhya, and refuting the self postulated by Nyāya.

### Refuting the self postulated by Sāṃkhya

The first is twofold: presenting the refutation, and rejecting their defense. The first is as follows. [9.60–61] If consciousness apprehending sound is permanent, then even when sound is not present, there would be consciousness perceiving sound. If you assent to this, then since consciousness perceiving sound depends on a sound, if there is no auditory object, what basis of perceiving and on what account could such consciousness be asserted to be "consciousness of sound"? If it can be consciousness of sound without perceiving sound, a block of wood could be asserted as consciousness of sound as well! Therefore it is determined that in the absence of an object, there can be no cognition perceiving it.

Rejecting their defense has two parts, the first of which is *the statement of their response*. [9.62a] You may respond, "It's not the case that when there is no sound, there can be no consciousness of sound. The very consciousness that perceived sound earlier would later, when there is no sound, come to perceive form and so on; the two are in fact one [consciousness]."

The second, *refuting this response*, has three parts: the previous consequence remains, how the aspects are incompatible, and refuting through the reasoning of nonperception of one as the other.

The first is as follows. [9.62b] In that case why, when perceiving form, is it not a consciousness of sound [for you]? It should be. [9.62cd] If you say sound is not heard because there is no sound, this would also establish that there is no consciousness perceiving sound [when there is a sound].

How the aspects are incompatible is twofold. The first is *stating the reasoning*. [9.63ab] Cognition whose nature is to perceive sound—how could it become a cognition perceiving form? The aspects of these [cognitions] are incompatible. The second is *how the analogy is not established*. [9.63c] You might assert that there is no contradiction in accepting two incompatible aspects of prior and later temporal stages as belonging to one [consciousness] in relation to two objects. It is just as, for example, how a single person can be both a father and a son. [Response:] [9.63d–9.64ab] According to your system, too, father and son are imputations and lack true existence. For you, truly existing matter refers to the state of equilibrium of lightness (*sattva*), mobility (*rajas*), and darkness (*tamas*), which is imperceptible, and so such an entity is neither a son nor a father.

Refuting through the reasoning of nonperception of one as the other is twofold: stating the argument, and rejecting the charge of nonestablishment. The first is as follows. [9.64cd] The cognition perceiving form is not endowed with the nature of consciousness of sound. If it were, this should be observable, but that is not the case.

The second, rejecting the charge of nonestablishment,[361] has two parts, of which the first is *the actual point*. [9.65ab] You may say, "Just as a single actor can appear in different and diverse guises, likewise, what was previously cognition perceiving sound is later seen in the guise of cognition perceiving a form." [Response:] In that case, your consciousness would not be permanent, for it changes into diverse forms.

The second, *rejecting the charge of no logical entailment*, is twofold. Of these the first, the opponent's objection, is as follows. [9.65c] "Even though it takes different forms, its nature remains permanent, the same as before."

The second, refuting this assertion, is twofold. The first is that *it is untenable for two incompatible aspects to share the same nature*. [9.65d–9.67b] This oneness [of yours] is indeed an unprecedented kind of oneness! You may say, even though [consciousness] is seen in diverse forms, these are unreal, so it is indeed one. In that case then tell us: what is the nature of this thing that is truly one? If you say it exists truly as unitary consciousness, then since the consciousnesses of all the people that share distinct mental continua are equal in being consciousness, it follows that they are all one. Furthermore, a self (*puruṣa*) that is conscious and a primal matter (*prakṛti*) that is unconscious would also be one, for insofar as being objects of cognition, they are the same.

The second is that *it is untenable for the universal to be real when its instances are unreal*. [9.67cd] When all the instances of consciousness, such as cognition perceiving form and cognition perceiving sound, are distorted and unreal, how can there be a truly existing one that serves as the basis for their similarity as cognitions? There cannot be.

### Refuting the self postulated by Nyāya

The Naiyāyika assert an eternal principle that is material and is within a person's continuum, endowed with mind that is separate from it. And it is this they take to be the self that is the enjoyer of the objects.

To refute this, there are three parts. First is *presenting the argument.* [9.68ab] An entity that is not conscious cannot be a self that enjoys the objects, for it lacks the nature of being conscious—just like a vase, for example.

Second, *rejecting any fault in the logical entailment.* [9.68c–9.69b] You may say that even though it does not exist in the nature of consciousness in an ultimate sense, it nonetheless possesses mind that is distinct from it, so it is indeed the enjoyer of the objects. [Response:] This is untenable. If a self that is by nature not conscious of objects can know by being endowed with mind, then it follows that this unknowing self would be subject to perishing and impermanence. And if self is devoid of such changes, how can you then draw the distinction of its becoming endowed with mind, turning something that does not perceive objects into one that perceives them? Such distinctions cannot be drawn.

The third is a *concluding summary.* [9.69cd] Thus if you accept a self that by virtue of being material has no consciousness of objects and by virtue of being permanent is devoid of the causal function of producing effects, you would be rendering space as the self; that is, [according to you] space would be self.

## Rejecting objections against the refutation of self

Rejecting objections against refutation of self has two parts:[362] rejecting that karmic causality would be untenable, and rejecting that compassion would be impossible.

The first is twofold, of which the first, the objection, is this: [9.70] You might argue, "If there is no permanent self, any connection between karma and its consequences would be impossible—that is to say, the agent who created the karma would not be the one who experienced the consequences. For if, once the karmic act is done, its agent perishes, he would no longer exist when the consequence is experienced. So whose karmic action would it be?"

The second, our response, has three parts. Of these, the first is *showing how the same objection applies to the opponent.* [9.71] On the [two points]—that the aggregates of this present life, the basis of the karmic action, and the aggregates of the future life that are the basis for experiencing the consequences are different, and that in both instances it's not self that commits the action and experiences its consequences—these are established for both of us, you who assert a self that is material and permanent and us who assert no self. So surely arguing about this here is pointless for both of us.

Second, *rejecting the opponent's rejoinder.* [9.72ab] You might assert, "When it comes to karmic actions whose consequences are experienced in this very life, there are not separates bases [for the karmic action and its consequences]." [Response:] Now, the aggregate at the time of the action occurring simultaneously with experiencing the consequence is something never seen, just as a father and his son can never be born simultaneously.

Third, *rejecting the charge of contradicting scripture.* [Opponent:] The following statement appears in scripture: "How can a karmic action done by one be experienced by another? O monks, a karmic action that has been done and accrued will not ripen upon external things like the earth element and so on. It will ripen upon the aggregates sustained by consciousness and so on."[363] Thus you would be contradicting such statements about how the consequence of karmic action is experienced by the same agent of that action.

[Response:] [9.72c–9.74] This is a statement made with a special intent. Holding the unity of the continuum of consciousness as the intention, and for the purpose of preventing denigration of the law of karma, it is taught that the very agent who created the karma is the one who experiences its consequence. In reality, this is not the case, for there is no eternal self.

Why is this? Neither the past nor the future mind is self, for they are either already ceased or not yet arisen, and thus non-existent. And if you say the present mind—which has arisen and has not yet ceased—is self, then, when it ceases in the subsequent moment, it would follow that the self would no longer exist. This same argument refutes self in all five aggregates. Just as, when chopped up, the trunk of a plantain tree has no core at all, in the same way the self, when subjected to a thorough analysis, has no true existence.

Next, rejecting the objection that compassion would be impossible has three parts: rejecting that there is no object [of compassion], rejecting that there is no result, and rejecting that compassion does not merit cultivation because it's an object to be abandoned.

The first is as follows. [9.75] You might argue, "If there are no sentient beings, for whom do you cultivate compassion?" [Answer:] Even though its objects, sentient beings, have no true existence, there is no contradiction in cultivating compassion for objects for whose sake one has taken the vow to lead them to the goal of liberation—that is, for beings projected by ignorance who appear within the deluded perspective.

Second is rejecting that there is no result [of compassion]. [9.76ab] You may ask, "If there are no sentient beings, who is it that would reap the benefits from one's cultivation of compassion?" [Answer:] This is indeed true from the ultimate perspective. But on the conventional level, we accept that through cultivating merely appearing compassion for merely appearing sentient beings within the deluded perspective of perceiving phenomena due to ignorance, merely appearing fruits would emerge.[364]

Third is rejecting that compassion does not merit cultivation because it's an object to be abandoned. [9.76c] You might say, "Compassion, too, since it takes on false objects, constitutes ignorance in relation to phenomena. So like the ignorance perceiving self, it is equally to be averted." [Response:] [9.76d–9.77] Since it is [cultivated] to bring an end to suffering, it should not be prevented, and neither can it be. So this effect of delusion that is mere appearance[365] is not something to be prevented, while the delusion pertaining to self is, because the latter increases the causes of suffering like conceit. If you say no method to prevent [grasping at self] exists, [we say] meditating on emptiness is the most excellent antidote against such [ignorance].

### The selflessness of phenomena

Next is engaging in the selflessness of phenomena. The *Sūtra Teaching the Nonorigination of All Things* states:

> Mañjuśrī, when one sees the *body* as space-like, one will establish the mindfulness viewing the body as body. Likewise, extending this to *feeling*, when one perceives no feeling, and one understands *mind* to be a mere name, one will perceive neither virtuous nor nonvirtuous *phenomena* and establish the mindfulness viewing phenomena as phenomena.[366]

In accord with the above sūtra, the four applications of mindfulness are presented.

### The application of mindfulness of the body

Of these, the first, the application of mindfulness of the body, has three parts: (1) how the body, the bearer of the limbs, is not established, (2) how the limbs themselves are not established, and (3) a summary of the points. The first is twofold: how the body, the object, is not established, and how apprehension of the body is deluded. The first, in turn, is twofold: refuting that the body is connected to the limbs, and refuting that the body is not connected to the limbs.

The first has three parts, the first of which is *refuting that individual body parts are the body.*

> The body is not the feet, not the calves;
> it is not the thighs and not the buttocks;
> it is not the stomach nor the back either;
> neither is it the chest or the arms. [9.78]
>
> The body is not the hands nor the sides;
> it is not the armpits, nor is it the shoulder area;
> the body is not the entrails;
> the neck or the head are also not the body. [9.79]

Among these parts, which is the truly existent body? None of them whatsoever.

Second, *rejecting that the body exists in each of these parts.* [9.80–81] If the body were to exist in each of these body parts, then even though the individual body parts might exist in those parts, where does the body that is said to be indivisible and real exist in itself? Now if you say that the whole indivisible body is present in its entirety in each of the parts, such as the hands, it would follow that there would be just as many bodies as there are parts.

Third, *a concluding summary*: [9.82ab] If the body is nowhere, neither inside nor outside, how does the body truly exist in the hands and so forth? It does not.

Next is refuting that the body is *not* connected to the limbs. [9.82cd] Since the body cannot be perceived apart from the hands and so forth—that is to say, it does not exist—how would the body that is a whole *not* connected to the body parts exist? It does not.

How apprehension of body is deluded is as follows. [9.83–84] Since there is no truly existing body, in the absence of a body, the deluded notion of body arises due to ignorance. However, the body apprehended by such a notion does not exist truly. For example, so long as the conditions are there for a post to be confused with a person, that post will be perceived as a person. Likewise, as long as the conditions remain for deludedly conflating the hands and so forth with the body, they will be perceived as the body.

Next, how the limbs themselves are not established. [9.85–86] Just as the whole body lacks true existence, in the same way, since it is an assemblage of fingers, how can a hand have any true existence? The same goes for the finger, since it too is an assemblage of joints and so cannot have true existence. A joint too, when analyzed into its constituents, is seen to have no such existence. Even those constituents can be deconstructed down to the atomic level, and the atom itself can be divided further into its directional parts, thus becoming many and not a truly existent one. These directional parts too, when divided, will turn out to be not truly existing; so just like space, they are empty. Thus atoms also lack true existence.

The summary of the points: [9.87] Thus, though appearing, it has no true existence—what discerning person would become attached to this dream-like body? It is illogical to do so. And since the body does not exist, what is a man's body and what is a woman's body? No such specific bodies exist.

### The application of mindfulness of feeling

The application of mindfulness of feeling has four parts: the nature of feeling, the cause contact, its object, and how the apprehending subject is not established. The first is twofold: how feeling lacks ultimate existence, and cultivating the antidote that counters such a notion.

The first, in turn, has two parts. Of these, the first, *the argument to refute*, is this. *Fundamental Verses* says:

> If something existed by intrinsic nature,
> there would not be the nonexistence of such a thing.
> Never is it logical that an intrinsic nature
> transforms into something else.[367]

[9.88] As this states, if painful feeling were truly existent, it would never discard its nature, and would it not then undermine its opposites, cheerfulness and pleasure? It would, in which case they could never arise at all. But that they do arise is obvious. Similarly, if the pleasurable truly existed as pleasurable, why would tasty food and its like not induce pleasure in someone afflicted by grief or illness? They should, but clearly they do not.

The second is *rejecting the opponent's rejoinder*. [9.89–91] Perhaps you say, "Pain does truly exist, but when a more forceful pleasure arises, it overpowers the former, so the pain is not experienced." [Response:] In that case, how can that which does not have the nature of an experience be a feeling? For it lacks that characteristic. Now you might say, "Surely the pain continues at a subtle level and is thus a feeling, and isn't it the case that its grossness is removed by the strong pleasure? And the character of this subtle feeling is such that it is distinct from the gross feeling of pleasure; it is a weak form of pleasure." [Response:] In that case, what is experienced as subtle [pain] would not belong to the category of pleasure. Alternatively, you may argue, "Because its opposite, pleasure, has arisen, pain does not arise in that mental continuum." [Response:] In that case, surely this would establish that what is conceived as "feeling" is in fact a symptom of grasping at something false?

Cultivating the antidote that counters such a notion is as follows. [9.92] Given that one is deluded by the notion of feeling, one should cultivate an antidote to this illusion: this wisdom analyzing all phenomena as devoid of intrinsic existence. The meditative absorption, the fruit that grows in the field of conceptualization projected by the mind, is indeed the nourishment that enhances the body—namely, the realization of the true nature of reality.

Next is the cause contact. Now *contact* is asserted to be the meeting of object, sense organ, and consciousness, so refuting this has three parts: refuting the meeting of the sense organ and the object, refuting contact for consciousness, and summarizing the key points.

The first is twofold, of which the first is *refuting [the possibility of] contact in general.* [9.93] When sense organs, like the eyes, and their objects, such as form, are separated by space, where can they meet each other? They are like the mountains in the east and the mountains in the west. And if there is no interval space, it would follow that they are in fact one, in which case what would be in contact with what? For there are no two distinct things, one that contacts and other being contacted.

The second is *refuting contact between atoms.* [9.94–95] The atoms in the sense organ and those in its object cannot come into contact with each other in their entirety. For one atom cannot enter into another atom—one atom cannot be absorbed into another. This is because, with no space in between, each would be exactly the same size. Here is the logical entailment: If one does not enter the other, there cannot be a fusion, and without fusion, there cannot be complete contact. As for those who assert that an atom is without parts, how could such a thing have partial contact? For in that case, the atom would have two parts—one in contact and another not in contact! Now if you do see such a thing that is without parts but has contact, then demonstrate it! You cannot.

Next is refuting contact for consciousness. [9.96] Contact is untenable for consciousness because consciousness has no body or matter. Now if you say that even though consciousness does not have contact in the physical sense, there is at least an assemblage [with other factors] to produce an effect. [Response:] This is untenable, for an assemblage itself does not exist as a real entity. This is the same as the analysis above in the lines "What is called continuum and collection . . ."[368]

Summarizing the key points is as follows. [9.97–98] In this way, when there is no contact, how can its effect, feeling, arise? Therefore, for what purpose is this struggle to seek pleasurable feeling? And what feeling of pain afflicts the mental continuum of whom? For there is nothing to attain and nothing that harms. Seeing that there is no such thing as a self that experiences feeling, and not even any feeling itself, wouldn't craving for attainment of pleasure and separation from pain then come to cease? It would.

The third topic [under mindfulness of feeling] is its object. [9.99ab] As for the objects [of the senses], from sight to tactile sensation, though appearing they are unreal, and thus their characters resemble dreams and magical illusions. Given this, feeling, which consists of a subject experiencing these objects, also has no true existence.

The fourth is how the apprehending subject is not established. [9.99c–9.101] Feeling is not perceived by the mind that is simultaneous with it, for arising simultaneously with the mind means that such feeling is not connected with it [as cause and effect]. As for the mind that has arisen before the feeling or has arisen after the feeling, they will either recollect it or anticipate it; they do not experience [the feeling], because during their time, the feeling is either yet to arise or already ceased. [Furthermore,] given there are not two things [within one's experience]—what is being felt and the feeling subject—it is not experienced by oneself on our own accord. Also when examined in terms of the three times, that it [the feeling] is experienced by something other remains untenable. Thus there is nothing whatsoever that experiences the feeling, and hence, in reality, there is no feeling. So, how can the feeling of pleasure help or the feeling of pain afflict this collection of aggregates that has no self? They do not exist as things that help or harm.

### The application of mindfulness of the mind

This has two parts: how the mind is not established, and how the five sensory cognitions are not established. The first is as follows. [9.102–3] The mental consciousness does not reside in the sense faculties, such as sight, nor does it reside in the objects, such as form. For there are occasions when even though the objects are present, mental consciousness does not arise. Nor does it reside in between—that is, elsewhere. The mind does not exist in the body nor outside it; neither is it found somewhere else. The mind is not the body; nor does it truly exist as something neither intermingled with the body nor existing separately elsewhere—such a thing does not have even the smallest degree of true existence. That this is so is stated in the *Heap of Jewels* collection:

> Kāśyapa, the mind is not inside, it is not outside, and neither is it in both; the mind is not perceived. Kāśyapa, the mind has no form, is not demonstrable, is without obstructive property, is not a basis, has no appearance, is incognizable, and is unlocated. Kāśyapa, the mind is something that even all the buddhas have not seen, do not see, and will not see [in the future].[369]

Therefore sentient beings are primordially liberated.[370]

The second, how the five sensory cognitions are not established, is as follows. [9.104–5b] You may say, "Even though this might be true with respect to mental consciousness, the five sense consciousnesses exist truly as subjects perceiving the five classes of objects." [Response:] Now if you assert that the five sensory consciousnesses exist prior to what is cognized—namely, the five classes of objects—then based on what kinds of objects do they come into existence? For at that time, the objects do not yet exist since they have not arisen. Now if you assert that the consciousness and its object are simultaneous, arising together at the same time, the question remains, "On the basis of perceiving what object does the consciousness arise?" For when it has not arisen yet, the object too would have not arisen yet, and when it has arisen, there would be no need for it to be produced by the object. Now if you say it [consciousness] exists after the thing to be cognized, then the question is, "On the basis of what object would that consciousness arise?" For at that time the object is no more; it has already ceased to exist.

## The application of mindfulness of phenomena

The application of mindfulness of phenomena is twofold. Of these, the first is stating how it is established that all phenomena are devoid of arising. [9.105cd] In this way—that is, through this reasoning showing how things do not arise in any temporal terms of prior, later, or simultaneously—it is established that with respect to all phenomena, no arising can be perceived in a true sense.

The second, repelling the objections, has two parts: The first, *repelling the consequence that there would be no conventional truth*, is twofold: [the objection and our response]. First is the objection: [9.106] Now if, as stated, all phenomena lack arising, there would be no conventional truth that possesses arising and disintegration. In that case, how can there be two truths according to the Madhyamaka system? There cannot be. Furthermore, if in this way all phenomena lack arising and disintegration, and conventional truth possessing arising and disintegration is posited by some other factor as a mere projection of delusory cognition, how then can a sentient being attain nirvāṇa? It would be impossible.

Second is our response. [9.107][371] Although phenomena do lack arising in reality, beings, not realizing this, conceive things as possessing arising and disintegration and take these as objects of cognition. It is from this perspective that conventional truth is posited; hence it is not the case that there would be no conventional truth. It is also not the case that there would be no nirvāṇa. [In general] it is [simply] not the case that someone else's delusion turns something into a conventional truth. The delusory conception [that posits nirvāṇa's existence] is not that of the one in nirvāṇa but that of someone else—it is not the conventional or delusory conception of the one in nirvāṇa himself. If later, at the time of nirvāṇa, there were indeed delusory conceptualization, then at that time there would be conventional truth as well. But since no such delusory conceptualization exists [at that time], there would be no conventional truth either. Here, the *Extensive Commentary* states, "The arising of phenomena from other phenomena is something that comes about later, but it does not exist. Therefore later, were there to be such phenomena, there would certainly be conventional truth then."[372] Thus it seems possible to interpret this phrase in terms of "if after nirvāṇa there is definitely the arising of one from another . . ."

The second, *repelling the consequence that no analysis would be possible*, has two parts: [stating the objection, and our response]. First, stating the objection: [9.108ab] Since [according to you Mādhyamika,] the pair—the examining mind and what it examines—are mutually dependent, so if the object is not established, there would be no cognition either. In this case, then, analysis would be impossible.

The second, our response, has three parts. Of these, the first is that *there is no need for a truly existing analyzer*. [9.108cd] Even though it is true that since objects have no true existence, the [analyzing] cognition also has no true existence, nevertheless this would not induce the consequence that analysis is impossible. This is because all analysis is expressed in terms of conventional cognition—in forms of reasoning commonly understood by the world.

The second is that *there would follow an absurd consequence if such a truly existing analyzer were necessary.* [9.109] If analysis required a truly existing analyzer, then that analysis, too, would require further analysis by means of another analysis, and so analysis would be endless. This would mean that the original analysis could never proceed.

The third is that *things are established to be empty even if not analyzed.* [9.110] Now if the object of analysis is established as empty after having been analyzed, then the analyzing mind, even if it is not analyzed, with no basis—no object [to ground it]—will arise no more. And this calming of both the object and its cognition is said to constitute nirvāṇa. This is as stated earlier in the line "With no object to focus, the mind is thoroughly calmed."[373]

## How to eliminate grasping at real entities, the object of elimination

This has three parts: a general presentation, refuting the proof arguments, and presenting the objections.

The first is as follows. [9.111ab] According to you realists, the two—object and cognition—have true existence. Thus you abide with great difficulty, for you have no [reliable] proofs and are open to injurious objections.

The second, refuting the proof arguments, is twofold. Of these, the first is *how because of their mutual dependence they are not established.* [9.111c–9.113] You may say, "It is on the strength of truly existing cognition, the faculty,[374] that a truly existing object is established." [Response:] What proof do you have that demonstrates that the object is supported by a truly existing cognition? If, instead, you claim that it is on the strength of the object that truly existent cognition is established, then what support is there for the existence of the object? If the two exist through mutual strengths, this would mean that when one is not established, the other would also be unestablished. This would make both nonexistent. For example, if there is no son, there cannot be a father, and without a father, from whom would the son come? So since there can be no father without a son and no son without a father, this means in the end that neither of them exists. In the same manner, neither of the two—object and cognition—can exist.

The second, *refuting the opponent's rejoinder*, is as follows. [9.114] You may say, "Even if something is dependent [on something else], there is no contradiction in it being established. For example, since a shoot arises from a seed and is hence dependent upon it, the existence of the seed can be deduced the strength of the shoot. Likewise, why cannot one verify the existence of the object on the strength of the cognition that arises from that object?" [Answer:] [9.115] The two cases are different. Granted that, in relation to the shoot, through it being seen by a cognition—something distinct from the shoot—the existence of the seed can be deduced. By what means—by what cognition—can that true existence of the object of cognition be known? There is no such cognizer.

The third, *presenting the objections*, has three parts: establishing emptiness from the point of view of the cause, establishing emptiness from the point of view of the effect, and a concluding summation.

### Establishing emptiness from the point of view of the cause

The first has two parts: how [phenomena] are unarisen in the ultimate sense, and establishing what has arisen conventionally to be empty.

### How [phenomena] are unarisen in the ultimate sense

The first, in turn, has three parts: refuting arising from no cause, refuting arising from a permanent cause, and a concluding summary.

### Refuting arising from no cause

The Cārvāka and Mīmāṃsā schools say:

> The shining of the sun and the downward flow of a river,
> the roundness of peas and the prickliness of long and sharp thorns,
> the striking colors of peacock feathers—all such phenomena
> are not created by anyone but emerge naturally by themselves.[375]

Thus they assert that things arise from no cause. Here is the refutation of this assertion: [9.116–17] Ordinary people, through direct perception, observe that effects arise from all sorts of causes, and they also establish this fact through inference. So the distinct features of an effect—such as a lotus blossom, its stalk, and so forth—arise from their distinct causes. You may ask, "What causes produce the distinct features of these effects?" The answer is that they result from a variety of preceding causes.

You may ask, "On what basis does the variety of the causes have the power to produce such a variety of effects?" It is through the power of their own preceding causes that they have the capacity to produce effects in such a manner.

### Refuting arising from a permanent cause

Refuting arising from a permanent cause has three parts: refuting arising from Īśvara (God), refuting arising from atoms, and refuting arising from primal matter. The first has three parts.

Of these, the first is that *Īśvara is not established.* [9.118a] The Nyāya and Vaiśeṣika assert an Īśvara that is endowed with the following five attributes—divine, pure and worthy of worship, eternal, unitary, and creator of everything—to be the cause of all beings. [9.118b–9.120] Against this, for now, we ask: "What exactly is this Īśvara? Do tell us." You may say, "It is the great elements." Indeed, the great elements are the cause of their derivatives, and if it's these you give the label Īśvara, then the dispute is really about semantics; so we will not partake in it. That said, the great elements do not possess the characteristics [of Īśvara] you assert, for the elements such as earth are multiple, impermanent, devoid of motivating thought, and not divine, for they can be walked over and are thus impure. So they cannot be Īśvara. Space too is not Īśvara, for it is devoid of movement. The self too is not Īśvara, for its existence was disproved above. Thus this so-called creator Īśvara cannot be conceived, so why do you assert something conceptually impossible to be the creator? This is pointless.

The second is that *there is nothing it has produced.* [9.121–22b] So when asked, "What is it that this Īśvara had created?" You may say, "It is self, the atoms of the elements, and the subsequent continuum of Īśvara itself." [Answer:] Don't you assert these to be permanent? If so, how can they be what is produced, for that would be contradictory? As to consciousness, it too arises from a cognizable object, and its character as mere awareness is something that arises from its preceding moment of awareness. Similarly, happiness and suffering arise from virtuous and non-virtuous karma. So tell us what is it that Īśvara produces?

The third, that *Īśvara cannot be the creator*, is twofold. Of these, the first is stating the consequence. [9.122cd] If the cause, the creator Īśvara, has no beginning, how could there be any beginning to its effects, such as happiness and suffering? There could not. Similarly, they could not have any end, in which case, why could they not exist continuously? They should. This is refuted, however, by the fact they are established as occasional.

Second is rejecting that there is no logical entailment [in our argument]: [9.123–25] You may argue, "Even though Īśvara is permanent, since producing the effect depends on other conditions, there is no logical consequence that the effects would exist continuously." [Response:] Īśvara cannot be dependent on something other than itself, for there is nothing that is not created by it. So on what could it depend to produce the effect? Now if it were to depend on the combination of conditions, then it would follow that the combination of conditions are the cause, not Īśvara. This is because when the combination of conditions is present, Īśvara would have no power to preclude the effect; yet, it has no power to produce the effect without such a combination either! Now if Īśvara produces the effect even without desiring to do so, it follows that it is subject to something other than itself. But if it produces the effect from desiring to do so, it would be subject to the desire. And if it produces the effect through being subject to desire, which is impermanent, how could it be Īśvara [i.e., omnipotent and eternal]?

Refuting arising from atoms is as follows. [9.126ab] Those such as the Vaiśeṣika assert that permanent atoms produce the entire container world and the sentient beings contained therein. But this is untenable. Permanent atoms were already refuted above in the line "The atom too can be divided in terms of the directions."[376]

The third, refuting arising from primal matter, has two parts: stating the assertion, and refuting the assertion. The first is as follows. [9.126c–9.127] Sāṃkhya subsumes all of reality in two categories: a conscious self (*puruṣa*) and primal matter (*prakṛti*). Of these, the self is, as explained above, endowed with five attributes[377] and is neither a cause nor an effect. The permanent primal matter, a substance that is not visible to anyone, alone is the creator of everything, and thus they assert a primal matter with five characteristics to be the cause of all beings.[378] Its nature is that of the equilibrium of three qualities of pleasure, pain, and neutrality bearing the names, respectively, lightness (*sattva*), mobility (*rajas*), and darkness (*tamas*). It is this nature that is called "the primary cause." From the disequilibrium of these [qualities, the world of] transformations emerge. Here too, what first emerges is called "the great one" [the intellect (*buddhi*)], clear as crystal. To this appear, internally, *puruṣa* (person) and, externally, the reflections of objects; the fusion of these two [sides] is what is referred to as "the person experiencing objects." Then ego arises, and from this emerge the following sixteen things: the eleven faculties—the five faculties such as the eyes; the five faculties of activity: mouth, legs, hands, and the organs for urine and excrement; and the shared mental faculty—and the five "mere thats" [i.e., sense objects]: form, sound, smell, taste, and texture. From the five "mere thats" emerge the five elements of space, wind, fire, water, and earth. These twenty-two categories, they assert, constitute the effects. It is stated:

> From the primary nature, the great; from that the ego;
> from that the grouping of sixteen;
> among these sixteen too,
> from the five "mere thats" emerge the five elements.[379]

The second, refuting this assertion, has four parts: refuting that nature is unitary, refuting that sense objects are pleasure and so forth, refuting [pleasure and so forth as] permanent entities, and refuting the arising of what already exists.

The first is as follows. [9.128–29b] Given that the nature that you assert is unitary cannot exist truly as possessing three natures, this primal matter is not existent. Similarly, the three qualities can have no true existence, for each of the three, in turn, would turn out to be composed of three qualities. The reasoning is established here by the fact that the opponent accepts the three [qualities] to share the same nature, and that everything material shares the nature of these three qualities. This latter point is made explicit in the *Extensive Commentary*.[380] Now if the cause, the three qualities, does not exist, the existence of other manifestations, such as sound, remains far away—that is to say, beyond possibility.

The second is refuting that sense objects are pleasure and so forth. [9.129c–9.131b] Pleasure and so forth cannot be present in the five sense objects, such as cloth, as a single nature because they are devoid of mind. You may argue that they exist truly as sharing the nature of causing pleasure and so forth, so pleasure and so forth do exist in them. [Response:] Entities such as cloth are similar to the body [with respect to being material entities], so the refutation of body through analysis, which was presented above, applies equally to them. Does it not? Furthermore, even though, in your system, the cause of cloth and so forth is also the three qualities, cloth and so forth do not emerge from pleasure and so forth. On the conventional level, it is in fact from cloth and so forth that pleasure and so on are seen to arise. Also, when analyzed, the cause, cloth and so forth, lack true existence, which would mean then that their effects, pleasure and so forth, also have no true existence whatsoever.

The third is refuting [pleasure and so forth as] permanent entities. [9.131c–9.134b] Pleasure and so forth can never exist as permanent entities because they are occasional. If manifestations such as pleasure and so forth were eternally existent, how come there is no apprehension of pleasure when pain arises? There should be. If you say that when pain arises, pleasure remains subtly and so it is not experienced, to this we ask, "How can something permanent be sometimes coarse and sometimes subtle?" If it sheds the state of being coarse and becomes subtle, that would mean that these coarse and subtle pleasures and so forth are indeed impermanent. In that case, why do you not accept that all transformations are similarly impermanent? The same argument applies to them too. Now if you say that although the coarse and subtle states of pleasure may be impermanent, their nature remains permanent, [we say] that since coarseness of pleasure is not something separate from pleasure and is impermanent, pleasure too would become an impermanent manifestation.

The fourth, refuting the arising of what already exists, has four parts. Of these the first is *uncertainty within the opponent's own view*. [9.134c–9.135b] You may say, "Something that has no existence whatsoever cannot arise, for it does not exist." [Response:] Although you do not assert the arising of a manifest thing that has no prior existence, the acceptance of this stands even according to your own tenet, for you assert that something that was not previously manifest comes to be manifest [later].

The second is *stating an absurd consequence*. [9.135cd] If the result exists in the cause, someone eating rice is eating feces! Also, you should buy cotton seeds at the price of cloth and wear them!

The third is *rejecting the opponent's rejoinder*. [9.136–37] You may say that although such is the actual reality, ordinary people do not see cloth in the cotton seeds, so they do not wear them. This is not true. The truth is that even those who supposedly understand this reality, such as the sage Kapila, do not wear the seeds but cloth. Also, according to you, this knowledge of reality, which is a result, should exist in its causal state—that is, it should be present even in ordinary people—so why is it that they do not see cloth in the seeds? They should. You might maintain that even though it is present in ordinary people, there is no validity in the knowledge of ordinary people with respect to the causal state, and because of this, they do not know this fact. In that case, what that cognition [of ordinary people] perceives clearly—the result—would also be unreal, for it would be an object of a deluded cognition.

The fourth is *rejecting that our own position is undermined.* [9.138] [Objection:] "According to your Madhyamaka system, the means of valid cognition through which objects are cognized are not valid but deluded, so wouldn't it the case that emptiness, which is ascertained through such means, is false as well? Since it is false, meditation on emptiness would be misguided."

[Response:] [9.139–40] Without contacting or bringing to mind as an object what is imputed by the mind, there is no apprehension of the nonexistence of that entity. For example, without there being a child of a barren woman, there cannot be the apprehension of his death. So, since nonexistence is contingent on existence, it follows that the negation of what is being negated—namely, the unreal entity—is clearly not real. Still it is fitting to meditate on emptiness because it serves as the antidote to grasping at true existence. For example, when in a dream a son dies, the thought "He does not exist" hinders the thought of his existence. Such an apprehension of nonexistence, though false, has the power to prevent [the arising of] the thought of the son's existence.

## The concluding summary

The concluding summary is as follows. [9.141–42] Therefore, with this kind of analysis through reasoning, nothing exists without a cause, and neither do things exist in individual or a combination of conditions. Nor do they come into existence anew from something other. Thus they have no arising at first, have no abiding in the middle, and do not go elsewhere in the end. Since an illusion does not exist when analyzed, what is the difference between an illusion and that which, though appearing, has no reality—and is grasped as real through ignorance?

## Establishing what has arisen conventionally to be empty

[9.143–44] As for magical horses and elephants conjured by illusion and as for forms and so forth created by causes, examine this: Where do they come from initially? Where do they endure in the middle? And where do they go in the end? When examined, they are equal in having no going and no coming. In a sūtra it says, "Form does not come from anywhere, it does not endure anywhere, and it will not go anywhere . . ."[381] An effect is seen when its cause is nearby and not when the cause is not present. As such it is a fabrication of causes and conditions, so how can such a thing, one that resembles a reflection, have true existence? It says in a sūtra:

> Whatever has arisen from conditions is unborn;
> it does not have the nature of arising.
> That which depends on conditions, I declare empty.
> One who understands emptiness is at ease.[382]

## Establishing emptiness from the point of view of the effect

Establishing emptiness from the point of view of the effect has three parts:[383] refuting arising from the two extremes, refuting the negation itself, and thus establishing phenomena to be empty. The first is twofold, of which the first, refuting the arising of what already exists, is as follows. [9.145ab] For an entity that already exists, because it exists already, what purpose would be served by a cause?

The second, refuting arising of what is nonexistent, has two parts. Of these the first is *how nonexistence itself is not something to be produced.* [9.145cd] For what is nonexistent also, because it is not an effect, what purpose would be served by a cause?

The second is *how it cannot be turned into an entity.* [9.146–48b] You may say, "Even though a cause would not produce something nonexistent, it can turn something into an entity." [Response:] This is untenable. Even hundreds of billions of causes will not produce any change in what is nonexistent, for nonexistence is permanent. Now if it could bring about such a change, we ask, is this change brought about in a way where the status of nonexistence is lost or not lost? If it is the latter, how can it be existent when the status of nonexistence is not lost? If it is the former, what else can, after losing its status of nonexistence, come into existence? This is impossible. Furthermore, if it does not lose its status of nonexistence, since it is impossible for something to exist while it is a nonexistent thing, when does the existent thing become existent? If it is asserted that, losing its status of nonexistence, it undergoes change, without it having arisen as an existent first, how can it lose its status of nonexistence? Since they are mutually dependent, both options are impossible.

Next, refuting the negation itself is as follows. [9.148cd] Likewise it is not the case that an entity becomes a nonexistent entity following its cessation. For at that time, if it has not lost its status of existence, then the nature of one and the same entity would become both existent and nonexistent, something impossible. Now if the entity were to lose its status of existence, in that case, it would be contradictory for that entity to be something real. This is as stated in the following:

> If something exists through an intrinsic nature,
> it would then not become nonexistent.[384]

Thus establishing phenomena to be empty is as follows. [9.149] Since there is neither cessation nor arising of entities, this entire universe is unborn, unceased, primordially pacified, and naturally liberated.

## Concluding summation

The concluding summation is as follows. [9.150] The universe, though appearing [as real], is unreal like a dream and, when analyzed, resembles the trunk of a plantain tree. The *King of Meditations Sūtra* states:

> Even though a person might cut open
> a plantain tree seeking to find some inner core,
> there is no core inside or outside.
> Understand all phenomena to be likewise.[385]

Therefore there is, in reality, no difference between nirvāṇa and non-nirvāṇa—cyclic existence. A sūtra states, "Since all phenomena are of equanimity, the perfection of wisdom too is of equanimity."[386]

## The activity of one who has attained wisdom

This has two parts: equalizing one's mind toward eight worldly concerns, and generating compassion for those who have not realized [emptiness].

The first is as follows. [9.151–54b] Since things are empty in this way, what gifts can be received, what taken away? Who—namely, what sentient beings can praise or honor you, who can humiliate you? From what help or harm can there be happiness or misery? What praise or disparagement is there to like or dislike? When examined as to its nature, who craves, and what is there to crave for? Upon analysis, since the world of living beings does not exist, who then will die in it? Who will come to exist in a future life? Who has existed in a previous life? Who is a relative, and who is a friend? So all those engaged in the analysis of ultimate reality like me, Śāntideva, accept these to be like space, having no existence in any specific terms.

Generating compassion for those who have not realized [emptiness] has two parts: the object and the aspect. The first is threefold, of which the first is *they live this present life miserably*. [9.154c–9.155] Those who desire happiness get angry and rejoice, respectively, through dispute and ostensible acts of service. Not finding happiness, they experience grief, and for the sake of happiness they strive hard with their three doors, argue with others, and inflict lacerations and amputations on each other. In this way, they appear to lead lives of misery.

The second is *they endure suffering in a future life*. [9.156] Even after repeatedly securing a good rebirth and enjoying pleasures over and over, they die and apparently plunge into the long and unbearable sufferings of the lower realms.

The third, *the faults of cyclic existence in general*, has three parts. Of these, the first is *how it [cyclic existence] is contradictory to liberation*. [9.157–58b] Cyclic existence has many suffering pitfalls. [In cyclic existence,] instead of the realization of suchness that is the means to liberation, there is the grasping at true existence of form and so forth. And since realization of suchness and grasping at real entities are mutually contradictory, in cyclic existence there is no realization of the truth of reality like this [emptiness]. Also, while there, beings experience an incomparable and unbearable ocean of suffering, beyond any limit.

The second is *how it is difficult to avoid this contradiction*. [9.158c–9.162] There [in cyclic existence] too, because of not having realized emptiness, one's cultivation of virtue remains weak, and the span of one's life endowed with leisure and opportunity is short. Even while alive, one is preoccupied with livelihood and health, assailed by such things as hunger, fatigue, and sleep, and absorbed in fruitless pursuits such as fraternizing with fools. In such a way, one's life passes quickly, pointlessly, making it so hard to analyze the apparent world [and recognize it] as devoid of true existence. So how could [cyclic existence] contain the method to avert the habitual distraction of grasping at real entities? Not only is there the lack of favorable conditions on one's own part, one also faces hindrances created by other forces. There, Māra strives to make beings fall into the great misfortune of the lower realms, showing them a profusion of false paths, and making it hard even to prevent doubt pertaining to the correct path. These factors are so powerful it becomes difficult to obtain a life of leisure again, and it makes the appearance of buddhas exceedingly rare and the flood of afflictions hard to prevent. "Oh, these beings in cyclic existence would experience a succession of suffering," exclaims [Śāntideva] out of compassion.

The third is *how, due to their distortions, beings grasp suffering as happiness.* [9.163–65] Alas! These sentient beings who, though living in extreme suffering, fail to see how they perpetuate its causes and remain in the ocean of suffering are indeed objects to feel deep sorrow for. Just as a person who douses himself with water again and again but each time must reenter a fire considers himself happy although living in pain, in the same way, [sentient beings] confuse suffering with happiness. People live like this, in suffering, pretending they will not grow old or die and continuing to live by indulging in the causes of suffering. First, they will be slain by the Lord of Death, and this will be followed by the unbearable suffering of falling into the lower realms. They are thus chained by the causes and effects of suffering. Such is [Śāntideva's] contemplation here.

The aspect [of generating compassion for those who have not realized emptiness] is twofold. Of these, the first is *aspiring for their happiness*. [9.166] "When might I bring relief to those tormented in the fire of such suffering, offering the happiness flowing perfectly from the clouds of my merit?"

The second is *aspiring for helpful conditions*. [9.167] "When might I, endowed with the wisdom realizing all phenomena are imperceptible, respectfully gather the collection of merit and, perfecting my two collections [of merit and wisdom], teach emptiness to those who are betrayed by their perception of objects?"

This concludes the explanation of chapter 9.

# 10. Dedication

THE CONCLUDING points[387] of the composition has two parts: dedicating the merit, and paying homage with gratitude. The first has three parts: dedicating the merit for the benefit of the trainees, for the author himself, and for the doctrine generally.

## DEDICATING THE MERIT FOR THE BENEFIT OF THE TRAINEES

The first is twofold: dedicating the merit to the benefit and happiness of beings in this world, and dedicating the merit to the realization of the aspirations of supramundane beings.

## DEDICATING THE MERIT TO THE BENEFIT AND HAPPINESS OF BEINGS IN THIS WORLD

The first, in turn, has two parts: dedicating the merit in general, and dedicating it specifically for the sake of those who have entered the order.[388]

## DEDICATING THE MERIT IN GENERAL

The first is threefold: a brief presentation, dedicating merit individually for specific beings, and dedicating it collectively.

The first is twofold. Of these, the first is *dedicating merit for the benefit [of all]*. It says: [10.1]

By whatever virtue I have amassed
from composing this
*Guide to the Bodhisattva Way*,
may every being enter the bodhisattva way.[389]

The second is *dedicating merit for happiness*. [10.2–3] "May beings everywhere who suffer torments of body and mind have oceans of joy and happiness by virtue of my merit. Until they attain the bliss of buddhahood, may their happiness never decline." This is as stated in *Ornament of Mahāyāna Sūtras*:

Giving by a steadfast compassionate one
produces such a joy in giving
that even a fraction of it is unmatched by the joys
of sense pleasures in the three realms.[390]

May the stream of such bodhisattva joys remain uninterrupted.

## Dedicating merit individually for specific beings

This has two parts: dedicating merit to benefit beings of the lower realms, and dedicating merit to benefit beings of the higher realms.

## Dedicating merit to benefit beings in the lower realms

This consists of three parts: dedicating merit for the benefit of hell beings, dedicating merit for the benefit of animals, and dedicating merit for the benefit of hungry ghosts. The first is twofold: praying that their sufferings disappear on their own accord, and praying that their sufferings be pacified due to external forces.

The first consists of a brief and a detailed explanation. Of these, the first is as follows. [10.4]

> In the realms of the world,
> however many hellish states there may be,
> may the beings in such realms enjoy
> the happiness and delight of Sukhāvatī heaven.

The detailed explanation is this: [10.5] May the eight types of destitute hellish beings, tormented by the freezing cold of the Blistering Hell, the Hell of Burst Blisters, the Hell of Lamentations, the Hell of Chattering Teeth, the Hell of Groans, the Hell of Cracks Like an Utpala, the Hell of Cracks Like a Lotus, and the Hell of Massive Cracks Like a Lotus, be warmed. May rivers flowing from great clouds of the bodhisattva's two accumulations cool the eight types of hell beings burning in the infernal fires of the Reviving Hell, the Black-Line Hell, the Rounding Up and Crushing Hell, the Howling Hell, the Great Howling Hell, the Burning Hell, the Intense Burning Hell, and the Hell of Ultimate Torment (Avīci). [10.6] May the sword-leaf forest become a splendid pleasure grove, and may the [thorny] *śālmalī* trees transform into wish-fulfilling trees. [10.7] May the very pits of hell become lovely ponds fragrant with lotuses, pleasing with the cries of white geese, swans, and other waterfowl so pleasing to the ear. [10.8] May heaps of fiery hot coals transform into heaps of jewels, the burning iron ground into a cool crystal floor. May the hills of the Crushing Hell transform into sublime abodes filled with tathāgatas. [10.9] May the downpour of burning lava, stones, and weapons from now on be a gentle rain of flowers. And may the mutual injury of one another with weapons be replaced by the playful tossing of flowers. [10.10] Through the power of my virtue, may those drowning in the fire-like river that has no ford, their flesh completely burned, bones bleached white like jasmine flowers, attain celestial bodies and rest gently with goddesses by the river Mandākinī.

Next, praying that the sufferings [of hell beings] be pacified due to external forces is as follows. [10.11] Thinking, "Why do the fire, crows, and vultures of the Lord of Death cause such unbearable fear? And what noble strength will dispel the dreadful darkness, filling us with joy and happiness? Whose strength is it?" May they [the denizens of the hells] look up to see the bodhisattva Vajrapāṇi in blazing splendor in the center of the sky, and may they, accompanied by Vajrapāṇi, be freed from negativity. [10.12] And when they see the seething lava floods of the hells extinguished in a perfumed rain of lotuses, may the hell beings be spontaneously filled with bliss and wonder. Wondering "How did this happen?" may the denizens of hell behold the one who is responsible for this—Avalokiteśvara in his Padmapāṇi aspect. [10.13] Some, having seen Mañjughoṣa, call out to others: "Friends, shun your fears and come here quickly! The one who banishes fear has come to us, this gleaming youth with bound-up hair, Mañjughoṣa, the bodhisattva who has the power to eliminate all pain and to bestow joy, who protects all beings, radiating light that removes the suffering of the hells, and who brings forth compassion that dispels all miseries. What need is there to run elsewhere? There is none!" [10.14] "O friends, behold the one at whose feet a hundred gods pay homage, with their crowns touching his lotus feet. Behold how a rain of flowers descends upon his head, which sports eyes moist with compassion. Behold the splendor of Mañjughoṣa residing in a mansion that echoes with the hymns of thousands of goddesses." In this way may friends call out to their fellow hell denizens, exclaiming "Look, look!" Seeing Mañjughoṣa in such a manner, may they erupt is shouts of joy. [10.15] Likewise, through my roots of virtue, may they see the bodhisattvas Samantabhadra, Maitreya, Kṣitigarbha, and Ākāśagarbha, stainless bodhisattvas like Nīvaraṇaviṣkambhin, who all produce with their respective magical powers beautiful clouds of bliss, raining down a cool and fragrant rain. Seeing that, may all hell beings experience utter delight.[391]

Dedicating merit for the benefit of animals is this: [10.16ab] "May animals be free from their fears, such as the fear of being eaten by one another."

Dedicating merit for the benefit of hungry ghosts is this: [10.16c–10.17] "May the hungry ghosts be as happy as the inhabitants of Uttarakuru, living without the suffering of hunger and thirst. And may the hungry ghosts be sated by streams of milk that pour from the noble lord Avalokiteśvara's hand, forever cleansing and cooling them."

## Dedicating the merit to benefit beings in the higher realms

[10.18] May the blind regain their eyesight and the deaf hear sounds. May women nearing their time give birth painlessly like Māyādevī. [10.19] May the naked be clothed, the hungry be fed, and the thirsty receive pure water and delicious drink. [10.20] May the poor find wealth, the weak and tormented find joy. May those in despair be whole in mind, undisturbed by suffering and sadness, and may they become an extraordinary, invincible support. [10.21] May all beings racked with sickness be immediately freed from every disease. May every sickness that afflicts the living be wholly and forever absent from the world. [10.22] May the frightened cease to be afraid, and may captives be unchained and now set free. May the powerless find strength. May they be kind and think of benefiting one another. [10.23] May travelers upon the road find happiness wherever they go. May they effortlessly attain the goals on which they set their hearts. [10.24] May travelers in boats and ships have their hearts' desires fulfilled and, after returning home, enjoy the company of friends and family. [10.25] May those who lose their way and wander in the wild find fellow travelers. Without fear of bandits, thieves, wild beasts, and the like, may their journeys be light and without fatigue. [10.26] May all those wandering in the highlands and solitary places, in fearful pathless wastes; the young, the elderly, and all without protections; and those who fall asleep, unconscious of their peril, have pure celestial beings as their guardians. [10.27] May they be freed from all eight unfree states. May they possess wisdom, faith, and love, complete with faultless sustenance and conduct, and may they always remember their former lives. [10.28] May the world and all sentient beings have unrestricted wealth, a treasury like space. May they enjoy it freely and without conflict or violence. [10.29] May those of little splendor be of great magnificence, and may those who suffer the hardship of deformity have beautiful and perfect bodies. [10.30] May all the females of the world attain the strength of masculinity. May the lowly be empowered and the haughty lose their arrogance.

## Dedicating the merit collectively

This has two parts: dedicating the merit for benefit, and dedicating the merit for happiness. The first is as follows. [10.31–32] "Through the merit I have collected, may every being without exception abandon all evil and engage in virtue forever." This indicates general benefit. Especially, may beings never be separate from the special intention, the mind of awakening (*bodhicitta*), and constantly engage in its application, the bodhisattvas' deeds. May they enjoy the favorable condition of being sustained by the buddhas, and may they discard the unfavorable conditions, the actions of Māra.

Dedicating the merit for happiness is twofold. Of these, the first is *dedicating it for the fulfillment of wishes*. [10.33] "May these beings enjoy unlimited longevity. May they always be content, and may the very word *death* be unknown to them." [10.34] May there be groves of wish-fulfilling trees in all directions, resounding with the sweet melody of the teachings of the buddhas and the buddhas' children. [10.35] And may the ground everywhere be free from rocks and pebbles, flat and even like the palm of one's hand and smooth like lapis lazuli. [10.36] For all the many beings in the maṇḍala of disciples, may there be multitudes of bodhisattvas in every land, adorning them with all their respective excellences, such as magic and the like. [10.37] May all beings constantly perceive the sound of Dharma from birdsong and the sighing of the trees, from shafts of light and from the sky itself. [10.38] And always may they meet the buddhas and their children, the bodhisattvas. Upon meeting them, may they worship those buddhas, lords of beings, with unsurpassable clouds of offerings. [10.39] May kindly spirits bring timely rains and bountiful harvests. May kings rule according to the Dharma, and may the world flourish. [10.40] May medicines be potent and evil spirits and negativity be pacified through the recitation of secret mantras, and may every need be fulfilled. May ḍākinīs, ogres, and malicious people adopt a spirit of compassion.

The second is *praying to be spared the undesirable.* [10.41] May no beings ever suffer anguish. May they not be overcome by fear or despised by others. May their minds always be free from sorrow.

## Dedicating the merit specifically for the well-being of those who have entered the order

This has two parts. Of these, the first is *making the dedication in general.* [10.42] "Texts" refers to the teachings, and where they are housed is a "monastery,"[392] which is also a residence for monastics. So in the monasteries, may the monastics' reading, reciting, and other Dharma activities flourish widely and be firmly upheld. May harmony prevail among the community, and may all their wishes be fulfilled just as they intend.

The second is *dedicating the merit for the well-being of specific [categories of monastics]*. [10.43] May the bhikṣus desiring to train on the path to liberation find perfect places for solitary retreat. Abandoning every distraction there, may they cultivate virtue with trained and serviceable minds that can pursue virtue in any way they wish. [10.44] May the bhikṣuṇīs obtain sustenance and be spared from quarreling within the community and from harm from without. May all who have embraced the monastic life observe it in a pure and unimpaired way. [10.45] May those who damage their vows always strive to cleanse their faults with remorse and determination. Through the power of their cleansing, may they attain in the future a fortunate rebirth and not impair their discipline there. [10.46] May the wise be revered and find alms. May their minds be pure, free from pride and so forth, and may their fame spread in all directions. [10.47] May all these beings never experience the lower realms; may the pain and hardship of the three doors be unknown to them. May they temporarily attain bodies greater than the gods and attain ultimate enlightenment swiftly. [10.48] May beings make offerings to all the buddhas time and time again. May the Buddha's inconceivable bliss bestow lasting happiness on them.

### Dedicating the merit to the realization of the aspirations of supramundane beings

[10.49–50] May all the bodhisattvas' intentions for beings be fulfilled just as they wish. May sentient beings now obtain all that their guardians, the buddhas, wish for them. Likewise, may śrāvakas and pratyekabuddhas be endowed with the perfect happiness of nirvāṇa.[393]

### Dedicating the merit for the author himself

> Until I attain the ground of Perfect Joy,
> may I too, through Mañjughoṣa's kindness,
> always remember my past lives
> and always become ordained. [10.51]

This is being stated for the benefit of trainees, showing them how to perform aspirational prayers. It does not establish that the master was an ordinary being [and not an ārya]. This is like when someone free of negative karma teaches the method to declare and purify negative karma. In the commentaries too, one finds references to "Ārya Śāntideva" and the statement that he had gained the supreme attainment.[394]

[10.52] May my body be sustained merely by simple foods and the bare necessities. And in all my lives, may I obtain a solitary dwelling place endowed with all excellences. [10.53] Whenever I wish to see him or put to him the slightest question, may I behold my own protector, Mañjughoṣa, with unobstructed sight. [10.54] To satisfy the needs of beings filling the limits of space throughout the ten directions, may I reflect the perfect instructions of Mañjuśrī in all my actions. [10.55] As long as space endures, as long as sentient beings abide, until then may I too remain, to dispel the miseries of the world. [10.56] The pains and sorrows of all wandering beings—may they ripen wholly on myself. And through the power of the virtuous company of bodhisattvas, may all beings enjoy happiness.

### Dedicating the merit for the Buddha's doctrine generally

[10.57] May the Buddha's teaching—the only medicine that heals the illness of wandering beings, the source of every temporary and ultimate happiness—be blessed with wealth, upheld with veneration, and remain for a long time!

## Paying homage with gratitude

Paying homage with gratitude [for Mañjuśrī's] kindness is as follows. [10.58] I pay homage to Mañjughoṣa, whose kindness stimulated my virtuous intention to compose this treatise. I also bow to my spiritual mentors, whose inspiration increased my virtue and caused it to grow. Thus I prostrate by remembering their kindness.

This concludes the explanation of chapter 10.

## Colophon

Through the virtue of explaining this treatise that
excellently presents the bodhisattva conduct of six
perfections—
the path traversed by all conquerors of the three times—
may all beings enter the way of the bodhisattva!

Becoming utterly free from the relentless sufferings of
lower realms
and having found the path to liberation,
may they swiftly enter the city of nirvāṇa,
adorned with the glory of the fulfillment of twin
collections.

May they never regress from the glory of higher rebirth,
and having realized saṃsāra's joys to be meaningless,
may they enjoy the glory of uncontaminated bliss,
wherein elaborations of subject and object are totally
calmed.

May the bright sun of the Sage's doctrine,
whose power dispels the darkness of suffering and its origin
and brings to bloom the lotus grove of benefit and happiness,
remain on this earth for a very long time.

May the lives of excellent spiritual mentors who uphold
the treasury of gems of the threefold training—
who with perfect wisdom, compassion, and skillful means
protect the Sugata's doctrine and sentient beings—remain eternal.

May those who have entered the Sugata's doctrine
be free from the bondage of indolence and distraction and,
abiding in discipline, always engage their three doors
in meaningful ways through listening, reflection, and meditation.

May the rains of the heavens fall in a timely manner;
may the great earth be richly adorned with grains, pulses, grasses, and trees;
may the people enjoy happiness and be kind to each other;
may they always engage in the ten virtuous deeds.

May I too, from now until I am enlightened,
never become attached to the pleasures of saṃsāra
and, not seeking liberation for my own self,
always strive for the welfare of sentient beings.

Those who feel attached to me or feel aversion for me,
those who praise me or deride me,
help me or even harm me—

whosoever sees me, hears of me, or thinks of me—
may they all quickly attain supreme enlightenment.

This commentary on *Guide to the Bodhisattva Way*, entitled *An Ocean of Excellent Discourses*, was composed by Thokmé, an utterer of scripture and reasoning, at the glorious monastery of É.

# Complete Outline

Homage

**1. The Benefits of the Awakening Mind**

The title

The text

- The way the author proceeds to compose the text
  - The actual point
    - The homage [1.1ab]
    - The promise to explain [1.1cd]
    - An expression of humility [1.2–3]
  - The purpose and interrelatedness indicated
    - The natures of the individual factors
    - The purpose of the teachings
    - How the treatise indicates its purpose
- The nature of the practice being engaged in
  - The person who engages in the discipline, the basis
    - Explaining how human existence endowed with leisure and opportunity, which is the basis, is difficult to obtain [1.4]
    - How the mental basis that is the meritorious thought is so rare [1.5]
  - The intention of the person engaging in the discipline
    - The benefits of generating the awakening mind
      - The actual benefits
        - The general benefits
          - The elimination of negative karma [1.6]
          - The creation of well-being and happiness [1.7]
          - The fulfillment of wishes [1.8]
          - The change of name and status [1.9]
          - Praising the benefits
            - Analogy of the alchemical transformation into gold [1.10]

Analogy of a jewel [1.11]
Analogy of a tree [1.12]
Analogy of a bodyguard [1.13]
Analogy of fire [1.14]
How other benefits are mentioned in the sūtras
The specific benefits
The divisions [of the awakening mind] [1.15]
Their difference in terms of nature [1.16]
Their difference in terms of benefits [1.17–19]
The proof that there are indeed such benefits
Proof through scriptures [1.20]
Proof through reasoning
The superiority of the intention
The vastness of the intention's object and aspect [1.21–22]
How it surpasses any worldly [intention] [1.23–25]
The superiority of the action
How the focus and aspect of the action are vast [1.26–27]
How they are the absent in others [1.28–30]
Praising individuals who have generated the awakening mind
For how they help others unconditionally [1.31]
For how they are outstanding benefactors [1.32–33]
For how they are an extraordinary field of merit [1.34–35a]
For how they are not overwhelmed by suffering [1.35bcd]
For how they are worthy of praise and are a source of refuge [1.36]

**2. The Confession of Negative Actions**

The way to uphold it
The general explanations
The generation of the awakening mind
Its defining nature
Its classification
In a general way
In terms of the accompanying factors or analogies
According to the way it is attained
By means of signs
Through the power of the nature of reality
According to their objects

            - The essence
            - The classification
                - Mundane
                - Supramundane
            - The specific natures of each [of the objects of refuge]
        - The practice
    - The corresponding verse [2.26]
- Confessing and purifying negative karma
    - The general meaning
        - The six aspects of negative karma that have to be purified
            - Based on the time
            - Based on the cause
            - Based on the doors
            - Based on the act itself
            - Based on the object
            - Based on its type
        - The four powers of the purifying antidote
        - The method of purification
            - The preparation
            - The main practice
            - The conclusion
    - The meaning in the text itself
        - The power of remorse
            - The general teaching on the confession of negative actions [2.27–29]
            - The confession of especially negative actions against superior objects [2.30–31]
        - The power of the support
            - The person's reason for seeking refuge
                - A brief explanation [2.32]
                - An elaboration
                    - Reflecting on the immediacy of death and generating the thought of going for refuge
                        - A brief presentation [2.33–34]
                        - An extensive explanation [2.35–37]
                        - A summation [2.38–39]

Reflecting on the great terror of having to die and generating the thought of going for refuge
A brief explanation [2.40–42]
An extensive explanation [2.43–46]
The objects of refuge
Seeking refuge in the Three Jewels in general [2.47–48]
And taking refuge in the bodhisattvas endowed with the great power of aspirational prayer [2.49–52]
What it means to go for refuge
The power of the antidote
The reason for exerting oneself in the antidotes
Illustrating using the analogy of illness [2.54–56]
Illustrating [the reason for exerting oneself in the antidotes] [2.57]
Making an immediate effort
One cannot rely on the lifespan [2.58–59]
One cannot rely on material resources [2.60]
One cannot rely on friends and family [2.61]
The manner of exerting oneself
The intention [2.62]
The action [2.63–64]
The power of turning away from error [2.65]

**3. Upholding the Awakening Mind**

Rejoicing
Rejoicing in mundane good deeds [3.1]
Rejoicing in supramundane good deeds [3.2–3]
Rejoicing in the virtue of the Lesser Vehicle
Rejoicing in the results
Rejoicing in the virtue of the Great Vehicle
Rejoicing in the cause
Requesting to turn the wheel of Dharma [3.4]
Supplicating [the buddhas] not to enter nirvāṇa [3.5]
Dedicating the merit
General dedication [3.6]
Specific dedication [3.7–9]
Training the mind to benefit others

- The general presentation of giving away everything
  - The objects to be given [3.10]
  - The reason for doing so [3.11]
- The specific explanation of giving one's body
  - Giving to those who accumulate karma because of me
    - Giving without reservation [3.12–14ab]
    - Dedicating it to becoming a cause of benefit
      - General presentation [3.14cd]
      - Specific presentation
        - Dedicating that one's intention may be meaningful [3.15]
        - Dedicating one's action to be meaningful [3.16]
  - Praying that it will become a cause of well-being for everyone [3.17–21]

The actual ceremony

The concluding rite

- A transitional statement [3.25]
- The actual ritual
  - Developing joy within oneself
    - Developing joy because one has accomplished one's own purpose [3.26–28]
    - Engendering because of accomplishing others' welfare [3.29–33]
  - Engendering joy in others [3.34]

**4. Conscientiousness**

- The practices by which the person engages [in the discipline]
  - Conscientiousness
    - Brief presentation [4.1]
    - Detailed explanation
      - Conscientiousness with respect to the training, the object of cultivation
        - Why we should not forsake [the awakening mind] [4.2–3]
        - The negative consequences of forsaking it
          - How, as its fruitional effect, one will fall to the lower realms
            - The extreme consequence [4.4–5]
            - The reason [why the consequence is so extreme] [4.6]

Refuting objections against this [4.7]
How one's altruistic activity will be undermined [4.8–11]
How one will be obstructed from the fruit, the attainment of liberation [4.12]
Hence the advice not to forsake the awakening mind [4.13–14]
Conscientiousness with respect to one's existence endowed with leisure and opportunity, the basis
The difficulty of obtaining it [4.15–16]
The disadvantages of not obtaining it
The actual point
Virtue remains unachievable in the lower realms [4.17–18]
Hence one will not obtain rebirth in the higher realms [4.19]
The substantiation
The substantiation through scripture [4.20]
The substantiation through logical reasoning [4.21–22]
Forswearing making no effort after having obtained it
A general presentation [4.23]
Its explanation
Reflecting on the results of such foolishness and ignorance [4.24–25]
Criticizing the course of action itself [4.26–27b]
Examining the cause thereof [4.27cd]
Conscientiousness with respect to the afflictions, what are to be discarded
Examining the afflictions that must be discarded
Reflecting on the faults [of the afflictions]
How they harm us even though this should not be the case [4.28–29]
How they cause great harm [4.30–32]
The advice to not embrace them [4.33]
Making up our mind not to embrace them [4.34–35]
Developing the determination to discard them
Donning armor by abandoning the afflictions [4.36]
Not becoming disheartened by suffering
The faults of what is to be abandoned [4.37–38]

Relying on spiritual mentors as support [5.102–3ab]
Reading the sūtras and so on to understand the ways of training [5.103c–5.107]
A concise definition of guarding meta-awareness [5.108]
Exhorting oneself to relate these [practices] to one's own mind [5.109]

**6. Forbearance**

Forbearance
The value of cultivating forbearance
The faults of anger
The consequences not [immediately] observable [6.1–2]
The object that will be destroyed
The agent that brings about the destruction
The specific way it destroys
The observable consequences [6.3–5ab]
The summary [6.5cd–6.6ab]
The benefits of forbearance [6.6cd]
The methods for cultivating forbearance
A brief presentation
Contemplating the faults of what is to be abandoned [6.7]
How it is therefore logical to avert it [6.8–10]
A detailed explanation
Presenting the objects of anger in general [6.11]
Controlling our anger about them
Controlling anger against those who create unwanted things for me
In relation to the four unwanted things done to myself
Controlling anger toward those who cause me suffering
Forbearance of voluntary acceptance of suffering
Forbearance through examining the nature of cyclic existence [6.12ab]
Forbearance through examining [suffering] as a cause of renunciation [6.12c–6.13]
Forbearance through examining how [suffering can be accepted] through habituation

A brief presentation [6.14]
A detailed explanation [6.15–18ab]
A summary [6.18c–6.19ab]
Bringing to mind positive qualities [of suffering] [6.19c–6.21]
Forbearance through gaining certainty in the Dharma
Overcoming anger against those who harm us
Since those who harm us lack autonomous power, it does not make sense to be angry with them
They lack autonomy [6.22–23]
They do not have the intention [6.24]
The summary [6.25–26]
Refutation of an autonomous aggressor
Refuting the primal matter and self in general [6.27–28ab]
Refuting a permanent self in particular
The refutation of the [self as] experiencer [6.28cd]
The refutation of the [self as] an agent that produces results [6.29–30]
The summary [6.31]
Abandoning false reasoning [6.32]
Summarizing the section [6.33–34]
Forbearance of being unperturbed by harm
Why it makes sense to have compassion for the perpetrator of harm [6.35–38]
Why it makes no sense to be angry with the perpetrator of harm
Examining the nature of the aggressor
Investigating the character [6.39–40]
Investigating how the harm is done [6.41]
Examining the harm in terms of one's own fault
How one has caused harm to others [6.42]

How it is the fault of my own body [6.43–44]

How it is the fault of my own karma [6.45–46]

Why the reasons for being angry are illogical [6.47–51]

Controlling anger toward those who commit humiliation, harsh words, and ill repute against me

Humiliation and so forth cannot harm me [6.52–54]

It is illogical to be angry because that will obstruct my material gains

The negative karma of anger weighs heavily [6.55–56]

Material possessions have no intrinsic value [6.57–59]

Refuting the notion that they possess intrinsic value [6.60–61]

It is illogical to be angry because people will lose respect for me [6.62–63]

Controlling anger in relation to the four misdeeds against my loved ones

How there can be no harm with respect to [certain] objects [6.64]

Controlling anger toward those who harm the vulnerable

Being certain of the Dharma [6.65]

Being fearless toward aggressors

Being angry toward an antagonist is not right

It is comparable to being injured through inanimate objects [6.66]

It is just as wrong as the faults of the aggressors [6.67]

Since it arises from having done harm, it is not right to be angry with antagonists [6.68]

Therefore giving up anger against them [6.69]

Giving up attachment [6.70–71]

Cultivating the forbearance of accepting suffering [6.72–75]
Controlling anger in relation to the four good things done to my enemy
Controlling my anger about the praises they receive
They [praises for my enemy] should be embraced because they could be causes of my own happiness [6.76–77]
They should not be rejected since they are causes of others' happiness [6.78]
They show how I am confused about what to adopt and what to reject [6.79]
Controlling my anger when they are happy [6.80]
Controlling my anger about their success
It is inappropriate to become angry at others for having achieved success
Anger is inappropriate because my own wishes are being fulfilled [6.81–83]
Anger is inappropriate because I am not getting hurt [6.84]
It is inappropriate to be angry at others for my not having achieved such success [6.85–86]
Controlling anger against those who obstruct my attainment of what I desire
Causing misfortune to my adversaries
The misfortune of my adversaries does not benefit me [6.87]
Wishing misfortune on them only harms me [6.88–89]
Controlling anger against those who obstruct my own success and that of my loved ones
Controlling anger against those who obstruct my worldly concerns
Those who prevent my gaining praise and who ruin my reputation are not evil
Praise and reputation bring neither spiritual nor temporal well-being [6.90–93]
It is pointless to be overjoyed by praise [6.94–97]

I should see them as helpers [6.98–101]
Controlling anger against those who obstruct my merit
Anger is the obstacle to merit [6.102–3]
Perpetrators of harm are conducive factors [6.104–5]
I should therefore control my anger and be respectful
I should be respectful on account of sentient beings' own qualities
Honoring them because they help me attain buddhahood
The reasoning why they should be respected [6.106–8]
Refuting any potential confusion about it [6.109–11]
Honoring them through establishing them as being equal to the buddhas
Citing scripture [6.112ab]
Establishing its meaning
The main argument [6.112cd–6.113]
Refuting others' objections [6.114–18]
I should be respectful out of faith in the buddhas
The Teacher embraces sentient beings as his own
Why it is appropriate to be respectful [6.119–23]
Rectifying the error of being disrespectful [6.124–25]
The Teacher identifies them as himself [6.126]
I should be respectful based on examining the effects
Demonstrating that making beings happy is the cause of all good things [6.127]
Pledging to put all my effort into [making others happy] [6.128–32]
The summary [6.133–34]

**7. Diligence**

- Diligence
  - An exhortation to cultivate diligence linked to the foregoing passage [7.1]
  - The actual explanation of diligence, the object of cultivation
    - Defining diligence [7.2]
    - Countering the opposing factors
      - Explaining laziness, what is being countered [7.2bcd]
      - Countering laziness
        - Countering indolence
          - Identifying the causes [7.3]
          - Relinquishing these causes
            - Setting the intention to be diligent
              - Contemplating this life to be transient
                - Contemplating the certainty of death [7.4–6]
                - Urging oneself through contemplating that one will die soon
                  - A brief presentation [7.7]
                  - Its elaboration [7.8–10]
              - Contemplating the suffering of future lives [7.11–13]
            - Applying [the intention to be diligent] in practice [7.14]
        - Countering indulgence in unhelpful behaviors [7.15]
        - Countering despondency
          - A brief presentation [7.16]
          - Its elaboration
            - Applying the antidote against the cause of despondency, the thought that I have no capacity [7.17–19]
            - Applying the antidote against the condition of despondency, [the thought] that it is difficult to cultivate diligence
              - There is no cause for discouragement
                - Abandoning the fear that the practice is difficult
                  - Stating the false notion
                  - Countering this [false notion]
                    - Countering this through appreciating its relative context [7.20c–7.24]

                - Criticism of the pride that is to be relinquished [7.56]
                - Praise for this curative form of pride [7.59]
            - Self-confidence in overcoming the afflictions [7.60–61]
    - The force of joy
        - A brief presentation [7.62]
        - Its elaboration
            - It is right to behave virtuously because its essence is happiness [7.63]
            - The fruit of happiness is what one should not be content with [7.64]
            - Therefore we should engage [in the bodhisattva conduct] with joy [7.65]
    - The force of letting go
        - Letting go temporarily when one does not have the ability [7.66]
        - Letting go permanently when tasks have been completed [7.67]
- Bringing dedication through the forces
    - Bringing dedication to [applying] the antidotes
        - Embracing conscientiousness with dedication [7.68]
        - Applying mindfulness with dedication [7.69]
    - Relinquishing the faults
        - Ensuring that no faults arise [in the first place] [7.70–71]
        - Counteracting it when faults do arise [7.72]
    - Engaging in the activities that accord with this [twin task of applying the antidotes and relinquishing the faults]
- Gaining self-mastery [7.74–75]

**8. Meditation**

- Meditation
    - An exhortation to cultivate meditative absorption linked [to the foregoing passage] [8.1ab]
    - Renouncing unconducive factors
        - A brief presentation [8.1c–8.2]
        - Its elaboration
            - Renouncing the mundane world

Renouncing distracting activities because of their shortcomings
- Developing the attitude of renunciation [8.3–4]
- Applying the methods that help renounce
  - Giving up "inner" attachment to people
    - The faults of attachment [8.5–7]
    - The faults of the objects of our attachment
      - The childish are not to be attached to and relied upon
        - A brief presentation [8.8cd]
        - The elaboration
          - We cannot benefit them [8.10–11]
          - They cannot benefit us [8.12–13]
        - The summary [8.14–15a]
      - How to interact with them when the context is right [8.15b–8.16]
  - Giving up attachment to external material possessions
    - Attachment gives rise to suffering [8.17–19ab]
    - The objects of attachment are meaningless
      - Material possessions and so forth are transient [8.19c–8.20]
      - It is inappropriate to be happy and unhappy for praise and criticism [8.21]
  - Giving up attachment to unachievable work for others [8.22–24]

Seeking a place of solitude because of its qualities
- Developing enthusiasm for the place of solitude
  - Companions [appropriate] in solitude [8.25]
  - The site [8.26–27]
  - The resources [8.28]
  - The state of mind to aspire for [8.29]
- Renouncing the causes that make us lack enthusiasm for solitude [8.30–33]
- The advice to seek such a place [8.34–37]

Discarding [extraneous] thinking
- A brief presentation [8.38]
- The elaboration
  - Developing disenchantment with [the objects of] desire

Examining the effects [of lust] as terrifying [8.39]
Examining how the nature [of the desired one] is unclean
  Examining it to be similar to a lifeless corpse
    It is not worth fretting about [8.40–42]
    It is not worth viewing with attachment [8.43–44]
    It is not worth jealously protecting [8.45]
    It is not worthy of great devotion [8.46]
    It is not worth touching with delight [8.47]
    It is not worth embracing with attachment [8.48]
  Examining how the living body itself is unclean
    Making its foulness evident
      Attachment to what is characterized by impurity is illogical
        Refuting attachment to saliva [8.49]
        Refuting attachment to touch [8.50–53]
        Refuting attachment to the flesh [8.54–55]
      A critique of the deluded [8.56–57]
    Ascertaining through reasoning
      Ascertaining [the body's foulness] in terms of cause and effect
        The actual point
          The body is the cause of impurity [8.58]
          The body is an impure result [8.59–60]
        A critique of attachment to it [8.61]
      Ascertaining [the body's foulness] through its function [8.62]
      Ascertaining [the body's foulness] through an analogy [8.63–64]
    Refuting the characteristics of purity
      It is illogical to be attached to the body because of some extrinsic qualities [8.65–67]
      Its very nature is not something to become attached to [8.68–69b]

It makes no sense to enjoy it [8.69c–8.70]
Examining how its causes bring harm
Brief presentation [8.71]
Its elaboration
There is no time to enjoy the [objects of] desire [8.72–73]
It entails other faults
One suffers physically [8.75–78]
It obstructs the opportunity for liberation [8.79]
Illustrating the disadvantages through analogy [8.80]
It wastes away a life of leisure and opportunity [8.81]
The suffering [through desire] would be meaningless [8.82–83]
How the suffering entailed transcends analogy [8.84]
Generating a delight in solitude
The brief presentation linked to the preceding section [8.85ab]
The explanation
[Identifying] the perfect factors [of solitude] [8.85c–8.86]
The characteristic of joy [8.87–88]
Cultivating discipline, the antidote
A general presentation linked to the preceding section [8.89]
Cultivating conventional awakening mind
Equalizing self and others
The advice to equalize self and others [8.90ab]
The extensive explanation of what is to be practiced
The actual point
A brief description [8.90cd]
The explanation
We can generate the attitude of equality [8.91–93]
It is logical to generate such an attitude
Presenting the reasoning
The equality of the objective, happiness and suffering [of self and others] [8.94]

The equality of the subject, the desire [to be happy and avoid suffering] [8.95–96]
Establishing the entailment
The actual point
The consequence that one should not protect the other since distinct entities lack truly existing oneness
The consequence that one should not protect oneself from suffering separated by time [8.97–98]
The consequence that one should not protect oneself from suffering separated by space [8.99]
It is therefore logical to relinquish grasping at self [8.100]
The rebuttal of the responses [8.101–2ab]
The summary
The actual point [8.102cd–8.103]
The rebuttal of the objections [8.104–6]
The benefits of the practice [8.107–9]
The summation [8.110–12]
Exchanging self and others
A brief presentation [8.113]
An extensive explanation
The defining characteristics
Embracing others
It is appropriate to engage in embracing others
The logic of embracing [others] [8.114]
One's capacity for embracing others [8.115]
The positive qualities of doing so [8.116]
The instruction on how to do this [8.117–18]
It is inappropriate to turn away from embracing others [8.119]
The summary [8.120]
Discarding one's own self
It is appropriate to discard because it engenders fear within this life [8.121]
It is appropriate to discard because it engenders suffering in the future [8.122–24]

Being envious in thought [8.160]
In action connecting [the self] to suffering [8.161ab]
Positing both [one's thought and action] as inferior [8.161cd–8.164]
Summarizing the points [8.165–66]
Gaining mastery over the mind through the practices
Mastering the antidotes
A brief presentation [8.167]
The elaboration [8.168–70]
Viewing what is to be abandoned as unconducive [8.171–72]
A brief explanation [8.173]
The elaboration
Renouncing attachment to the body
The faults of having such attachment
The actual point [8.174–76ab]
Presenting, as an aside, the benefits of contentment [8.176cd–8.177]
The inappropriateness of such attachment [to the body]
It is lowly [8.178–80]
It is inappropriate to be attached to it for it does not know what is beneficial and what is harmful [8.181–83]
Upholding it for others' welfare [8.184]
Being skilled in the methods of applying the antidotes
The practices common to both equalizing and exchanging self and others
Dispelling the obscurations [8.185]
Striving in the antidotes [8.186]
Cultivating ultimate awakening mind [8.187]

**9. Wisdom**

Wisdom
Linking [to the preceding section] and advising to cultivate wisdom [9.1]
The method to cultivate wisdom

- How to identify the nature of wisdom
  - Establishing the two truths, the objects
    - Setting forth the nature of the two truths
      - The division [9.2]
      - Their natures
      - The characteristics of the mind cognizing them
        - Types of persons [9.3ab]
        - The stages of impairment [9.3cd–9.4ab]
        - The reasoning that undermines [9.4cd]
    - Rebutting the objections
      - Rebutting objections pertaining to conventional truth
        - Rebutting the objection that no one will enter the path [9.4d]
        - [Rebutting the objection] that the dispute is not about the objects [themselves] [9.5–6]
        - [The perception of objects as real] is negated by valid cognition [9.7ab]
        - [Rebutting the objection] that it contradicts the scriptures [9.7c–9.8]
        - Rebutting the charge of an absurd consequence
          - Rejecting that there would be no obtaining of merit [9.9ab]
          - Rejecting that there would no connecting to a new birth [9.9c–9.10]
          - Rejecting there would be no positive or negative karma [9.11–13b]
          - Rejecting that engaging in the deeds would be pointless [9.13c–9.15b]
      - Rebutting objections pertaining to ultimate truth
        - Rejecting the objection that if there is no delusory cognition, there would be no apprehension
          - The objection [9.15cd]
          - The response
            - The same objection applies equally to both parties [9.16ab]
            - Refuting the opponent's rejoinder
              - Asserting the appearance to be the mind
                - Stating the opponent's view [9.16cd]
                - Refuting this view

- The selflessness of persons
  - A summary linked to the preceding section [9.56]
  - The extensive explanation
    - General refutation of self based on deconstructing the aggregates [9.57–59]
    - Refuting specific postulations of self
      - Refuting the self postulated by Sāṃkhya
        - Presenting the refutation [9.60–61]
        - Rejecting their defense
          - The statement of their response [9.62a]
          - Refuting this response
            - The previous consequence remains [9.62bcd]
            - How the aspects are incompatible
              - Stating the reasoning [9.63ab]
              - How the analogy is not established [9.63cd–9.64ab]
            - Refuting through the reasoning of nonperception of one as the other
              - Stating the argument [9.64cd]
              - Rejecting the charge of nonestablishment
                - The actual point [9.65ab]
                - Rejecting the charge of no logical entailment
                  - The opponent's objection [9.65c]
                  - Refuting this assertion
                    - It is untenable for two incompatible aspects to share the same nature [9.65d–9.67b]
                    - It is untenable for the universal to be real when its instances are unreal [9.67cd]
      - Refuting the self postulated by Nyāya
        - Presenting the argument [9.68ab]
        - Rejecting any fault in the logical entailment [9.68c–9.69b]
        - Concluding summary [9.69cd]
    - Rejecting objections against the refutation of self
      - Rejecting that karmic causality would be untenable

How nonexistence itself is not something to be produced [9.145cd]
How it cannot be turned into an entity [9.146–48b]
Refuting the negation itself [9.148cd]
Thus establishing phenomena to be empty [9.149]
Concluding summation [9.150]
The activity of one who has attained wisdom
Equalizing one's mind toward eight worldly concerns [9.151–54b]
Generating compassion for those who have not realized [emptiness]
The object
They live this present life miserably [9.154c–9.155]
They endure suffering in a future life [9.156]
The faults of cyclic existence in general
How [cyclic existence] is contradictory to liberation [9.157–58b]
How it is difficult to avoid this contradiction [9.158c–9.162]
How, due to their distortions, beings grasp suffering as happiness [9.163–65]
The aspect
Aspiring for their happiness [9.166]
Aspiring for helpful conditions [9.167]

**10. Dedication**

The concluding points
Dedicating the merit
Dedicating the merit for the benefit of the trainees
Dedicating the merit to the benefit and happiness of beings in this world
Dedicating the merit in general
A brief presentation
Dedicating merit for the benefit [of all] [10.1]
Dedicating merit for happiness [10.2–3]
Dedicating merit individually for specific beings
Dedicating merit to benefit beings of the lower realms
Dedicating merit for the benefit of hell beings
Praying that their sufferings disappear on their own accord

# Notes

1. Parts of this introduction have been adapted from my introduction in Jinpa, *Bodhisattva Ideal.*
2. On the suggestion, based on an ancient recension of the text found in the Dunhuang caves, that "originally" chapters 2 and 3 may have been merged, see Crosby and Skilton's "Translators' Introduction" in Śāntideva, *The Bodhicaryāvatāra.* While the Tibetan canon's version of the *Guide* contains ten chapters and 912 verses, the Dunhuang recension contains only 721 verses in nine chapters. As mentioned below, Kṛṣṇapa's Indian commentary on the *Guide* also adopts this nine-chapter model. Here we follow the ten-chapter structure in the Tibetan canonical version, which accords with Prajñākaramati's commentary.
3. Toh 44 Kangyur, phal chen, *'a,* 309b2.
4. *Śikṣāsamuccaya.* For the key points of this text, see Tsongkhapa's *Concise Summary of the Compendium of Training* in Jinpa, *Bodhisattva Ideal.*
5. That this story is Indian in origin is testified by the fact that it appears in Vibhūticandra's (thirteenth-century) commentary *Distinctive Illumination* (*Viśeṣadyotanī,* Toh 3880 Tengyur, dbu ma, *sha*), 194a2. Vibhūticandra was one of nine Indian paṇḍitas who accompanied the Kashmiri master Śākyaśrībhadra when he visited Tibet in the early thirteenth century.
6. As attested to by the translators' colophon, the *Guide* was first translated in the ninth century by Kawa Paltsek with the assistance of the Indian paṇḍita Sarvajñādeva. It was revised, around two centuries later, by Rinchen Sangpo (958–1055) with the assistance of Indian master Dharmaśrībhadra on the basis of an Indian manuscript of the root text and its commentary (possibly Prajñākāramati's). Still later, this translation was again carefully revised by Ngok Loden Sherab (1059–1109) with the assistance of the Indian master Sumatikīrti.

7. In *Grains of Gold* (53), Gendun Chopel reports seeing numerous commentaries on the *Guide* by early Tibetan masters such as Chumikpa and Yangönpa and states that, during his time, "even the names of these [commentaries] are unknown." Thanks to the discovery of many early Kadam texts at Drepung Monastery and other places and their compilations through the Collected Works of the Kadampas series (*Bka' gdams gsung 'bum pyogs bsgrigs*), we now have access to some of these early Tibetan commentaries on the *Guide*, such as the one by Chapa Chökyi Sengé (1109–69).
8. On Tibetan *lojong* (spelled *blo sbyong*) and its connection with Śāntideva's equalizing and exchanging of self and others, see Jinpa, "*Bodhicaryāvatāra* and Tibetan Mind Training (*Lojong*)."
9. Palden Yeshé, *Drops of Nectar: Biography of Bodhisattva Thokmé Sangpo*, 2b5; the author of this first biography was a student of the master himself. Lechen, *History of Kadam*, 592. Judging by available biographies of Thokmé Sangpo and the master's own writings, the master appeared to have identified more with the Kadam tradition than with Sakya, despite his early education. In any case, this is how later Tibetan historians such as Lechen seemed to have viewed the master's sectarian affiliation, if any.
10. Palden Yeshé, *Drops*, 5a1; Lechen, *History of Kadam*, 593.
11. Lechen, *History of Kadam*, 594.
12. Yongzin Yeshé Gyaltsen, *Biographies of the Masters of the Lineage of the Stages of the Path*, 854. This volume contains a lengthy entry on Thokmé Sangpo (pp. 849–90), containing both the life of the master as well as selected verses from his writings.
13. For an example of such a guide to the heart of dependent origination, see Jinpa, *Mind Training*, 423–30.
14. Lechen, *History of Kadam*, 594. Lechen, however, gives the impression that the *Thirty-Seven Practices* was composed when the master was at Bodong É Monastery, which cannot be the case. In the colophon of the text, it explicitly mentions that it was composed at the Ngulchu retreat. For my translation of the *Thirty-Seven Practices*, see Jinpa, *The Bodhisattva Ideal*.
15. Collected Works of Thokmé Sangpo, vol. *ka*, 49b1 and 50b6. "Maṇipa" alludes to the famous six-syllable mantra of Avalokiteśvara, *Oṃ maṇi padme hūṃ*. By referring to himself as Maṇipa, the master is probably stating how he is a proponent and practitioner of Avalokiteśvara and his mantra.

16. "How to Bring Sickness and So on into the Path," Collected Works, 1:194b1.
17. Lechen, *History of Kadam,* 603. According to the biography by the nineteenth-century author Ngedön Tengyé, *A Joyful Mahāyāna Feast* (47b1), Thokmé Sangpo was admired within the Yuan imperial court, and one of the Yuan Mongol princes, in fact, authored a commentary on his *Thirty-Seven Practices.* The same prince is also said to have taught Maitreya's *Ornament of Mahāyāna Sūtras* on the basis of Thokmé Sangpo's commentary.
18. Ngedön Tengyé's biography (41b3) speaks of how the great Jonang master Dölpopa (1292–1361) felt that, with Thokmé Sangpo's mastery of bodhisattva practice, were he to embrace Dölpopa's perspective on the view, he would then be excellent both with respect to view and practice. So Dölpopa went to the Ngulchu retreat, but as Thokmé Sangpo was in a strict retreat at the time, the two did not meet. Later, Dölpopa sent a letter containing some questions pertaining to the view, to which Thokmé Sangpo wrote back saying he did not know the answers. This same biography speaks of how, when Thokmé Sangpo visited Central Tibet, he did not meet with Karmapa Rangjung Dorjé because the Karmapa had already left for China by that time.
19. Ngedön Tengyé, *Joyful Mahāyāna Feast,* 48b3. Yongzin Yeshé Gyaltsen (*Ornament of Losang's Intent: A Guide to Mind Training,* 34), for example, identifies the two distinct lineages of transmission of the *Seven-Point Mind Training* within the Geluk tradition, both stemming from Thokmé Sangpo: one from the master to Rendawa, who passed it to Tsongkhapa, and the other from the master to Gyamapa Yönten Ö, who transmitted it to Phakpa Lophel, reaching eventually to the Fifth Dalai Lama's teacher Khöntön Paljor Lhundrup, who conferred it to Sur Trinlé Rabgyé, from whom the Great Fifth received the transmission.
20. Tib. *slob dpon blo gros mi zad pa 'phags pa 'jam dpal gyi dngos grub brnyes pa.* Kṛṣṇapa, 331a5. A close reading of Kṛṣṇapa's commentary, extant only in Tibetan, could shed important light on the textual history of Śāntideva's text in India.
21. "On the Rites of Generating Aspiring and Engaging Minds According to Śāntideva's Tradition," Collected Works of Thokmé Sangpo, vol. 1, 92b5.
22. Since I have benefitted deeply in my own understanding of the *Guide* by comparing Thokmé Sangpo's commentary with that of Gyaltsab

Darma Rinchen (1364–1432), I have offered Gyaltsab's reading in the notes where I felt could be helpful to the reader, especially in the difficult ninth chapter.

23. In conformity with how the title of Śāntideva's famed text is known in Tibet, Thokmé Sangpo's Sanskrit title includes the word *sattva*. In extant Sanskrit versions of the text, however, as well as in references to it in other Sanskrit works, the title appears as simply *Bodhicaryāvatāra*.
24. The Tibetan *dge ba'i lha* could translate the names Kṣemadeva, Kalyāṇadeva, or Sudeva; we have chosen Kṣemadeva as the Sanskrit name of the author of the commentary *Excellent Exposition on Guide to the Bodhisattva Way* (*Bodhisattvacaryāvatārasaṃskāra*), Toh 3874. This commentary was translated from the Sanskrit into Tibetan by Śrīkumāra and Gewai Lodrö. When referring to this commentary, Thokmé Sangpo calls it simply the *Exposition* (*rnam bshad*). From here on in the notes, we cite it by the author's name, Kṣemadeva.
25. Kṣemadeva, 91b3.
26. The Tibetan *nag po pa* could also be the translation of the Sanskrit names Kṛṣṇapāda or Kānapa, or even the short form of Kṛṣṇācārya (*nag po spyod pa*). It is difficult to determine if this Indian master who wrote a major commentary on Śāntideva's text is the same as the mahāsiddha Kṛṣṇācārya, also known as Kāṇha. In any case, the commentary cited here is not the major *pañjikā* commentary by this author (Toh 3873) but the much shorter *Clarification of the Difficult Points*, Toh 3875.
27. As explained in the preface, these notations in brackets refer to the relevant verses from the *Bodhicaryāvatāra*. Thus here, [1.4a] refers to chapter 1, verse 4, with the *a* indicating the first line of the verse.
28. These are chapters 4 and 5 of Śāntideva's work. Only the first two perfections are correlated with specific chapters here because the remaining four perfections—forbearance, diligence, meditation, and wisdom—each have a chapter dedicated to them. Kṛṣṇapa, *Clarification of the Difficult Points* (*Duravabodhananirṇaya*), Toh 3875, 91b3.
29. Vairocanarakṣita (*snam snang 'tsho*) was an Indian paṇḍita who came to Tibet sometime in the eleventh century (see Roerich, *Blue Annals*, 844–45). In addition to his commentary on Śāntideva's *Guide* (Toh 3876), he also composed a verse summary of Śāntideva's *Compendium on Training* (*Śikṣākusumamañjarī*, Toh 3943).
30. In Tibetan, the modifier in all these instances, such as "well shaped," is the same, *legs par*. These modifiers express three features of the

abandonment dimension of buddhahood, *sugata* ("gone to bliss"), that the obscurations are excellently eliminated, they are eliminated in their entirety, and in a manner that they can never arise again.

31. Kṣemadeva, 1a4.
32. Asaṅga, *Bodhisattvabhūmi*, book I, chap. 7, Toh 4037, 49b3.
33. Maitreya, *Uttaratantra*, 1.148 (1.145 in Skt. ed.), Toh 4024, 61a7.
34. Its *natural purity*—its emptiness—and its *purity of adventitious stains* attained through the realization of the path.
35. Maitreya, *Uttaratantra*, 1.34, Toh 4024, 56b6.
36. Thokmé Sangpo is referring here to the conjunctive particle *te* (in Tibetan) at the end of the second line of the salutation verse, which connects the next two lines expressing what he wishes to do after having paid homage to the Three Jewels.
37. Thokmé Sangpo cites this as from a sūtra, *Sangs rgyas kyi yon tan bsngags pa'i mdo*, but we have not been able to identify the source.
38. Thokmé Sangpo is referring to the Tibetan word *re zhig* (Skt. *tāvad*, translated here as "for now") in *Bodhicaryāvatāra* 1.3b. He is saying that, according to the two Indian commentators, the benefit of others is also a motivation for composing the text.
39. Thokmé Sangpo is referring here to four factors that the Tibetan commentarial tradition understands to stem from the promise an author makes to compose a text. They are the *subject matter* of the text, the *purpose* of the text, the *interrelatedness*, or dependence, of the realization of the purpose on the text, and the *ultimate goal* of the text, which here is to enable the reader to attain buddhahood.
40. *Duravabodhananirṇaya*, Toh 3875, 91a7.
41. Kṣemadeva, 1a4.
42. This verse is found in Kṛṣṇapa, 97a4, which is most probably our author's source.
43. This verse appears in Vibhūticandra's commentary on *Guide to the Bodhisattva Way* (*Distinctive Illuminator* [*Viśeṣadyotanī*], Toh 3880, 197b4), where he includes these lines alongside those on the eight opposites of leisure referred to by Kṛṣṇapa in the preceding note.
44. *Gaṇḍavyūhasūtra*, Toh 44, *ga*, 381a7.
45. A source for this exact sūtra citation was not identified.
46. Candragomin, *Śiṣyalekha*, verse 40, Toh 4183, 40a2.
47. This verse is from Thokmé Sangpo himself, composed in the style of what is known as "intermediate verses" (*bar skabs kyi tshigs bcad*), often written as a respite before moving onto the next major topic.

48. General (*thun mong*) benefits here are benefits common to both the aspiring and engaging awakening minds, while specific (*khyad par*) benefits are not common to both.
49. *Gaṇḍavyūhasūtra*, Toh 44, *'a*, 319b5.
50. *Gaṇḍavyūhasūtra*, Toh 44, *'a*, 317a5.
51. *Gaṇḍavyūhasūtra*, Toh 44, *'a*, 315a6.
52. *Ratnakaraṇḍasūtra*, Toh 117, 254b6.
53. This exact quote could not be located in the *Akṣayamatinirdeśasūtra*. However, a similar quote is found in the *Array of Trees Sūtra* (*Gaṇḍavyūhasūtra*), Toh 44, *'a*, 320b5.
54. In Buddhist texts, the universe is envisioned in terms of three realms of existence—the desire realm, form realm, and the formless realm. Since the first meditative absorption (*dhyāna*) is the threshold of the form realm, "below the realm of the first meditative absorption" indicates the entire desire realm.
55. *Gaṇḍavyūhasūtra*, Toh 44, *'a*, 310a7.
56. Kṣemadeva, 6a5. By "great patience," he is here referring probably to the advanced stage of the third phase of the path of preparation that is called *patience*, within the fourfold division of heat, peak, patience, and supreme dharma.
57. *Gaṇḍavyūhasūtra*, Toh 44, *'a*, 298b2. This and the previous verse are contiguous in the sūtra.
58. *Gaṇḍavyūhasūtra*, Toh 44, *'a*, 309b2. Thokmé Sangpo quotes here a selection rather than a full contiguous passage from the sūtra.
59. *Gaṇḍavyūhasūtra*, Toh 44, *'a*, 312a1. Thokmé Sangpo is here identifying the point where the extensive explanation of the virtues of the awakening mind ends in this sūtra.
60. *Gaṇḍavyūhasūtra*, Toh 44, *ga*, 323b7. Śāntideva quotes this in his *Compendium of Training* as the key source for this twofold division of the awakening mind, but the wording of the engaging mind in the Kangyur version of the sūtra itself is a little different from the one cited in the *Compendium* (and from its citation in Kamalaśīla's *Stages of Meditation*). Instead of "engage" (*'jug pa* or *chas pa*), the sūtra reads *'tshol ba* ("to seek or search").
61. *Gaṇḍavyūhasūtra*, Toh 44, *ga*, 323a5.
62. *Subāhuparipṛcchā*, Toh 70, 164a7.
63. The story of Maitrakanyaka ("Daughter of Mitra," Tib. *mdza' bo'i bu mo*) speaks about a merchant who named his son Daughter to protect him from his karma, which proves futile. In the passage relevant to

this verse, Maitrakanyaka's head is being tortured by a burning iron wheel as a karmic result of having kicked his mother in the head. From wishing to take upon himself the bad karma of everyone who might otherwise suffer his fate, he is instantly released from the wheel. The story is found in the *Avadānaśataka* and translated from Sanskrit in Appleton, *Many Buddhas, One Buddha*.

64. Maitreya, *Mahāyānasūtrālaṃkāra* 9.14, Toh 4020, 8a3.
65. *Vīradattagṛhapatiparipṛcchā*, Toh 72 Kangyur, dkon brtsegs, *ca*, 202b6.
66. *Samādhirājasūtra*, chap. 34, Toh 127, 114b6.
67. Kṣemadeva (9b3) contains this phrase, which is the source for Thokmé Sangpo here. It's not clear if it is a line being cited from elsewhere or Kṣemadeva is simply giving examples of what is inexhaustible. In Kṣemadeva, the line is preceded by another that reads, "All wishes would be accomplished" (*yid la bsam pa thams cad rdzogs byed cing*).
68. Prajñākaramati, *Extensive Commentary on Guide to the Bodhisattva Way*, Toh 3872, 56a7; and Kṣemadeva, 9b2. Throughout the text, Thokmé Sangpo refers to Prajñākaramati's commentary simply as the *Great Commentary* (*'grel chen*). From here on, when citing this text, we refer to it by its author's name, Prajñākaramati.
69. *Praśāntaviniścayaprātihāryasamādhisūtra*, Toh 129, 209a3.
70. *Sūtra Evaluating Whether Progress Is Certain or Uncertain* (*Niyatāniyatgatimudrāvatārasūtra*), Toh 202, 76a6.
71. Āryaśūra, *Pāramitāsamāsa*, 3.13; Toh 3944, 225b1.
72. *Kāśyapa Chapter* (*Kāśyapaparivarta*), Toh 87, 136b3.
73. Maitreya, *Abhisamayālaṃkāra*, 1.19ab, Toh 3786, 2b5.
74. Maitreya, *Mahāyānasūtrālaṃkāra*, 5.2, Toh 4020, 4b2.
75. Maitreya, *Abhisamayālaṃkāra*, 1.20–21, Toh 3786, 2b5.
76. *Bodhisattvaprātimokṣacatuṣkanirhāra*, Toh 248, 53b4.
77. Candragomin, *Twenty Verses on the Bodhisattva Vow* (*Bodhisattvasaṃvaraviṃśaka*), verse 2cd; Toh 4081, 166b2.
78. *Bodhicaryāvatāra* 5.102.
79. Asaṅga, *Bodhisattvabhūmi*, book I, chap. 10, Toh 4037, 82b7. "Support" (*rten*) refers to representations of the enlightened beings such as the Buddha in the form of an image.
80. Śāntideva, *Śikṣāsamuccaya*, chap. 1, Toh 3940, 9b1.
81. Atiśa, *Bodhipathapradīpa*, verse 20, 239a4. The seven prātimokṣa, or "individual liberation," vows are (1–2) fully ordained male and female vows, (3) probationary nun's vow, (4–5) male and female novice vows,

and (6–7) male and female lay vows. Sometimes, the day-long lay vow is added, making a list of eight individual liberation vows.

82. This is Kṛṣṇapa's *Exposition of Guide to the Bodhisattva Way* (Toh 3873), where we find this critical discussion on 301b4. Hereafter, this work will be cited by the author's name, Kṛṣṇapa.
83. *Bodhimārgapradīpapañjikā*, Toh 3948, 258a7.
84. *In Clear Words* (*Prasphuṭapadā*), Toh 3796, 38b5.
85. Kṛṣṇapa, 301b1.
86. Prajñākaramati, 51a5.
87. *Bodhicaryāvatāra* 5.11.
88. Asaṅga, *Bodhisattvabhūmi*, book I, chap. 10, Toh 4037, 85b5–86a7. On these infractions, including the defeats, see the texts by Tsongkhapa, Changkya, and Dza Paltrul in Jinpa, *Bodhisattva Ideal.*
89. On these eighteen and their enumeration in Śāntideva's *Compendium of Training*, see Tsongkhapa's summary explanation in his commentary on that work in Jinpa, *Bodhisattva Ideal.*
90. Śāntideva, *Śikṣāsamuccaya*, chap. 4, Toh 3940, 43a5.
91. Śāntideva, *Śikṣāsamuccaya*, chap. 4, Toh 3940, 43a7.
92. Śāntideva, *Śikṣāsamuccaya*, chap. 4, Toh 3940, 43a7.
93. Abhayākaragupta, *Munimatālaṃkāra*, chap. 1, Toh 3903, 86b2.
94. Candragomin, *Bodhisattvasaṃvaraviṃśaka*, verse 4; Toh 4081, 166b3.
95. That is, when the intention is nonvirtous, then even if an action might seem virtuous, this is a false impression.
96. Candragomin, *Bodhisattvasaṃvaraviṃśaka*, verse 8, Toh 4081, 166b5. Śāntarakṣita, in his commentary on the text (Toh 4082, 172b5), explains the final line as saying that if no one is around, one can confess minor infractions within one's own mind.
97. Śāntideva, *Śikṣāsamuccaya*, chap. 4, Toh 3940, 43b3.
98. *Bodhicaryāvatāra* 5.98.
99. This section pertains to the seven-limb worship presented in the *Guide to the Bodhisattva Way*. Thokmé Sangpo lists "going for refuge" as a distinct item instead of subsuming it in the second limb, that of prostration, as part of its preliminary. Hence there are eight limbs here instead of the usual seven.
100. The three spheres are the three key elements of a given act—the object of the act, the doer, and the act itself—and their "purification" refers to bringing to awareness their essential character of emptiness so that there is no grasping at any of the three spheres.

101. The text here is presented as a quote, but it has not been found in the Tibetan edition of the sūtra in the Kangyur.
102. In Indian cosmology, this is the northern continent among the four main continents.
103. This verse seems to be a summary by the author himself rather than a citation from some other text.
104. Vasubandhu, *Abhidharmakośa*, 3.72, Toh 4089, 9b4. That is, universes comprised of, respectively, a thousand, a million, and a billion world systems.
105. *Ratnolkādhāraṇī*, Toh 145, 67b5. This English translation is by David Jackson at https://read.84000.co/translation/toh145.html.
106. *Banner's Crest Great Sūtra* (*Dhvajāgramahāsūtra*), Toh 293, 267a3. The wording in the sūtra itself is slightly different.
107. *Great Nirvāṇa Sūtra* (*Mahāparinirvāṇasūtra*), Toh 119, 120a5.
108. It's difficult to infer the source for this list of six aspects in relation to negative karma. In the *Main Treatise on the Grounds* (*Bhūmivastu*, Toh 4035, 81a2), Asaṅga lists nine aspects when presenting the topic of affliction through karma: nature, divisions, cause, states, doors, weight, distortion, enumeration, and faults.
109. *Caturdharmanirdeśasūtra*, Toh 249, 59b1.
110. The Skilton and Crosby translation includes the following additional verse before verse 32: "How can I escape it? I am continually in a state of alarm, O Leaders. Let death not come too soon for me, before my mass of evil is destroyed!" Hence from this point onward, there is a variance of one in the numbering of the verses in this chapter between ours and that translation.
111. This seems to be a versified text from the author himself rather than a citation from another source.
112. The line is not found in the *Discourse on the Meaning of Impermanence* (*Anityārthaparikathā*, Toh 4174), whose title (*Mi rtag pa'i don gyi gtam*) is closest to the title cited by Thokmé Sangpo here.
113. *Sūryagarbhasūtra*, Toh 257, 215b3.
114. This is the second of the two divisions of "preparatory activities," listed above on page 53.
115. Prajñākaramati, 72a2. On this version, *Bodhicaryāvatāra* 3.15ab would read, "Should thoughts of anger and distrust arise in some on my account. . . ," a reading that accords with the extant Sanskrit version of the text.
116. Most probably, the text by Jitāri that Thokmé Sangpo is referring to is

his *Rite for Generating the Awakening Mind and Adopting the Pledge* (*Bodhicittotpādasamādānavidhi*, Toh 3968, 243a2).

117. This and the subsequent verse are from Thokmé Sangpo presenting the two stages of taking the vow of aspiring mind and the engaging mind separately, modifying the actual vow-ceremony lines of 3.23–24.
118. This is the third among three major outlines enumerated on page 29 after (1) the person who engages in the discipline, the basis, and (2) the intention of the person engaging in the discipline. Together, these three outlines cover the entire text.
119. Morality, forbearance, diligence, meditative absorption, and wisdom.
120. Asaṅga, *Abhidharmasamuccaya*, chap. 1, Toh 4049, 49a2.
121. *Samādhirājasūtra*, Toh 127, 87b6. As translated in the 84000.co translation, *The King of Samādhis Sūtra*, 26.18.
122. Exact source for this statement in the sūtra not located.
123. *Kanakavarṇapūrvayoga*, Toh 350, 52b6. The story of Kanakavarṇa is translated in Rotman, *Divine Stories: Divyāvadāna, Part 2*, 83–93.
124. Kṣemadeva, 24a4.
125. Vibhūticandra, *Distinctive Illumination* (*Viśeṣadyotanī*), Toh 3880, 214b3.
126. *Prajñāpāramitāsaṃcayagāthā*, Toh 13, *ka*, 18b3.
127. *Praśāntaviniścayaprātihāryasamādhi*, Toh 129, 196b2. English translation adapted from https://read.84000.co/translation/toh129.html, 1.122.
128. The *Connected Discourses* are known in the Pāli canon as the *Saṃyuttanikāya* and have not been translated into Tibetan. In Sanskrit the texts are known as *Saṃyuktāgama*. The above quotation is found in Nāgārjuna's *Compendium of Sūtras* (*Sūtrasamuccaya*, Toh 3934, 149b1), which is probably Thokmé Sangpo's source here.
129. Prajñākaramati, 85b6. The reference in the *Extensive Commentary* is to 4.43cd, "Except against the kind of afflictions/ that are related to the destruction of the afflictions."
130. The Sanskrit text has the reading "I do not care if my guts ooze out! Let my head fall off!" (English translation by Crosby and Skilton).
131. Prajñākaramati, 86a6.
132. Kṛṣṇapa, 308b7.
133. This is the third, alongside a brief presentation and a detailed explanation, presented as the main framework for chapter 4 at its outset.
134. Śāntideva, *Śikṣāsamuccayakārikā*, verse 3, Toh 3939, 1a3. This verse presents in summary the main outline of the *Compendium of Train-*

*ing*: the giving away, protecting, purifying, and enhancing of one's body, material resources, and roots of virtue.

135. This relates to the second of the two prongs, the other being conscientiousness, that Thokmé Sangpo identified at the start of chapter 4 as the core of the training in the perfection of morality. Earlier, however, he only mentioned meta-awareness (*shes bzhin*), while here he includes mindfulness (*dran pa*) as well.
136. Āryaśūra, *Jātakamālā*, chap. 1, Toh 4150, 2b5.
137. *Ratnameghasūtra*, Toh 231, 82a2.
138. *Dharmasaṃgītisūtra*, Toh 238, 63a7.
139. Prajñākaramati, 89a4; and Vairocanarakṣita, 109b6.
140. Kṣemadeva, 29a2.
141. Thokmé Sangpo is likely referring here to a commentary by Pang Lotsāwa on *Guide to the Bodhisattva Way* to which we have had no access.
142. *Application of Mindfulness Sūtra* (*Saddharmasmṛtyupasthāna*), Toh 287, *ya*, 146b3.
143. *Akṣayamatinirdeśasūtra*, Toh 175, 92b6.
144. The Tibetan text reads "In the *Perfection of Morality Sūtra* it says" (*tshul khrims kyi pha rol du phyin pa'i mdo las*). This I take to be a scribal error, and it should read *tshul khrims kyi pha rol du phyin pa ni mdo las*.
145. *Teachings of Akṣayamati* (*Akṣayamatinirdeśasūtra*), Toh 175, 92b6.
146. Kṛṣṇapa, 310b3.
147. Tib. *tsangs par skye ba*, literally "being born as a brahma"; it refers to being reborn in form or formless realms.
148. Source not located.
149. What specific Perfection of Wisdom scripture Thokmé Sangpo has in mind remains unidentified.
150. Prajñākaramati, 91a5.
151. Prajñākaramati, 91a5; and Kṛṣṇapa, 310b6.
152. *Condensed Perfection of Wisdom in Verse* (*Prajñāpāramitāsaṃcayagāthā*), Toh 13, 6b5.
153. Despite efforts, we have not located this in the *Array of Trees Sūtra*. In Śāntideva's *Compendium of Training* (*Śikṣāsamuccaya*, Toh 3940, 70a4) too, this is cited as being from this sūtra, and that is probably Thokmé Sangpo's source.
154. Vairocanarakṣita, 111a2
155. Kṣemadeva, 31a4; Prajñākaramati, 88b3. What Kṣemadeva means by

"the ten aspects of the awakening mind" (*byang chub kyi sems rnam pa bcu*) can be discerned from what he says in his commentary on chapter 1, 3b6, where he lists the ten chapters of Śāntideva's *Guide to the Bodhisattva Way* and identifies them as the ten aspects.

156. *Rājāvavādakasūtra*, Toh 221, 84a6.
157. Kṛṣṇapa, 311b2; Prajñākaramati, 92b1.
158. Kṛṣṇapa, 311b6; and Kṣemadeva, 31b1.
159. Prajñākaramati, 93b2.
160. Although Thokmé Sangpo does not specify it here, he reads 5.30–32b as presenting three main conditions for mindfulness: (1) associating with one's teacher and receiving instructions from one's preceptors and practicing colleagues, (2) ensuring respect for the precepts through fear of negative consequences, and (3) always remembering the presence of the buddhas, who bear witness to one's actions and thoughts. The discussion of the conditions that give rise to or help sustain mindfulness presented in the *Guide* should be read in comparison with the one surrounding *kārikā* 8 at the start of chapter 6 of Śāntideva's *Compendium of Training*.
161. Āryaśūra, *Jātakamālā*, chap. 13, Toh 4150, 49b7. The wording of the stanza here is slightly different from the one in the Tengyur.
162. The four are sitting, standing, lying down, and walking.
163. *Akṣayamatinirdeśasūtra*, Toh 175, 99b4.
164. Kṛṣṇapa, 313b2.
165. Tib. *shes bzhin ma yin pa* (*asamprajanya*), one of the twenty secondary afflictions according to Asaṅga's Abhidharma system.
166. Thokmé Sangpo is saying that Kṣemadeva (34b2) reads the two words "evasive" (*skyor 'byin*) and "deceiving" (*slu sems*) as equivalents of "pretense" (*gyo*) and "dissimulation" (*sgyu*).
167. Vairocanarakṣita, 315a1.
168. Maitreya, *Mahāyānasūtrālaṃkāra* 6.10, Toh 4020, 6b4.
169. The sense of integrity forbids you to commit wrong actions for your own sake, whereas decency forbids it in the regard of others. Kṛṣṇapa, 315a1.
170. Prajñākaramati, 89a2; Vairocanarakṣita, 111a1; Kṣemadeva, 34b6.
171. Kṣemadeva, 34b4.
172. The Tibetan text has *gcom skyung zhing dga' bar 'gyur* for the Sanskrit *syān niḥśabdaruciḥ sadā*. Whereas the Tibetan *gcom* is an archaic word for pride, or arrogance, and *skung ba* means reduce, diminish (i.e., "curb pride"/"practice humility"), we follow here the meaning

of the word in its Sanskrit form, "delight in silence," as it fits more logically in the context of being mindful of the mind and practicing gentle, calm behavior.

173. Nāgārjuna, *Suhṛllekha*, verse 42, Toh 4182, 42b4. "Five attributes" refer to the execution of the act (engaged in constantly), the state of mind, the absence of opposing forces, and the basis or the object of the act, with the last differentiated in terms of objects of kindness, such as one's parents, and objects of great virtue, such as the Three Jewels.
174. Vairocanarakṣita, 372b3.
175. *Sarvabuddhamahārahasyopāyakauśalya*, Toh 82, 60a6–61a2.
176. Nāgārjuna, *Suhṛllekha*, verse 38ab, Toh 4182, 42b2.
177. An alternative title for the *King of Meditations Sūtra. Samādhirājasūtra*, chap. 9, Toh 127, 28a7.
178. *Bodhisattvaprātimokṣacatuṣkanirhāra*, Toh 248, 54a3.
179. Āryadeva, *Catuḥśataka*, 2.1, Toh 3846, 3a2.
180. Śāntideva, *Śikṣāsamuccaya*, chap. 3, Toh 3940, 34a6.
181. Thokmé Sangpo is saying that some versions of the root text have the additional line *bsam pa mnyam pas de gtang bya* after 5.87ab. As is clear from the what follows, Thokmé Sangpo is referring to Vairocana's commentary (Vairocanarakṣita, 114b5), which glosses a line of the root text as "*With the mind of equanimity*—that is, if one's mind is equal [to the task], there would then be no danger of being undermined. Enlightenment too would not be undermined."
182. Kṛṣṇapa, 318a2.
183. These types of behavior and posture are described as disrespectful when attending a teaching, suggesting that the student should be seated with full attention assuming a reverent bodily posture.
184. *Sarvavaidalyasaṃgraha*, Toh 227, 186a6.
185. Alternative translation: the Dharma of vast activity.
186. *Kāśyapa Chapter* (*Kāśyapaparivarta*), Toh 87, 123a5.
187. Śāntideva, *Śikṣāsamuccayakārikā*, verse 11, and *Śikṣāsamuccaya*, chap. 6, Toh 3940, 71b3.
188. *Ratnameghasūtra*, Toh 231, 90a4.
189. Maitreya, *Mahāyānasūtrālaṃkāra* 12.64, Toh 4020, 14b4. The five areas of knowledge, or five sciences, are inner science (i.e., the Dharma) and the sciences of logic, language, medicine, and arts and crafts.
190. Maitreya, *Mahāyānasūtrālaṃkāra* 20.59–60, Toh 4020, 35a5.
191. *Gaṇḍavyūhasūtra*, Toh 44, *'a*, 286b1.

192. The blockprint edition reads: "and the ways to confess and purify them."
193. Prajñākaramati reads 5.105–6, as do most Indian and Tibetan commentators, as advising that one reads constantly Śāntideva's *Compendium of Training* and his shorter *Compendium of Sūtras*; furthermore, one should also read Nāgārjuna's two similar texts. Prajñākaramati (109b7) writes: "Alternatively, one should read with effort—that is, with care—both the *Compendium of Training* and the *Compendium of Sūtras* composed by Ārya Nāgārjuna." Whether Nāgārjuna indeed composed a compendium of training remains open to question; Śāntideva's *Compendium of Sūtras* is no longer extant.
194. Prajñākaramati, 110a1.
195. *Mañjuśrīvikrīḍitasūtra*, Toh 96, 231b4.
196. For an in-depth discussion stemming from 6.1, especially on what type of virtue is destroyed by anger and what such "destruction" means, see Jinpa, *Illuminating the Intent*, 135–40.
197. Vasubandhu, in his *Treasury of Knowledge Autocommentary* (*Abhidharmakośabhāṣya*, Toh 4090, 94b5), cites this as from an authoritative source but does not specify who that is. Thokmé Sangpo here identifies the actual source as the elder (*sthavira*) Rahula.
198. This sūtra is cited also in Prajñākaramati's commentary as part of a larger quote, which must be the source for Thokmé Sangpo here.
199. In other words, these twelve unwanted situations are suffering, humiliation, harsh words, and ill repute inflicted on myself; suffering, humiliation, harsh words, and ill repute inflicted on my loved ones; and pleasure, honor, praise, and renown bestowed on my enemy.
200. Thokmé Sangpo, instead of taking *dka' bzlog* as Durga, reads it as *bkha thub bzlog pa*—"preventing asceticism"—combining it with the word Śiva to form the phrase "who obstructs Śiva's asceticism." Hence the need to add the name of Śiva's consort as the object of worship by her devotees. In Śāntideva's text itself, the relevant lines read: "The devotees of Durga and the people of Karṇāṭa/ willingly endure the pains/ of burns, cuts, and the like./ Why then am I a coward when my goal is liberation?"
201. Thokmé Sangpo seems to be thinking here of the possessiveness that involves taking measures to guard one's wealth, something that many might find a pain but the miserly see as a form of happiness.
202. Tib. *chos thams la bde bar 'gro ba'i ting nge 'dzin* (Skt. *sarvadharmasukhākrānta*).

203. Prajñākaramati, 114a1.
204. Although a more detailed critique of Sāṃkhya theory appears later in chapter 9, here the phrase "as will be explained below" seems to point to what immediately follows. In the Sāṃkhya school, *primal matter* (*prakṛti* or *pradhāna*) is the eternal and unitary cause of the world and its various manifestations. As it is only a cause and is never an effect, it is the autonomous agent *par excellence*. It is itself nonmanifest, but it pervades all phenomena. As such, it is sometimes equated with *ātman*, the permanent, partless, and independent self that is accepted by most of the non-Buddhist Indian schools but rejected by Buddhists.
205. Thokmé Sangpo is referring here to line 6.28d, which reads, "it cannot attempt to cease to exist either."
206. Kṣemadeva, 42b; Kṛṣṇapa, 322a6.
207. Prajñākaramati, 115a2.
208. Skilton and Crosby read the first two lines of the verse as "On account of them, because I am patient, my evil is considerably decreased." Thokmé Sangpo's reading here accords with all extant versions of the text in the Tengyur.
209. Tib. *dge sbyong gi spyod pa bzhi*. Most probably the reference here is to what are known as "the four attributes of a paragon of virtue" (*dge sbyong gi chos bzhi*): not responding to abusive words with abuse, not responding to anger with anger, not responding to being hit with hitting back, and not responding to slander with slander.
210. The woodblock edition presents this outline as "Refuting the arrogance that they possess intrinsic value" (*snying po yod pas drags pa dgag pa*). By "woodblock edition," we are referring to a single-volume xylograph edition of Thokmé Sangpo's writings at the library of the Central Institute for Higher Tibetan Studies, Sarnath, containing three texts: the biography of Thokmé Sangpo, his miscellaneous writings (*gsung thor bu*), and his commentary on Śāntideva's *Guide to the Bodhisattva Way*. The edition on which our critical edition was based is the modern book edition of the commentary published by the Sakya Students' Welfare Association, Sarnath, 1992.
211. These two lines are cited in Prajñākaramati's *Extensive Commentary*, which must be the source for Thokmé Sangpo here. The actual source unidentified.
212. Prajñākaramati, 125b3. Thokmé Sangpo is making the point that his reading here, which deviates from the root text, is based on Prajñākaramati. The Tibetan version of the root text reads, "Because of my

attachment, I have brought myself/ to burn in the hells a thousand times. . ."

213. Kṣemadeva, 47b7.
214. Prajñākaramati, 126b3, and Kṛṣṇapa, 331a1.
215. Vairocanarakṣita, 121a4.
216. *Dharmasaṃgītisūtra*, Toh 328, 63b1.
217. Thokmé Sangpo, following Prajñākaramati and other Indian commentators, views despondency (*sgyi lug*) as a form of *self-contempt* (*bdag nyid brnyas pa*) in the context of laziness, and Gyaltsab identifies this third type of laziness in exactly the same way. Crosby and Skilton (63) list *despondency* (*viṣāda*) and *self-contempt* (*ātmāvamanyanā*) as distinct forms of laziness.
218. Prajñākaramati, 138b5.
219. Āryaśūra, *Jātakamālā*, chap. 32, Toh 4150, 128b3.
220. Nagarjuna, *Suhṛllekha*, verse 55, Toh 4182, 43a6. This translation follows Jinpa, *Mind Training*, 327.
221. Nagarjuna, *Letter to a Friend* (*Suhṛllekha*), verse 84, Toh 4182, 55b3.
222. Tib. *rgyal po rnams chos bzhi*. Thokmé Sangpo does not specify what these four attributes are. Quite possibly, he is referring to the so-called four arms or four divisions that make up a fighting force in ancient India: infantry, calvary, chariots, and elephants.
223. *Subāhuparipṛcchāsūtra*, Toh 70, 165b4.
224. *Svapnanirdeśasūtra*, Toh 48, 235b6.
225. Maitreya, *Uttaratantra*, 1.27, Toh 4024, 56a2.
226. Prajñākaramati, 141a4; Vairocanarakṣita, 124b8.
227. Prajñākaramati, 142a1; Kṣemadeva, 51a5.
228. Vibhūticandra (*Distinctive Illumination* [*Viśeṣadyotanī*], Toh 3880, 239a3) asserts that the inclusion of 7.31 is problematic and opines that it might have been added later. The signaling of the shift from the negative aspect, examining the opposites of diligence and how to overcome them, to the more proactive section on fortifying diligence through cultivating the powers is done in 7.32. At best, according to him, 7.31 is a repetition, and at worst, it creates unnecessary confusion because of the use of two lists—"four forces" (*dbung bzhi*) and "six powers" (*stobs drug*). On the problem of how to relate the two sets we see in the text—the four divisions of force (*dpung gi tshogs bzhi*) and the six powers (*stobs drug*)—see also Crosby and Skilton (pp. 63–65). Tsongkhapa (Lamrim Chenmo Translation Committee, *Great Treatise*, 2:195–206) offers a clear and insightful explanation of how these

"four forces" (*dbung bzhi*) are related to the two additional powers of *dedication* (*lhur len*) and *self-mastery* (*dbang 'gyur*). In brief, the development of the four forces entails gathering the forces to apply diligence, the power of *dedication* involves being single-pointed in one's diligence, and the power of *self-mastery* pertains to making one's body and mind tractable in the pursuit of the bodhisattva's altruistic ideal and conduct.

229. Prajñākaramati, 142a6.
230. Pang Lotsāwa is, to be precise, referring to the Sanskrit word *canda*, whose Tibetan equivalent is *'dun pa. Mos pa*, on the other hand, is the Tibetan equivalent of the Sanskrit *adhimokṣa*, which connotates decisiveness, resolve, appreciation, and conviction. Incidentally, they are both part of the group of "five object-determinate factors" within the taxonomy of mental factors. Asaṅga, in his *Compendium of Abhidharma*, defines the two like this: *Aspiration* "is the very wish to be endowed with this or that attribute of a desired thing; its function is to act as a basis for generating diligence." *Appreciation* "apprehends the ascertained thing to be just as it is ascertained, so it functions to prevent diversion."
231. Vairocanarakṣita, chap. 7, 125a6.
232. Prajñākaramati, chap. 7, 143a4.
233. Prajñākaramati, 143a4; Vairocanarakṣita, 125a7.
234. This is a reference to 7.37c, *bstan la bya ba ma byas dang*.
235. *Sāgaramatiparipṛcchāsūtra*, Toh 152, 49a4.
236. *Mañjuśrībuddhakṣetraguṇavyūhasūtra*, Toh 59, 279a4.
237. Three entries in the Kangyur have *rājāvavādaka* (*rgyal po la gdams pa*) as part of their title, but we have been unable to locate this verse in any of these sūtras.
238. The root text reads "the Sugata's children" (*bde gshegs sras*).
239. *Avataṃsakasūtra*, chap. 30, Toh 44, *kha*, 76b5.
240. When explaining in detail these three types of self-confidence in what follows, the text reverses the order of the second and the third forms of self-confidence. That is to say, it explains self-confidence in our abilities prior to that of overcoming the afflictions.
241. The text uses the same word, *nga rgyal* (Skt. *mana*), in both its positive sense of "self-confidence" and its negative sense of "arrogance."
242. Prajñākaramati, chap. 7, 147v4; Kṣemadeva, chap. 7, 5315.
243. In all Tibetan editions of the text in the Tengyur, there is an additional six-lined stanza here that reads, "Let me be burned to death,/

or let me be beheaded,/ but never will I bow/ to my enemy, the afflictions./ Similarly, in all situations/ I will do nothing but what is appropriate.//" See note 200 and notice how the first four lines of this stanza appear in fact in chapter 4 as well. Interestingly, Thokmé Sangpo seems to raise questions only about the last two lines of the stanza rather than the stanza in its entirety. Gyaltsab Jé (124), on the other hand, treats its appearance here as unproblematic, assigning it, in fact, a distinct heading: "Generating a distinctive state of mind ensuring the stability of the antidote." To maintain the integrity of the stanza numbers, we have numbered this verse as 7.61(a).

244. See the previous note.

245. Prajñākaramati, 148a3.

246. Thokmé Sangpo reads this verse as making a crucial psychological point that if we do not let go of tasks that have been completed and remain fixated on them, this will impede dedication to new tasks. Such fixation on past projects prevents us from bringing our full attention and dedication to the new task.

247. When this subheading was first enumerated above, it was phrased simply as "Bringing dedication" (*lhur blang ba*). Here, the topic is phrased more fully as *dpung gis lhur blang bar bya ba.*

248. Prajñākaramati, chap. 7, 150a1. The reference here is 5.73d, "and accept the appropriate tasks" (*rigs pai'i las ni dod par bya*).

249. Śāntideva, *Śikṣāsamuccayakārikā*, verse 20ab, Toh 3939, 2b4. The woodblock edition of Thokmé Sangpo's text cites the two remaining lines of the stanza as well: "Strive in meditative equipoise;/ meditate on repulsiveness and so forth."

250. Maitreya, *Mahāyānasūtrālaṃkāra* 19.67, Toh 4020, 31a2.

251. Kṣemadeva, 54b6.

252. Āryaśūra, *Jātakamālā*, chap. 7, Toh 4150, 23a3.

253. *Maitreyamahāsiṃhanāda*, Toh 67, 75r6.

254. Thokmé Sangpo is quoting here directly from Vairocanarakṣita (128b5) in relation to 8.18cd: *de dang de sdongs stong 'gyur du/ sdug bsngal nyid du 'gyur zhing ldang//.*

255. The monk Sunakṣatra, one of the attendants of the Buddha, did not have faith in the Buddha and is said to have held only wrong views, causing him to take birth as a hungry ghost.

256. Prajñākaramati, chap. 8, 154a5.

257. *De bzhin gshegs pa thams cad kyi yul la 'jug pa.* Source not located.

258. This verse is cited in Asvabhāva, *Interlinear Explanation of Survey of*

*the Mahāyāna* (*Mahāyānasaṃgrahopanibandhana*, Toh 4051, 253b3), which is probably the source here for Thokmé Sangpo.

259. This is probably from the *Great Nirvāṇa Sūtra* (Toh 119, *nya,* 164b4), where the wording is quite different.

260. *Candrottarādārikāvyākaraṇasūtra*, Toh 191, 292a3. The quotation in the Dergé Kangyur does not correspond entirely to the verse here.

261. *Lalitavistarasūtra*, Toh 95, 71b5.

262. *Smṛtyupasthānasūtra*, Toh 287, *nya*, 259a5. The wording here is different from how it appears in the Dergé Kangyur.

263. Prajñākaramati, 157b2. According to Prajñākaramati, the first part, pertaining to another's wife, refers to 8.40–42, and "subsequent lines," pertaining to one's own wife, refers to 8.43–48.

264. Prajñākaramati, 152b3.

265. There is a major variance here between the edition that is the basis of the critical edition of the Tibetan text and the woodblock edition of Thokmé Sangpo's text. In the latter, the outlines appear as the following: (1) criticizing attachment to the body in general, and (2) criticizing attachment to specific types of body in particular. The first is twofold: (1) criticizing attachment to another's body, and (2) criticizing not perceiving the impurity of one's own body. Here, we have followed the outline as in the critical edition of the text.

266. A *torma* is a ritual cake offered to spirits to appease them so they do not cause harm and also offered to the protectors so they help protect the practitioner, especially from unseen forces. The point here is that just as the *torma* and the harmful spirits are made for each other, a man's lust for a woman's body is natural. Furthermore, if the woman's body is unclean, so is the man's, so it is natural and appropriate for the one to lust after the other. So the opponent argues here.

267. Candragomin, *Śiṣyalekha*, verse 64, Toh 4183, 50a2. Garuḍas, vidyādharas, kinnaras, and mahoragas are various nonhuman life forms according to ancient Indian cosmogeny.

268. Candragomin, *Śiṣyalekha*, verses 68–69, Toh 4183, 50a6.

269. Thokmé Sangpo is contrasting the discussion of the qualities of physical solitude in verses 8.25–29 with the discussion of mental solitude here in verses 8.85–88.

270. When Thokmé Sangpo laid out the main outlines at the beginning of the chapter, this was phrased slightly differently, as "Cultivating discipline, the antidote" (*gnyen po sdom pa bsgom pa*).

271. Prajñākaramati, 166a1.

272. Prajñākaramati, 166a5. Thokmé Sangpo is stating that Prajñākaramati reads 8.95–96 as part of the substantiation of the reasoning in 8.94 (which Thokmé Sangpo reads as actually beginning at 8.97), rather than presenting a new point about the equality from the subjective point of view of the desire to be happy and avoid suffering.
273. E.g., Prajñākaramati, 167a6.
274. *Samādhirājasūtra*, Toh 127, 126b4.
275. Tib. *ro bral bde bas ci zhig bya.* Thokmé Sangpo seems to be querying the Tibetan translation of the root text here, suggesting, per the Indian commentaries, that line 8.108d should read: "What would be point of happiness [liberation] that is devoid of sweetness?" In the Sanskrit text the word for "taste" does appear in the line, and in the parallel verse in Śāntideva's *Compendium of Training* (193a2), the line reads, "What is the use of liberation devoid of taste?" (*ro bral thar pas ci zhig bya*).
276. This verse is cited in Prajñākaramati, 171b1, which must be Thokmé Sangpo's source.
277. This is the summation of the section on equalizing self and others first laid out on page 191.
278. Prajñākaramati, 170b7.
279. Prajñākaramati, 171a3.
280. Kṣemadeva, 60a3.
281. Vairocanarakṣita, 332b1. The reference here is to 8.17cd, "so an attitude of protection and of compassion/ should be practiced toward the world." Vairocana interprets "protection" as referring to compassion and suggests that the word "compassion" should in fact be read as referring to lovingkindness.
282. Precise source not located.
283. The Tibetan version of 8.124 reads: "What wise person would desire/ protect, and venerate this body?" (*mkhas pa su zhig lus 'di la/ 'dod dang bsrung dang mchod byed kyi/*). Where the Tibetan version has "body" (*lus*), the Sanskrit has *ātman* ("self") and hence reads instead as "desire, protect, and venerate this self."
284. Thokmé Sangpo is noting here a variance between the Tibetan root text of 8.138c—*de don mig la sogs pa yis*—where it says "eyes and so forth," and the Indian commentaries on *Guide to the Bodhisattva Way*, which read "hands and so forth" (*lag pa sogs*).
285. The meditation instructed here involves putting yourself in the shoes of those others you are arrogant, competitive, and envious toward,

and imagining how they see you and feel about you—that is, you take on their envy, competitiveness, and arrogance toward your "old self." The practice undermines the solidity and superficiality of our perceptions of others, helping us develop empathy, and it helps puncture the blind spots we have about ourselves, giving us a less self-centered assessment.

286. Thokmé Sangpo is saying that the context of this thought experiment, the word "self" refers to the other whom you have identified as your "self," and "other" refers to your own self, the practitioner of the bodhisattva path.
287. "Him" (*de la*) refers to your old self that has been otherized for the sake of this three-stage series of meditation cultivating envy, competitiveness, and pride.
288. Thokmé Sangpo is stating that the series of meditations that began in 8.140—i.e., the thought experiments wherein you "otherize" your own self as the target of envy, competitiveness, and pride—ends here at 8.155.
289. Tib. *thod rgyal*. The lexicon on archaic Tibetan terms, Ngawang Tsultrim's *Golden Mirror: Unraveling the Terms*, 303, explains the expression as a word for "going over the hierarchy or a conflation of the hierarchical order," hence the choice of the word "upstart."
290. The Tibetan text reads here as *rang don gyi bsam sbyor gnyis po*, which is to say, without the instrumental case. We have treated this as a scribal error, adding the instrumental case so that it reads as *rang don . . . gnyis pos*.
291. This stanza, 8.169, echoes the poignant lines in the *Collection of Aphorisms* 31.7, where we read, "Now I have seen you, the housebuilder;/ I have dismantled the great beams;/ I have destroyed all the rafters;/ and I will not allow you to build the house any longer." Incidentally, this is *Dhammapada* 11.10 as well.
292. Nāgārjuna, *Staff of Wisdom* (*Prajñādaṇḍa*), Toh 4329, 107a7.
293. Nāgārjuna, *Suhṛllekha*, verse 34, Toh 4182, 42a6.
294. This is the third of the three main outlines laid out right at the beginning of the presentation of the conventional awakening mind on page 191, the first two being (1) equalizing self and others and (2) exchanging self and others.
295. Nāgārjuna, *Suhṛllekha*, verse 44, Toh 4182, 42b5.
296. This stanza 8.186 appears only in the Tibetan edition of the root text, not in the Sanskrit version. Hence all translations based on the Sanskrit

version of the text have 186 stanzas in chapter 8, as opposed to 187, as here. Among the Indian commentaries in Tengyur, only Kṛṣṇapa (138a6) refers to this verse, suggesting that the version of the root text he is using is different.

297. *Dharmasaṃgītisūtra*, Toh 238, 52a6. In the sūtra itself, it reads: "One whose mind is in meditative equipoise knows the perfect truth as it is."

298. Śāntideva, *Śikṣāsamuccayakārikā*, verse 9ab, Toh 3939, 2a2. This sūtra passage echoed in the *Compendium of Training* is cited also in Gyaltsab's commentary on Nāgārjuna's *Precious Garland*, with a slightly different wording; see Jinpa, *The Bodhisattva Ideal*, 437.

299. Nāgārjuna, *Yuktiṣaṣṭikā*, verse 46, Toh 3825, 22a3. In the Dergé edition, the lines read, "If one has the thesis of real entities,/ relentless and vicious views arise,/ giving birth to attachment and aversion."

300. *Prajñāpāramitāsaṃcayagāthā* 32.4, Toh 13, 19b3.

301. Nāgārjuna, *Bodhicittavivaraṇa*, verse 73, Toh 1801, 41a3. In the Dergé edition of Tengyur, the verse reads: "When this emptiness [as explained]/ is thus meditated upon by yogis,/ no doubt there will arise in them/ a sentiment attached to others' welfare."

302. Candrakīrti, *Madhyamakāvatāra* 6.28, Toh 3861, 205b2. The Sanskrit word *saṃvṛti*, which is rendered here as "conventional" in the context of conventional truth, carries also the meaning of a "concealer," something that obstructs one's vision like a veil.

303. Tib. *snang med ye shes*. This is very likely an abbreviation of "gnosis free of dualistic appearance," *gnis snang med pa'i ye shes*, a key characteristic of an ārya's meditative equipoise on emptiness.

304. Maitreya, *Madhyāntavibhāga*, 1.16, Toh 4021, 40b5.

305. *Saṃvṛtiparamārthasatyanirdeśa*, Toh 179, 247a4. The wording in the Dergé Kangyur is a little different from what Thokmé Sangpo cites here.

306. Kṣemadeva, 66b7. The Tibetan word translated here as "intellect" is *blo* (pronounced *lo*), whose Sanskrit equivalent is *buddhi*. In Tibetan texts, the word *blo* is often used in a more general sense equivalent to mental states or awareness (*shes pa*). It is clear from the context that, as read by Thokmé Sangpo and the Indian commentaries he consults, the term is not being used in this wider sense.

307. Prajñākaramati, 193b3; Vairocanarakṣita, 137b7.

308. Maitreya, *Madhyāntavibhāga*, 1.9, Toh 4021, 40a5.

309. *Ajātaśatrukaukṛtyavinodanā*, Toh 216, 55b6.

310. Thokmé Sangpo is pointing out that there is no contradiction in saying that the ārya's gnosis does not apprehend phenomena in the terms of positive determination that our sensory cognitions employ, and that such gnosis also sees the ultimate truth.
311. That is, the Indian commentaries on *Guide to the Bodhisattva Way*.
312. The reference is to the three levels of understanding of selflessness—derived from study, from critical reflection, and from meditative cultivation.
313. The two realist Buddhist schools are Vaibhāṣika and Sautrāntika, both accepting the real existence of external objects.
314. Vasubandhu, *Twenty Verses* (*Viṃśatikā*), verse 12, Toh 4056, 3b3.
315. That is, in *Bodhicaryāvatāra* 9.17–23.
316. *Bodhicaryāvatāra* 9.4cd: "by means of analogy accepted by both parties,/ irrespective of what they aim to prove." In the Tibetan text, 9.4d reads *'bras bu'i don du ma dpyad phyir*, containing the key word *'bras bu*, which can be translated either as "aim" or as "result." If this line is read as presenting a response to the charge of denigrating conventional truth, as interpreted by Vairocana and adopted by Thokmé Sangpo, then the line should read, "One engages [in generosity and so forth], without analysis, for the sake of a result."
317. Kṣemadeva, 67a6.
318. Thokmé Sangpo offers two distinct readings of 9.4d, the second under a separate outline heading.
319. *Samādhirājasūtra*, chap. 26, Toh 127, 26b5.
320. Nāgārjuna, *Sixty Stanzas of Reasoning* (*Yuktiṣaṣṭikā*), verse 39, Toh 3825, 21b4.
321. Thokmé Sangpo seems to be drawing here a distinction between those who realize selflessness of person only and those who realize the selflessness of phenomena as well, thus suggesting a difference of subtlety between the two forms of selflessness.
322. Thokmé Sangpo has in mind here a monastic yogi meditating on the impurity of the body as an antidote to lust and desire, hence the specification of a woman's body as the object.
323. Kṣemadeva, 67a6.
324. The reference here is to 9.14a, "Then, in that case, even a buddha would revolve in cyclic existence" (*sangs rgyas kyang ni 'khor 'gyur bas*).
325. Starting from "Alternatively" (*yang na*), Thokmé Sangpo presents the divergent interpretations of this difficult part of the text (9.14–15a)

offered by three Indian commentators—Kṣemadeva, Prajñākaramati, and Vairocanarakṣita.

326. Prajñākaramati, 201a7.
327. Vairocanarakṣita, 140b1.
328. Thokmé Sangpo is reading the line 9.16a, "When, according to you, illusion itself does not exist, what is perceived?" as a Madhyamaka response to the Cittamātra's objection, "When even delusory cognition does not exist, by what is illusion perceived?" where it is being pointed out that the same question can be raised to the Cittamātra's own position.
329. Tib. *gzung cha sgyu ma lta bu.*
330. *Laṅkāvatārasūtra*, Toh 107, 179b4.
331. *Ratnacūḍaparipṛcchā*, Toh 91, 227a3.
332. Nāgārjuna, *Mūlamadhyamakakārikā*, 7.9, Toh 3824, 5a1.
333. Thokmé Sangpo is likely referring here to some earlier Tibetan commentators of Śāntideva's text. See, for example, Sönam Tsemo's commentary (Collected Works, 3:298a6).
334. Prajñākaramati, 204b4.
335. Like most Tibetan commentators, Thokmé Sangpo reads the phrase "rodent's poison" (*byi ba'i dug*) as a poison caused by a rodent's bite, suggesting that the animal infected with poison is some type of hibernating animal. This reading of a rodent's poison seems to accord with all the Indian commentaries. Kṣemadeva, however, speaks of the rodent's poison being active during summer, and when one sees a bite mark that resembles a snake bite when no snake has been around, one comes to "remember" having been bitten by a rodent and, through this inference, being infected by poison. This suggests he understands the one bitten to be a human rather than a hibernating animal.
336. Prajñākaramati and Kṣemadeva give a different reading of stanza 9.24. They read it as a response to yet another rejoinder from the opponent, who asserts, "Even though, as you say, cognition does not arise as self-cognizing by itself, when cognitions such as visual perceptions arise, they do so as in the nature of something endowed with the perception of other conditions, such as form and so forth." In response, the Mādhyamika says, for example, just as without other conditions such as a salve, one does not see vases and so forth, similarly, merely being endowed with other conditions is not sufficient for something to be conscious.
337. This is cited in Dharmamitra's commentary on the *Abhisamayālaṃ-*

*kāra*, *In Clear Words* (*Prasphuṭapadā*, Toh 3796, 97b4), which is probably Thokmé Sangpo's source here. There, too, Dharmamitra does not identify the author of the text.

338. Thokmé Sangpo is reading 9.29, "If the mind is devoid of objects,/ then everyone would be a tathāgata./ In that case, what virtue is gained by asserting 'mind only'?" as demonstrating the following undesirable consequence of the Cittamātra denial of external reality: If there is no external reality, then mind has no object whatsoever, and thus the mind remains alone, free of any objectification, which would mean all beings are already enlightened buddhas. What then is gained by being partial to the mind, stating that it alone has real existence?
339. By "two cases," Thokmé Sangpo means the magician who lusts after his own creation and the person who has realized that all phenomena, including emptiness itself, are empty of true existence.
340. Thokmé Sangpo interprets this stanza (9.33) as presenting the Madhyamaka view, a reading that accords with Prajñākaramati and Kṣemadeva. Crosby and Skilton, along with Wallace and Wallace, read this stanza as presenting an objection from the Cittamātra.
341. Candrakīrti, *Madhyamakāvatāra*, 11.17, Toh 3861 Tengyur, dbu ma, *'a*, 216b3.
342. Prajñākaramati, 213a6. The Tibetan Tengyur text of Prajñākaramati has the reading *me bzhin du 'das pa*, literally, "something past like a flame," which I think is a typographical error. I have read it as *med bzhin du 'das pa*.
343. *Jñānālokālaṃkārasūtra*, Toh 100, 279a1.
344. This is cited in Prajñākaramati, 215b6, which is probably the source here for Thokmé Sangpo.
345. Tib. *kun rdzob kyi sems dang bral ba'i bcom ldan 'das*. Prajñākaramati, 214b5.
346. *Perfection of Wisdom in Twenty-Five Thousand Lines* (*Pañcaviṃśati*), Toh 9, 169a4.
347. *Condensed Perfection of Wisdom in Verse* (*Prajñāpāramitāsaṃcayagāthā*), Toh 13, 3b4.
348. The four meanings of term *śrāvaka* being referred to here are: (1) emanation śrāvakas, referring to emanations of the buddhas in the guise of śrāvakas, (2) śrāvakas who are likely to move to the Mahāyāna path and attain buddhahood, (3) those who will pursue the śrāvaka path to the end, and (4) finally, those of the śrāvaka schools—namely, the Vaibhāṣika and Sautrāntika. The śrāvaka identified as the opponent

questioning the authenticity of Mahāyāna scripture is the fourth kind.

349. As Thokmé Sangpo's notes, there appeared to be a divergence of opinion on the status of stanzas 9.49–51, with Prajñākaramati rejecting them as later additions not by Śāntideva, while commentators like Kṣemadeva accepted them to be from the master but placed them slightly later in the text. Thokmé Sangpo himself prefers an approach that addresses the three stanzas here after verse 9.43 as part of refuting the opponent's assertion that Mahāyāna sūtras cannot be accepted as sacred words of the Buddha. Since the canonical version of Śāntideva's *Guide to the Bodhisattva Way* in the Tengyur, as well as extant Sanskrit, places these verses later, as stanzas 49–51, we have retained that numbering for these verses. Gyaltsab Jé (192), while acknowledging Prajñākaramati's questioning of these verses, commences his explanation with the statement, "Be that as it may, the meaning is. . ." Unlike Thokmé Sangpo, the latter's commentary retains the placement of these verses found in the current canonical version of the root text.

350. Prajñākaramati, 224a6.

351. "The training of the mind" (*sems kyi bslab pa*) is often used as a synonym for "training in meditative absorption" (*bsam tsan gyi bslab pa*) and "training in concentration" (*ting nge 'dzin gyi bslab pa*), referring to the second within the threefold training.

352. Maitreya, *Mahāyānasūtrālaṃkāra*, 2.5, Toh 4020, 2b1.

353. Maitreya, *Mahāyānasūtrālaṃkāra*, 2.13, Toh 4020, 3a1.

354. Thokmé Sangpo is here presenting an alternative interpretation of verse 9.51.

355. Thokmé Sangpo, having moved up verses 9.49–51 to be part of the defense of the authenticity of Mahāyāna scripture, now returns to the earlier sequence.

356. Thokmé Sangpo is simply reproducing here what is found in Prajñākaramati. The latter does not provide any scriptural source.

357. Tib. *'du shes med pa'i snyoms 'jug*; Skt. *asaṃjñisamāpatti*. A state of deep meditative absorption wherein all conscious thought processes have ceased through the power of meditation.

358. Thokmé Sangpo reorders the sequence of verses 9.53 and 9.54, reading the former as a concluding summary for the section on the fruits of meditating on emptiness.

359. This echoes Nāgārjuna's *Precious Garland* 1.76: "Persons who are terrified of this no-locus truth/ delight in [seeking haven in an] objec-

tive locus;/ not transcending "existence" and "nonexistence,"/ those unwise are ruined."

360. The Tibetan word being translated here as "deconstructing" is *rnam par dbye ba*, which can also mean to differentiate, dissect, or separate. This rendering is chosen to convey the key idea of dismantling the solidity of the notion of self through undoing its basis, the aggregates.

361. Thokmé Sangpo seems to be using "nonestablishment" (*ma grub pa*) here more as a general characterization of a flawed argument, and "no logical entailment" (*ma nges pa*) as the specific flaw of a lack of entailment between the reason and the probandum. In Indo-Tibetan epistemological texts generally, "nonestablishment" pertains to a logical fault in the connection between the reason (*rtags*) and the subject (*chos can*), while "no logical entailment" pertains to a fault in the connection between the reason and the probandum (*bsgrub bya'i shos*).

362. This is the last of the three main topics in the extensive explanation of the selflessness of persons introduced on page 238 above.

363. The citation is clearly from a non-Mahāyāna sūtra, but its exact source has not been located.

364. In reading 9.75cd, Kṛṣṇapa speaks of "four reasons" (*dgos pa bzhi*) why speaking of generating compassion for sentient beings is not contradictory even though there are no intrinsically real beings. Speaking of sentient beings such as Devadatta helps facilitate expedient conventions, it accords with the conventions of the world, it accords with the scriptures, and it enables the discernment of faults and virtues of beings.

365. Tib. *'bras bu rmongs pa snang tsam*. In glossing 9.76d, "the delusion of what has to be done is not prevented" (*'bras bu'i rmongs pa bzlog mi bya, kāryamoho na vāryate*), like most Tibetan commentators, Thokmé Sangpo reads the Sanskrit *kārya* in the phrase *kāryamoho* as "effect" rather than as "what has to be done." In such a reading, it is activity such as compassion cultivation that is referred to by the phrase "the effect of delusion," which, unlike the delusion of self, is not to be prevented. Gyaltsab Jé (*Entryway*, 201) reads this line as "the nonafflictive delusion of the post-meditative equipoise, which is a condition for attaining the result buddhahood, should not be prevented, nor can it be for now." This reading of *kārya* as "effect" seems to be based on Prajñākaramati, 225a4, which characterizes conventional truth, such as compassion for suffering sentient beings, as an effect of delusion but one that supports the cessation of suffering.

366. *Sarvadharmāpravṛttinirdeśasūtra*, Toh 180, 277b3.
367. Nāgārjuna, *Mūlamadhyamakakārikā*, 15.8, Toh 3824, 9a1.
368. *Bodhicaryāvatāra* 8.101ab. The full sentence reads: "What is called continuum and collection/ are unreal, like a rosary or an army." Gyaltsab Jé (*Entryway*, 207) identifies this cross reference in the text as stanza 9.85, where the unreality of the hand is demonstrated by analyzing it in terms of fingers and the latter into joints, a reading that accords with Prajñākaramati, 252a6: "This is as established above, where the author states 'Likewise the hand is a collection of fingers' and so on."
369. *Kāśyapa Chapter* (*Kāśyapaparivarta*), Toh 87, 139a2.
370. Tib. *sems can gdod nas nya ngan 'das.* This reflects line 9.103d of Śāntideva's text as *sems can rang bzhin mya ngan 'das*, though the Dergé edition reads *sems nyid rang bzhin mya ngan 'das*, which would make this line read, "The mind itself is by nature liberated." This latter reading accords with Prajñākaramati, 254b3, which glosses the line "There is no mind that has even the smallest degree of ultimate reality . . . For this reason, the mind and life faculty are by nature liberated; they share the nature of being utterly free; and this natural nirvāṇa, whose character is the absence of intrinsic existence, is always present in the mental continua of sentient beings."
371. There seem to be significant divergence among the commentaries on how to interpret stanza 9.107. All agree that the verse presents the Madhyamaka response to the objection that if all phenomena lack arising, there would be no two truths, since conventional truth would be rendered untenable. Furthermore, given that according to Madhyamaka, conventional truth is defined from the perspective of deluded cognition, there would be no sentient beings who attain nirvāṇa. Tsongkhapa (*Notes on the Wisdom Chapter*, 579) offers a more straightforward reading of the Madhyamaka response when he writes, "This conventional truth [you are speaking of] that has no existence, something purely imagined by the deluded conceptual mind of another, is not our own conventional truth. If it were, then we would be vulnerable to your objection. As for our own [conventional truth], if in the aftermath of realizing the view, one can ascertain or posit it as a conventional truth, such a conventional truth would then exist. If not, then it would not exist as a truth even conventionally."
372. Prajñākaramati, 257b1.

373. *Bodhicaryāvatāra* 9.34d.
374. Thokmé Sangpo reads the phrase *shes dbang* as the faculty of cognition rather than "the force of cognition."
375. This verse is cited in Prajñākaramati's commentary, which is the likely source here. Thokmé Sangpo's inclusion of Mīmāṃsā alongside Cārvāka as proponents of origination from no cause is most probably based on *Excellent Explanation of the Treatise Systems* (*Gzhung lugs legs par bshad pa*), a doxographical work attributed to Sakya Paṇḍita.
376. See commentary on *Bodhicaryāvatāra* 9.86b above.
377. Nowhere in the text does Thokmé Sangpo identify these five attributes (*khyad chos lnga*). Most probably he has in mind the five as identified in Candrakīrti's *Entering the Middle Way* (6.121ab). They are that it is the enjoyer [of the fruits of action], eternal, not an agent, devoid of qualities, and inactive. See, for example, Jinpa, *Illuminating the Intent*, 422–25.
378. Most probably Thokmé Sangpo has in mind the five listed as characteristics of primal matter in Bhāviveka's *Blaze of Reasoning* (*Tarkajvālā*, 443): (1) material and unconscious, (2) unarisen and permanent, (3) object of experience by self (*puruṣa*), (4) unitary, and (5) pervasive. See also note 204 on *prakṛti* above.
379. Īśvarakṛṣṇa, *Īśvarakṛṣṇatantra*, verse 22.
380. Prajñākaramati, 270a4.
381. *Questions of Nāga King Anavatapta* (*Anavataptanāgarājaparipṛcchāsūtra*), Toh 156, 237a7.
382. *Questions of Nāga King Anavatapta* (*Anavataptanāgarājaparipṛcchāsūtra*), Toh 156, 230b2.
383. This is the second of the three headings introduced on page 255 under the topic "presenting objections."
384. Nāgārjuna, *Fundamental Verses on the Middle Way* (*Mūlamadhyamakakārikā*), 15.9, Toh 3824, 9a1.
385. *Samādhirājasūtra*, Toh 127, 26b5.
386. For example, *Perfection of Wisdom in Eighteen Thousand Lines* (*Aṣṭādaśasāhasrikāprajñāpāramitā*), Toh 10, 203b5.
387. Thokmé Sangpo introduced this heading on page 24 as the third of three primary sections of the text.
388. Tib. *bstan pa la zhugs pa*. The choice of translation here is driven by the content of the section indicated—dedicating merit for the well-being of monastics.

389. Where Thokmé Sangpo simply provides the lines from the root text with no gloss, we have formatted them as verse so they can be easily recognized.
390. Maitreya, *Mahāyānasūtrālaṃkāra*, 18.47, Toh 4020, 27a6.
391. The Sanskrit version of the text contains an additional stanza at the end of the section dedicating merit to benefit hell beings. In Crosby and Skilton, this verse reads: "May the intense pains and fears of those in hell be allayed. May those dwelling in all evil realms be freed from those states of woe." So from here on, the numbering of the stanzas between the Tibetan and Sanskrit editions differ by one. Judging from Kṣemadeva's statement that verse 10.15, "In this way, through my roots of virtue. . . ," indeed appears to be the conclusion of dedicating merit to benefit hell beings, the Tibetan translation may have been based on a Sanskrit original that does not include this extra verse.
392. Thokmé Sangpo is glossing here on the Tibetan word *gtsug lag khang* (rendering the Sanskrit word *vihara* here), which is composed of two words: *gtsug lag*, referring to texts, and *khang*, short for *khang pa* ("a house"). Though etymologically, the Tibetan word *tsug lag khang* means "a house of texts," it is used widely to refer to a temple or a monastery, since another word, *dpe mbdzod khang*, is used to refer to a library.
393. The Tibetan edition of the root text features only two lines for this stanza. The final two lines are rendered in Crosby and Skilton as: "ever worshipped with great respect by gods, titans, and men."
394. For example, Prajñākaramati, 41a5, where he refers to "Ārya Śāntideva."

# Glossary

**affliction(s)** (*nyong mongs, kleśa*). Dissonant mental states, both thoughts and emotions, which have their root in ignorance. They are called *afflictions* because they disturb the individual from deep within. The term has been translated elsewhere as "delusion" or "defilement." Classical Buddhist texts list six root afflictions—attachment, aversion, conceit, afflicted doubt, ignorance, and afflicted view—out of which attachment, aversion, and ignorance are referred to also as the *three poisons* of the mind. Associated with these root afflictions, especially the three poisons, Abhidharma lists twenty secondary or derivative afflictions.

**aggregates** (*phung po, skandha*). A class of phenomena with a group of five—that of form, feelings, discrimination, mental formations, and consciousness. Together they serve as a basis for the arising of the notion of a "self" or personal identity, according to Buddhism.

**arhat** (*dgra bcom pa*). One who has eliminated all the afflictions and has thus attained nirvāṇa. In Sanskrit, it is a term of respect that means "worthy" or "venerable," while the Tibetan term, rendered with a different etymology, means "foe destroyer." An arhat is necessarily an ārya being.

**ārya** (*'phags pa*). In all Buddhist traditions, this is a practitioner whose enlightenment is certain, usually because of his or her direct insight into the ultimate nature of things with a mind that is deeply concentrated. In the five-path schema, whether of Hīnayāna or Mahāyāna, the point at which one becomes an ārya (literally, a "noble one") is one's entrance into the third path, the path of seeing. The term is often contrasted with *ordinary being* (*so so'i skye bo*, *pṛtagjana*), one who has not yet attained such direct insight.

**awakening mind** (*byang chub kyi sems*, *bodhicitta*). In the Mahāyāna, a particular state of mind cultivated by a bodhisattva. The *conventional* awakening mind is the generation of the aspiration to attain enlightenment for the sake of all beings, and the *ultimate* awakening mind is the direct realization of emptiness of all phenomena, including especially the enlightened mind. The first type, conventional awakening mind, is characterized as twofold: *aspiring* awakening mind and *engaging* awakening mind, with their differentiation analogous, respectively, to that of the setting the intention of going and the actual act of going.

**bodhisattva grounds**. *See* ground.

**buddhafield** (*sangs rgyas kyi zhing*, *buddhakṣetra*). The expanse of specific, enlightened experience proper to a particular buddha, just like the kingdom of a monarch. According to Mahāyāna literature of the bodhisattva ideal, cultivating a buddhafield is one of the three things—along with gathering the two collections of merit and wisdom, and bringing sentient beings to maturity—before the completion of which a bodhisattva is said to shun attainment of liberation.

**Cittamātra** (*sems tsam*). Literally, "mind only," this is the name of a well-known Mahāyāna Buddhist philosophical school that is also called Yogācāra or Vijñānavāda. Its founding figures include the fourth-century brothers Asaṅga and Vasubandhu. The standpoint of Cittamātra features prominently as an object of critique in the ninth chapter of Śāntideva's *Guide to the Bodhisattva Way*.

**cessation** (*'gog pa*, *nirodha*). The third among the four noble truths, referring to the result of the path. It is a state defined as the ending of specific factors through applying their antidote, such as the elimination of ignorance through the wisdom of emptiness, and the highest such cessation is nirvāṇa. When it refers to one of the three characteristics of a condition—its arising, enduring, and cessation—*cessation* (rendered also as *disintegration*) conveys that conditioned phenomena never remain static but undergo moment-by-moment change, which entails the cessation of preceding instances. In Tibetan texts, this second meaning of the word is captured by a distinct rendering of the Sanskrit *nirodha*—as *'gag pa* rather than *'gog pa*.

**compassion** (*snying rje, karuṇā*). A mental state that wishes for others to be free from suffering. While compassion itself is innate, meaning it arises naturally as a response in the face of a suffering of a fellow sentient being, *great compassion* (*snying rje chen po*)—a universal, nondiscriminatory compassion that wishes all beings to be free of suffering—needs to be cultivated systematically by the Mahāyāna practitioner. *See also* four immeasurables.

**concentration** (*ting nge 'dzin, samādhi*). In the Abhidharma taxonomy of mental factors, concentration is one of the five object-determinate factors and is defined as the mind's natural capacity for single-pointedness and focus. Used in this sense, the term refers to an aspect of mind that is present when one's mind remains focused on any given subject or object, irrespective of meditation practice. However, the Sanskrit term *samādhi* is used also to refer to a meditative state in which one's mind abides in deep equipoise. When used in this sense, we have rendered the term as "meditative concentration." Often used interchangeably with *meditative absorption* (*bsam gtan, dhyāna*), a key feature of meditative concentration is the heightened quality of focus and absorption and absence of distraction.

**conqueror** (*rgyal ba, jina*). Traditional epithet of a fully awakened buddha, so called because buddhahood marks the total conquering of the four māras—those of the aggregates, the afflictions, death, and the desire for sense gratification.

**concept/conceptualization** (*rtam rtog, vikalpa*; *rtog pa, kalpana*). The constructive mental activity that dominates the inner life of sentient beings and obstructs them from seeing things as they really are. For humans in particular, such activity entails processes of interpreting their experience of the world shaped by language-based thought, perspectives, and attitudes. Like conceptual elaboration, it involves a process of superimposition on reality that must be eliminated before enlightenment can be attained. Sometimes, *rtog pa* could simply mean "thought" or "thinking," which, according to Buddhist thought, necessarily involves conceptual processes, or "discursivity." Though often used interchangeably, *rnam rtog* (*vikalpa*) and *rtog pa* (*kalpana*) are sometimes differentiated, where the former connotes a greater degree of habitual rumination, fabrication, or even fantasizing, while the latter merely conveys states that belong to the category of thought.

**conceptual elaboration** (*spros pa, prapañca*). Conceptual elaborations occur in the domain of thought and language and include all forms of dichotomizing conceptualization, such as subject-object duality and grasping at objects and their characteristics. The ultimate truth and its direct realization are marked by total freedom from such conceptual elaborations. Some render this term as "fabrication."

**conventional truth** (*kun rdzob bden pa, saṃvṛtisatya*). *See* two truths.

**defeat** (*pham pa, pārajayīka*). The term is used in the contexts of both the prātimokṣa and bodhisattva vows. It refers to the transgression of a root precept, such as the infraction of one of the root precepts of the bodhisattva vow.

**dependent origination** (*rten 'brel, pratītyasamutpāda*). The general causal law in Buddhist thought that asserts that whatever arises does so in dependence upon causes and conditions. Sometimes taken to be the essential Buddhist teaching, it is given specific instantiation in the twelve links of dependent origination, which explains how it is we continually take birth in cyclic existence. Dependent origination is also explained by Nāgārjuna as equivalent to, and as a major proof of, emptiness.

**dharmadhātu** (*chos dbyings*). In Madhyamaka writings, this is an epithet for emptiness and used as a synonym for *suchness* and *thatness*.

Emptiness is an "expanse" (*dhātu*) in that it is a "field," "sphere," "realm," or "element" in which (metaphorically, at least) all phenomena, of both saṃsāra and nirvāṇa, naturally reside.

**dharmakāya** (*chos sku*). *Dharmakāya* is contrasted with the buddha's *form body* (*rupakāya*)—namely, the dimension of buddhahood that is endowed with form. In earlier traditions, the dharmakāya is the corpus of the Buddha's teaching; in the Mahāyāna, it the aspect of buddhahood that is equivalent to the enlightened mind and the basis of the two form bodies. Literally "truth body," it is sometimes singular and sometimes divided into a *natural* dharmakāya (*ngo bo nyid chos kyi sku*, *svabhāvikadharmakāya*), which is the buddha's emptiness or suchness, and a *gnostic* dharmakāya (*ye shes chos sku*, *jñānadharmakāya*), which is the buddha's perfected knowledge, compassion, power, and other qualities. When dharmakāya is differentiated into these two dimensions, a buddha's embodiment (*kāya*) is explained to be fourfold: natural dharmakāya and gnostic dharmakāya (the two truth bodies), and enjoyment body and emanation body (the two form bodies).

**emptiness** (*stong pa nyid*, *śūnyatā*). According to the Madhyamaka school, all things and events, including our own existence, are empty or devoid of any independent, substantial, and intrinsic existence. This emptiness of intrinsic existence is the ultimate truth, the ultimate mode of being of all phenomena—the way they actually are—and hence it is referred to by such epithets as *suchness* or *thatness*. As such, according to Madhyamaka, the realization of emptiness is indispensable for the attainment of enlightenment.

**five acts of immediate retribution** (*mtshams med lnga*, *pañcānantaryāṇi*). This refers to five heinous acts whose karmic fruition with birth in the lower realms would ripen in the immediately succeeding rebirth with no interruption of any other type of rebirth. They are the evil deeds of killing one's mother, one's father, or an arhat; causing schism in the sangha of bhikṣus; and drawing blood from a tathāgata with evil intent.

**four applications of mindfulness** (*dran pa nyer bzhag bzhi, catuḥ-smṛtyupasthāna*). An important system of meditation practice entailing the application of mindfulness in a progressive manner on the body, feelings, the mind, and phenomena, or mental objects. The term is sometimes rendered as "the four foundations of mindfulness." The four are part of the thirty-seven factors of enlightenment. Śāntideva employs this meditation for his presentation of the formal meditative practice of emptiness, especially in the form of meditation on selflessness of phenomena, in both his *Guide to the Bodhisattva Way* and *Compendium of Training*.

**four continents** (*gling bzhi, caturdvīpa*). The four main continents that lie in the four cardinal directions of Mount Meru in ancient Buddhist cosmology: Videha (*shar lus 'phags po*) in the east, Jambudvīpa (*lho 'dzam bu'i gling*) in the south, Godanīya (*nub ba blang spyod*) in the west, and Kuru (*byang sgra mi snyan*) in the north.

**four immeasurables** (*tshad med bzhi, catvaryapramāṇāni*). Immeasurable lovingkindness, immeasurable compassion, immeasurable sympathetic joy, and immeasurable equanimity. Known also as "four abodes of brahma" (*tshangs pa'i gnas bzhi, brahmavihāra*).

**generation of the mind** (*sems bskyed, cittotpāda*). *See* awakening mind.

**grasping.** *See* self-grasping.

**ground** (*sa, bhūmi*). Invoking the imagery of earth as the basis supporting all beings and the natural world, the term is used in the Buddhist texts to refer to the "states of attainment" that, like the earth, support the great qualities that are attained. In Mahāyāna texts, the term is used in connection with "path" (*lam, marga*), the main road on which specific stations, such as the ten stages traversed by the bodhisattva, are characterized as "grounds." Asaṅga especially employs the term to refer to specific levels, such as that of the śrāvaka, pratyekabuddha, and the bodhisattva. Derivatively, he also uses the term as part of the title of works pertaining to such levels, e.g., the *Bodhisattva Ground* (*Bodhisattvabhūmi*) and the *Śrāvaka Ground* (*Śrāvakabhūmi*).

**gnosis** (*ye shes*, *jñāna*). In contrast to wisdom (*prajñā*, *shes rab*), which may be either worldly or transmundane, gnosis usually connotes a realization of the nature of things that is profound and liberating. The "accumulation" of gnosis on the bodhisattva path eventuates in the attainment of a buddha's dharmakāya. While Tibetan authors differentiate between *ye shes* and *shes pa* ("cognition"), the latter a generic term referring to all mental events, including those of ordinary people, both Tibetan terms are used to translate Sanskrit *jñāna*. *See also* wisdom.

**Hīnayāna** (*theg dman*). Literally "Lesser Vehicle," the term is used by the Mahāyāna tradition to refer to the systems of Buddhist practice based exclusively on the teachings expounded by the Buddha in his first turning of the wheel of Dharma. Such a vehicle sets as its ideal the attainment of nirvāṇa, the arhat's state of freedom from personal suffering, while the Mahāyāna upholds as its vision the attainment of buddhahood for the benefit of all beings. When the term is used in the context of philosophical schools, the first two—Vaibhāṣika and Sautrāntika—are recognized as Hīnayāna schools, while Yogācāra and Madhyamaka are Mahāyāna schools.

**identity view** (*'jig tshogs lta ba*, *satkāyadṛṣṭi*). Literally "view of the transitory collection," the term refers to our innate sense of self-identity as individuated beings. This identity view can take the form of the thought "I am" when it is based on an underlying assumption of an intrinsically existing self that is the referent of such a "self" or "I." By extension, the identity view can take the form of the thought "mine" in relation to people and things that we appropriate as part of our identity. According to Buddhist thought, the identity view—an important subclass of grasping at self-existence—constitutes a fundamental ignorance and hence a root of all our afflictions.

**infraction** (*ltung ba, āpatti*). The generic terms used in the context of all three vows—the prātimokṣa, the bodhisattva, and tantric—for a transgression of a precept. The Tibetan term *ltung ba* (and its Sanskrit equivalent) explicitly conveys the defining characteristic of an act that represents "falling down" from a formal vow the practitioner has made. The term covers the transgressions of both the root precepts as well as the secondary precepts. By definition, an "infraction" is incurred only by those who have taken a vow and hence is different from negative karma, which can be incurred irrespective of any vows.

**insight** (*lhag mthong, vipaśyanā*). An advanced meditative state, sometimes rendered as "superior" or "penetrative" insight, in which the meditator has successfully attained physical and mental pliancy as a result of having applied analytic meditation on a basis of *tranquil abiding* (*śamatha*). Sometimes the term is also used to embrace all analytic (as opposed to absorptive) meditation practices.

**intrinsic existence** (*rang bzhin gyis grub pa, svabhāvasiddhi*). Existence by virtue of some kind of intrinsic nature, something categorically rejected by Nāgārjuna and major Madhyamaka thinkers, including Śāntideva.

**intrinsic nature** (*rang bzhin, svabhāva*). Chapter 15 of Nāgārjuna's *Fundamental Verses on the Middle Way* defines intrinsic nature as "unfabricated" and "not dependent on something else." There are two senses in which the term is used in the Madhyamaka context: (1) something intrinsic in things, an essence by virtue of which a given thing obtains its existence and identity, and (2) a thing's absence of intrinsic existence—its emptiness—which, in an objective sense, is the only true nature that things have. In the first sense, intrinsic nature is categorically rejected, while in the second sense, intrinsic nature is accepted.

**Jambudvīpa** (*'dzam bu'i gling*). Within Buddhist Abhidharma cosmology, Jambudvīpa ("land of the jambu fruit") is the name given to our world. *See also* four continents.

**lojong** (*blo sbyong*). Lojong, or "mind training," is a special genre of teachings within Tibetan Buddhism. Tracing its origin to the Indian Bengali master Atiśa, who spent his final years in Tibet in the eleventh century, a central theme of lojong is the profound reorientation of our basic attitude both toward our own self and toward fellow sentient beings, as well as toward the events in our lives, so that self-cherishing no longer inflicts suffering on ourselves and others. Lojong is cherished particularly for is practical approach to transforming even adversities into the path of enlightenment. The *Seven-Point Mind Training* by Chekawa is one of the most well-known lojong texts."

**Madhyamaka** (*dbu ma*). Literally "the Middle Way," it is, with Cittamātra, one of the two major philosophical schools of Mahāyāna Buddhism. Founded by Nāgārjuna (second century CE), it focuses on the doctrine of emptiness as expounded in the Perfection of Wisdom literature. Madhyamaka was the most influential single philosophical tradition in Tibet and spread throughout the Mahāyāna world as well. The Tibetan tradition recognizes two subschools of Madhyamaka philosophy—the Svātantrika and the Prāsaṅgika—and recognize Śāntideva to be a proponent of the latter.

**Mādhyamika** (*dbu ma pa*). One who propounds the Madhyamaka philosophical standpoint.

**māra/Māra** (*bdud*). Personification of "evil" or obstacle in Buddhist thought typically enumerated in terms of the following four: the māra of death, the māra of the aggregates, the māra of the afflictions, and the devaputra māra, literally "the māra of god's son," referring to the forces of temptation such as lust and jealousy.

**meditative absorption** (*bsam gtan, dhyāna*). Meditative absorption, generally speaking, is single-pointed focus of the mind. A paradigmatic example is the state of *tranquil abiding* (*zhi gnas, śamatha*), where the person has attained a deep state of effortless focused attention marked by absence of mental excitation or laxity. When used technically in the context of the "four meditative absorptions," however, the term refers to four progressively subtler states of mind defined by progressive diminishing of feelings and discriminations, with tranquil abiding being the gateway into such states. *Meditative absorption* is also the term used for one of the six perfections in Mahāyāna Buddhism. The term is often used interchangeably with *concentration* (*ting nge 'dzin, samādhi*).

**meditative attainment** (*snyoms 'jug, samāpatti*). Advanced meditative states characterized by single-pointed focus, absence of distraction, and tranquil abiding accompanied by physical and mental pliancy. Typically, three distinct types of such meditative attainments are mentioned in the texts: (1) meditative attainment in the form of states of absorption (*bsam gtan snyoms 'jug*), (2) meditative attainment devoid of discrimination (*'du shes med pa'i snyoms 'jug*), and (3) the meditative attainment of cessation (*'gog pa'i snyoms 'jug*).

**misdeed** (*nyes byas, duskṛta*). Literally meaning "a wrong act"—with the verb (*byas, kṛta*) in the past tense. When used in the technical sense in the context of Buddhist vows, as is the case in this volume, the term refers to an infraction of a precept belonging to the secondary class. Within the bodhisattva vow, for example, there are forty-six such misdeeds.

**nāga** (*klu*). In Indian cosmogeny, snake-like water and tree spirits.

**nyungné** (*smyung gnas*). A Tibetan Buddhist rite of fasting and other purifying austerities, typically based on the worship of Avalokiteśvara, the bodhisattva of compassion.

**obscuration** (*sgrib pa, avaraṇa*). Sometimes rendered also as "defilement" or "obstruction," the term refers to factors that obscure and block our attainment of enlightenment. Typically, two classes of obscuration are identified—*afflictive obscurations* (*nyon sgrib, kleśāvaraṇa*), which refers to all the afflictions and their seeds, and *knowledge obscurations* (*shes sgrib, jñeyāvaraṇa*), the subtle residue of dualistic thinking that obstructs perfect wisdom and omniscience and thus is eliminated only by buddhas. The latter is thus sometimes called the *obstructions to omni-*

*science*. Sometimes, two additional classes of obscurations are added: (3) *obscurations to concentration* (*ting nge 'dzin gyi sgrib pa, samādhyāvaraṇa*), referring to the five hindrances to meditation—sense desire, ill will, excitation and regret, lethargy and sleep, and doubt—and (4) *karmic obscurations* (*las kyi sgrib pa, karmāvaraṇa*).

**prātimokṣa vow** (*so sor thar pa*). The precepts of "individual liberation" are one of the three sets of vows (the others being bodhisattva vows and tantric vows), those that are concerned primarily with restraining outward activity. Described typically in seven categories for seven different types of practitioners, they include the levels of monastic discipline and the vows for lay Buddhists.

**pratyekabuddha** (*rang sangs rgyas*). Literally "solitary realizer" or "self-enlightened one," a pratyekabuddha is an adept who seeks liberation on the basis of autonomous practice. Along with the Śrāvaka Vehicle, the Pratyekabuddha Vehicle belongs to the Hīnayāna path, requiring a thorough realization of the truth of dependent origination. *See also* śrāvaka.

**precept** (*bslab bya*). Literally meaning "the object of training" or "what is to be trained in," the Tibetan word rendered here as *precept* connotes specific codes of conduct one who has taken a vow needs to observe. Hence "the precept of taking refuge" (*skyabs 'gro'i bslab bya*), "the precept of mind training" (*blo sbyong gi bslab bya*), and, of course, "the bodhisattva precepts" (*byang sems kyi bslab bya*). When contrasted with its cognate term *bslab pa* ("training"), the term connotes greater specificity, while *training* (*bslab pa*) can refer more broadly to a set of practices. Incidentally, the Sanskrit word for both these Tibetan terms is *śikṣā*.

**sādhana** (*sgrub thabs*). Literally "method of attainment," a sādhana is a structured tantric practice, the heart of which consists of visualization of a meditation deity and chanting its mantra.

**Sautrāntika** (*mdo sde pa*). A Hīnayāna school whose name means "followers of the sūtras." The Sautrāntikas emerged as a reaction to the Vaibhāṣika, preferring to follow the original discourses of the Buddha rather than the great Abhidharma compendium the *Mahāvibhāṣa*.

**self** (*bdag, ātman*). The Sanskrit term *ātman* and its Tibetan equivalent *bdag* have multiple overlapping senses so require different renderings in different contexts. In two distinct but related senses of the term, it is rendered as "self": the sense of an individual, as in "self and others," and the sense of an enduring personal identity, like an eternal soul. This latter sense is rejected by all Buddhists. When the term is used as a more broad ontological concept, attributing objective existence to both persons and things, the term is rendered as "selfhood" or "self-existence." In this sense, the term then becomes synonymous with true existence, intrinsic existence, and objective independent existence, all of which are categorically rejected by Madhyamaka.

**self-cherishing** (*rang gces 'dzin*). The deeply ingrained thought that cherishes the welfare of one's own self and makes one oblivious to others' well-being. This is one of the "twin demons" (*'gong po gnyis*), according to the Tibetan *lojong* teaching, that lie within our heart and serve as the source of all misfortune and downfall (the other demon being grasping at selfhood). These two thoughts—self-cherishing and self-grasping—are the primary target of Mahāyāna mind training, such as the teachings presented in Śāntideva's *Guide to the Bodhisattva Way*.

**self-grasping** (*bdag 'dzin, ātmagraha*). Holding on to the self-existence of one's own self, one's physical or mental aggregates, or the external world. *Self* or *self-existence* (*bdag*) here connotes a form of existence whereby one accords substantial, true existence and identity to one's own self and the world. The cultivation of the wisdom of emptiness eliminates this grasping at self-existence.

**selflessness** (*bdag med, anātman*). The absence or negation of self-existence. The negation of such self-existence in relation of persons is called the *selflessness of persons*, and its negation in relation to phenomena other than persons is called the *selflessness of phenomena*. These two forms of selflessness, according to Candrakīrti, are the two basic divisions of emptiness taught by the Buddha. *See also* self.

**spiritual potential** (*rigs*, *gotra*). While the Sanskrit term *gotra* connotes "lineage," as in family lineage, its Tibetan equivalent *rigs* has multiple meanings—"lineage," "family," "kind or type," or even "germinal seed." In its generic sense, as used in Mahāyāna literature, the term refers to a living being's potential for enlightenment. Typically, the spiritual potential is differentiated in terms of "naturally abiding" (*rang bzhin du gnas pa*) and "the developed" or "transformational" (*rgyas 'gyur*) spiritual potentials, with the former being innate and the latter being acquired or developed. In Maitreya's *Sublime Continuum*, the concept of spiritual potential is intimately connected with that of buddha nature (*tathāgatagarbha*).

**śrāvaka** (*nyan thos*). Literally "hearers," śrāvakas are disciples of the Buddha whose primary objective is to attain liberation from cyclic existence. They are often paired with pratyekabuddhas as spiritual trainees on the Hīnayāna path, as distinct from the bodhisattvas, who embark on the Mahāyāna path to full enlightenment.

**suchness** (*de kho na nyid*, *tathatā*). The reality of things as they are. Having the same meaning as *thatness* (*de bzhin nyid*, *tattva*) and *ultimate nature* (*chos nyid*, *dharmatā*), the term is often a synonym for emptiness.

**tathāgata** (*de bzhin gshegs pa*). Literally "thus gone," it is an epithet for a buddha alongside *sugata* ("gone to bliss").

**three spheres** (*'khor gsum*, *trimaṇḍala*). A technical term referring to three key elements of an action—the object of the action, the agent of the act, and the act itself. The Mahāyāna practitioner is advised to not grasp at any of these "three spheres" when engaging in altruistic conduct, such as when practicing the perfection of generosity.

**tīrthika** (*mu stegs pa*). The Sanskrit *tīrthika* means "one who fords" and was used non-pejoratively by Indian traditions to refer to their own founders, but in classical Buddhist texts it came to mean an expounder of an Indian philosophical system outside the Buddhist tradition. The term in its Tibetan equivalent, *mu stegs pa*, literally means "upholder of an extreme."

**tranquil abiding** (*gzhi gnas, śamatha*). An advanced meditative state where the meditator has attained physical and mental pliancy derived from the channeling of the mind. It is characterized by the stability of single-pointed attention on a chosen meditation object with the calming of mental distractions. Tranquil abiding is an essential basis for cultivating insight (*vipaśyanā*), a profound understanding of the subtler aspects of the chosen object, such as its impermanence or emptiness, through refined analysis. *See also* concentration; meditative absorption.

**true existence** (*bden par grub pa, satyasiddhi*). *See* intrinsic existence; self.

**two truths** (*bden pa gnyis, dvayasatya*). Conventional truth (*kun rdzob bden pa, saṃvṛtisatya*) and ultimate truth (*don dam bden pa, paramārthasatya*). According to the Madhyamaka school, *ultimate truth* refers to emptiness—the absence of intrinsic existence of all phenomena. In contrast, *conventional truth* refers to the empirical aspect of reality characterized by diversity and differentiation and experienced through perception, language, and thought.

**ultimate nature** (*chos nyid, dharmatā*). A term defined in contrast with *dharma* (phenomena) to refer to the true nature of things, hence *dharma* and *dharmatā*. In Mahāyāna thought, the term is used invariably as a synonym for other similar terms like *suchness* (*tathatā*) and *thatness* (*tattva*) and, like those terms, refers to emptiness.

**ultimate truth** (*don dam bden pa, paramārthasatya*). *See* two truths.

**Vaibhāṣika** (*bye brag smra ba*). Literally "the proponents of differentiation," the school derives its name from its emphasis on the authority of the great Abhidharma compendium the *Mahāvibhāṣa*. Alongside Sautrāntika, Cittamātra, and Madhyamaka, it is one of the four Indian Buddhist philosophical schools.

**wisdom** (*shes rab*, *prajñā*). The Sanskrit term and its Tibetan equivalent can also be translated as "discerning wisdom" (or "insight") or as "intelligence," depending on context. In the Abhidharma taxonomy of mental factors, *prajñā* refers to a specific mental factor that helps evaluate the properties or qualities of an object. The term can refer simply to intelligence or mental aptitude. In the context of the Mahāyāna path, *prajñā* refers to the wisdom aspect of the path, consisting primarily of deep insight into the emptiness of all phenomena. It is also the name of the sixth perfection. *See also* gnosis.

**yakṣa** (*gnod byin*). A class of fierce spirits depicted often with a stocky body, a large round belly, and thick limbs. Many of the worldly protectors in the Indian and Tibetan Buddhist pantheon belong to the *yakṣa* family.

# Bibliography

## Canonical Scriptures (Kangyur)


*Account of Kanakavarṇa. Kanakavarṇapūrvayoga. Gser mdog gi sngon gyi sbyor ba.* Toh 350, mngo sde *a.*

*Adornment of the Illumination of Gnosis Sūtra. Jñānālokālaṃkārasūtra. Ye shes snang ba'i rgyan gyi mdo.* Toh 100, mdo sde *ga.*

*Advice to a King Sūtra. Rājāvavādakasūtra. Rgyal po la gdams pa zhes bya ba.* Toh 221, mdo sde *dza.*

*Ajātaśatru Sūtra. Ajātaśatrukaukṛtyavinodanā. Ma skyes dgra'i 'gyod pa bsal ba.* Toh 216, mdo sde *tsha.*

*Ākāśagarbha Sūtra. Ākāśagarbhasūtra. Nam mkha'i snying po'i mdo.* Toh 260, mdo sde *za.*

*Application of Mindfulness Sūtra. Saddharmasmṛtyupasthānasūtra. Dam pa'i chos dran pa nyer bar gzhag pa'i mdo.* Toh 287, mdo sde *ya–sha* (4 vols.).

*Array of Trees Sūtra. Gaṇḍavyūhasūtra. Sdong po bkod pa'i mdo / Sdong po rgyan pa'i mdo.* Toh 44, phal chen *ga* and *'a* (chap. 45 of *Flower Ornament Sūtra*).

*Banner's Crest Great Sūtra. Dhvajāgramahāsūtra. Mdo chen po rgyal mtshan dam pa.* Toh 293, mdo sde *sha.*

*Bodhisattva Collection. Bodhisattvapiṭaka. Byang chub sems dpa'i sde snod.* Toh 56, dkon brtsegs *kha* and *ga.*

*Bodhisattvas' Individual Liberation: Cultivating the Sets of Four Qualities. Bodhisattvaprātimokṣacatuṣkanirhāra. Byang chub sems dpa'i so sor thar pa chos bzhi sgrub pa.* Toh 248, mdo sde *za.*

*Collection of Aphorisms. Udānavarga. Ched du brjod pa'i tshoms.* Toh 326, mdo sde *sa.*

*Condensed Perfection of Wisdom in Verse. Prajñāpāramitāsaṃcaya-gāthā. Shes rab kyi pha rol tu phyin pa sdud pa tshigs su bcad pa.* Toh 13, shes phyin sna tshogs *ka.*

*Descent into Laṅkā Sūtra. Laṅkāvatārasūtra. Lang kar gshegs pa'i mdo.* Toh 107, mdo sde *ca.*

*Display of the Qualities of Mañjuśrī's Buddha Realm. Mañjuśrībuddha-kṣetraguṇavyūhasūtra. 'Jam dpal gyi sangs rgyas kyi zhing gyi yon tan bkod pa'i mdo.* Toh 59, dkon brtsegs *ga.*

*Flower Ornament Sūtra. Avataṃsakasūtra. Sangs rgyas pal po che'i mdo.* Toh 44, phal chen, *ka–a* (4 vols.).

*Gathering All Fragments Sūtra. Sarvavaidalyasaṃgraha. Rnam par 'thag pa thams cad bsdus pa'i mdo.* Toh 227, mdo sde *dza.*

*Great Lion's Roar of Maitreya Sūtra. Maitreyamahāsiṃhanāda. Byams pa seng ge sgra chen po.* Toh 67, dkon brtsegs *ca.*

*Great Nirvāṇa Sūtra. Mahāparinirvāṇasūtra. Mya ngan las 'das pa chen po'i mdo.* Toh 119, mdo sde *nya* and *ta.*

*Heap of Jewels. Ratnakuṭa.* The Dkon brtsegs sūtra collection in the Kangyur, Toh 45–93. Most references to the *Heap of Jewels*, if not further specified, are to the *Kāśyapa Chapter* (Toh 87). Other sūtras in the collection are generally cited by their respective titles.

*Jewel Casket Sūtra. Ratnakaraṇḍasūtra. Dkon mchog za ma tog gyi mdo.* Toh 117, mdo sde *ja.*

*Jewel Cloud Sūtra. Ratnameghasūtra. Dkon mchog sprin gyi mdo.* Toh 231, mdo sde *wa.*

*Jewel Torch Dhāraṇī. Ratnolkādhāraṇī. Dkon mchog ta la la'i gzungs.* Toh 145, mdo sde *pa.*

*Kāśyapa Chapter Sūtra. Kāśyapaparivarta. 'Od srung gi le'u.* Toh 87, dkon brtsegs *cha.*

*King of Meditations Sūtra. Samādhirājasūtra/Candraprabhasūtra. Ting nge 'dzin rgyal po'i mdo / Zla ba'i sgron me.* Toh 127, mdo sde *da.*

*Many Elements Sūtra. Dhātubahutakasūtra. Khams mang po pa'i mdo.* Toh 297, mdo sde *sha.*

*Meditative Concentration on the Miraculous Ascertainment of Peace Sūtra. Praśāntaviniścayaprātihāryasamādhi. Rab tu zhi ba rnam par nges pa'i cho 'phrul gyi ting nge 'dzin.* Toh 129, mdo sde *da.*

*Meeting of Father and Son Sūtra*. *Pitāputrasamāgamanasūtra*, Toh 60, dkon brtsegs *nga*.

*Miraculous Play of Mañjuśrī Sūtra*. *Manjuśrīvikrīḍitasūtra*. *'Jam dpal rnam par rol pa'i mdo*. Toh 96, mdo sde *kha*.

*Moon Lamp Sūtra* (*Candrapradīpasūtra*). See *King of Meditations Sūtra*.

*Perfection of Wisdom in Eighteen Thousand Lines*. *Aṣṭādaśasāhasrikāprajñāpāramitā*. *Shes rab kyi pha rol tu phyin pa khri brgyad stong pa*. Toh 10, khri brgyad *ka*, *kha*, *ga*.

*Perfection of Wisdom in Twenty-Five Thousand Lines*. *Pañcaviṃśatisāhasrikāprajñāpāramitā*. *Shes rab kyi pha rol tu phyin pa stong phrag nyi shu lnga pa*. Toh 9 nyi khri *ka*, *kha*, *ga*.

*Perfectly Gathering the Teachings Sūtra*. *Dharmasaṃgītisūtra*. *Chos yang dag pa sdud pa*. Toh 238, mdo sde *zha*.

*Play in Full Sūtra*. *Lalitavistarasūtra*. *Rgya cher rol pa'i mdo*. Toh 95, mdo sde *kha*.

*Prophecy of the Girl Candrottarā Sūtra*. *Candrottarādārikāvyākaraṇasūtra*. *Bu mo zla mchog lung bstan pa'i mdo*. Toh 191, mdo sde *tsa*.

*Questions of the Householder Vīradatta*. *Vīradattagṛhapatiparipṛcchā*. *Khyim bdag dpas byin gyis zhus pa*. Toh 72, dkon brtsegs *ca*.

*Questions of Nāga King Anavatapta*. *Anavataptanāgarājaparipṛcchāsūtra*. *Klu'i rgyal po ma dros pas zhus pa'i mdo*. Toh 156, mdo sde *pha*.

*Questions of Ratnacūḍa*. *Ratnacūḍaparipṛcchā*. *Gtsug na rin po ches zhus pa*. Toh 91, dkon brtsegs *cha*.

*Questions of Sāgaramati*. *Sāgaramatināgarājaparipṛcchā*. *Blo gros rgya mtshos zhus pa*. Toh 152, mdo sde *pha*.

*Questions of Subāhu*. *Subāhuparipṛcchā*. *Lag bzangs kyis zhus pa*. Toh 70, dkon brtsegs *ca*.

*Skillful Means with the Secrets of All Buddhas: The Chapter on the Questions of Bodhisattva Jñānottara*. *Sarvabuddhamahārahasyopāyakauśalya-Jñānottarabodhisattvaparipṛcchāparivarta*. *Sangs rgyas thams cad kyi gsang chen thabs la mkhas pa byang chub sems dpa' ye shes dam pas zhus pa'i le'u*. Toh 82, dkon brtsegs *cha*.

*Sūtra Evaluating Whether Progress Is Certain or Uncertain*. *Niyatā-*

*niyatagatimudrāvatārasūtra. Nges pa dang ma nges par 'gro ba'i phyag rgya la 'jug pa*. Toh 202, mdo sde *tsha*.
*Sūtra Teaching the Nonorigination of All Things. Sarvadharmāpravṛttinirdeśasūtra. Chos thams cad 'byung ba med pa bstan pa'i mdo*. Toh 180, mdo sde *ma*.
*Sūryagarbha Sūtra. Sūryagarbhasūtra. Nyi ma'i snying po'i mdo*. Toh 257, mdo sde *za*.
*Teaching on Dreams Sūtra. Svapnanirdeśasūtra. Rmi lam bstan pa'i mdo*. Toh 48, dkon brtsegs *ka*.
*Teaching on the Conventional and the Ultimate Truth. Saṃvṛtiparamārthasatyanirdeśa. Kun rdzob dang don dam pa'i bden pa bstan pa*. Toh 179, mdo sde *ma*.
*Teaching the Four Factors Sūtra. Caturdharmanirdeśasūtra. Chos bzhi bstan pa zhes bya ba*. Toh 249, mdo sde *za*.
*Teachings of Akṣayamati Sūtra. Akṣayamatinirdeśasūtra. Blo gros mi zad pas bstan pa'i mdo*. Toh 175, mdo sde *ma*.
*Three Heaps Sūtra. Triskandhakasūtra. Phung po gsum pa'i mdo*. Toh 284, mdo sde *ya*.
*Unraveling the Intent Sūtra. Saṃdhinirmocanasūtra. Dgongs pa nges par 'grel pa'i mdo*. Toh 106, mdo sde *ca*.

## Canonical Treatises (Tengyur)

Abhayākaragupta (tenth century). *Ornament of the Sage's Intent. Munimatālaṃkāra. Thub pa'i dgongs pa'i rgyan*. Toh 3903, dbu ma *a*.
Āryaśūra (fourth century). *Condensed Presentation of the Perfections. Pāramitāsamāsa. Pha rol tu phyin pa bsdus pa*. Toh 3944, dbu ma *ki*.
———. *Garland of Birth Stories. Jātakamālā. Skyes pa rabs kyi rgyud*. Toh 4150, skyes rabs *hu*.
Asaṅga (fourth century). *Bodhisattva Ground. Bodhisattvabhūmi. Byang chub sems dpa'i sa*. Toh 4037, sems tsam *wi*. (English translation in Engle, *The Bodhisattva Path to Unsurpassed Enlightenment*.)
———. *Compendium of Abhidharma. Abhidharmasamuccaya. Chos mngon pa kun las btus pa*. Toh 4049, sems tsam *ri*.
———. *Main Treatise on the Grounds. Bhūmivastu. Sa'i dngos gzhi*. Toh 4035–37 Tengyur, sems tsam *chi*. That is, the *Multiple Grounds*

(*Bahubhūmika*), the *Śrāvaka Ground*, and the *Bodhisattva Ground* from the *Grounds of Yogic Practice* (*Yogācārabhūmi*).

Asvabhāva (d.u.). *Interlinear Explanation of Survey of the Mahāyāna. Mahāyānasaṃgrahopanibandhana. Theg pa chen po bsdus pa'i bshad sbyar*. Toh 4051, sems tsam *ri*.

Atiśa Dīpaṃkara (982–1054). *Commentary on the Difficult Points of Lamp for the Path to Enlightenment. Bodhimārgapradīpapañjikā. Byang chub lam gyi sgron ma'i dka' 'grel*. Toh 3948, dbu ma *khi*.

———. *Lamp for the Path to Enlightenment. Bodhipathapradīpa. Byang chub lam gyi sgron me*. Toh 3947, dbu ma *khi*.

Bhāviveka (sixth century). *Blaze of Reasoning. Tarkajvālā. Critical edition in Dbu ma snying po'i 'grel pa rtog ge 'bar ba* (*Tarkajvālā: An Autocommentary on the Madhyamakahṛdaya*), edited and introduced by Thupten Jinpa. New Delhi: Institute of Tibetan Classics, 2019.

Candragomin (ca. eighth century). *Letter to a Student. Śiṣyalekha. Slob ma la springs pa*. Toh 4183, spring yig *nge*.

———. *Twenty Verses on the Bodhisattva Vow. Bodhisattvasaṃvaraviṃśaka. Byang chub sems dpa'i sdom pa nyi shu pa*. Toh 4081, sems tsam *hi*.

Candrakīrti (ca. eighth century). *Entering the Middle Way. Madhyamakāvatāra. Dbu ma la 'jug pa*. Toh 3861, dbu ma *'a*.

Dharmamitra (fl. 800–850) *In Clear Words: Commentary on Ornament for the Clear Realizations. Abhisamayālaṃkāraprasphuṭapadā. Mgnon par trogs pa'i rgyan gyi 'grel bshad tshig rab tu gsal ba*. Toh 3796, shes phyin *nya*.

Jitāri (tenth century). *Rite for Generating the Awakening Mind and Adopting the Pledge. Bodhicittotpādasamādānavidhi. Byang chub kyi sems bskyed pa dang yi dam blang ba'i cho ga*. Toh 3968, dbu ma *gi*.

Kṛṣṇapa (eleventh century). *Clarification of the Difficult Points of Guide to the Bodhisattva Way. Bodhisattvacaryāvatāraduravabodhananirṇaya. Byang chub sems dpa'i spyod pa la 'jug pa'i dka' ba'i gnad gtan la dbab pa*. Toh 3875, dbu ma *sha*.

———. *Exposition of Guide to the Bodhisattva Way. Bodhicaryāvatāravivṛtipañjikā. Byang chub sems dpa'i spyod pa la 'jug pa'i rnam par bshad pa'i dka' 'grel*. Toh 3873, dbu ma *sha*.

Kṣemadeva (ca. eleventh century). *Excellent Exposition on Guide to the Bodhisattva Way. Bodhisattvacaryāvatārasaṃskāra. Byang chub sems dpa'i spyod pa la 'jug pa legs par sbyar ba.* Toh 3874, dbu ma *sha.*

Maitreya (fourth century). *Differentiation of the Middle and Extremes. Madhyāntavibhāga. Dbus dang mtha' rnam par 'byed pa.* Toh 4021, sems tsam *phi.*

———. *Ornament of Mahāyāna Sūtras. Mahāyānasūtrālaṃkāra. Theg pa chen po mdo sde rgyan.* Toh 4020, sems tsam *phi.*

———. *Ornament for the Clear Realizations. Abhisamayālaṃkāra. Mngon rtogs rgyan.* Toh 3786, shes phyin *ka.*

———. *Sublime Continuum. Uttaratantra* (a.k.a. *Ratnagotravibhāga*). *Theg pa chen po rgyud bla ma.* Toh 4024, sems tsam *phi.*

Nāgārjuna (second century). *Commentary on the Awakening Mind. Bodhicittavivaraṇa. Byang chub sems kyi 'grel pa.* Toh 1801, rgyud 'grel *ngi.*

———. *Compendium of Sūtras. Sūtrasamuccaya. Mdo kun las btus pa.* Toh 3934, dbu ma *ki.*

———. *Letter to a Friend. Suhṛllekha. Bshes pa'i springs yig.* Toh 4182, springs yig *nge.*

———. *Fundamental Verses on the Middle Way* (a.k.a. *Root Wisdom; Treatise on the Middle Way*). *Mūlamadhyamakakārikā. Dbu ma rtsa ba'i tshig le'ur byas pa* (*Rtsa ba'i shes rab*). Toh 3824, dbu ma *tsa.*

———. *Precious Garland. Ratnāvalī. Rin po che'i phreng ba.* Toh 4158, springs yig *ge.*

———. *Sixty Stanzas of Reasoning. Yuktiṣaṣṭikā. Rigs pa drug cu pa.* Toh 3825, dbu ma *tsa.*

———. *Staff of Wisdom. Prajñādaṇḍa. Shes rab sdong po.* Toh 4329, lugs kyi bstan bcos *ngo.*

Prajñākaramati (950–1030). *Extensive Commentary on Guide to the Bodhisattva Way. Bodhicaryāvatārapañjikā. Byang chub sems pa'i spyod pa la 'jug pa'i dka' 'grel.* Toh 3872, dbu ma *la.* (a.k.a. the *Great Commentary, 'grel chen*).

Śāntarakṣita (ca. 725–88). *A Commentary on Twenty Verses on the Vow. Saṃvaraviṃśakavṛtti. Sdom pa nyi shu pa'i 'grel pa.* Toh 4082, sems tsam *hi.*

Śāntideva (eighth century). *Compendium of Training. Śikṣāsamuccaya. Bslab pa kun las btus pa.* Toh 3940, dbu ma *khi.*

———. *Compendium of Training Verses. Śikṣāsamuccayakārikā. Bslab pa kun las btus pa'i tshig le'ur byas pa.* Toh 3939, dbu ma *khi.*

———. *Guide to the Bodhisattva Way. Bodhicaryāvatāra. Byang chub sems dpa'i spyod pa la 'jug pa.* Toh 3871, dbu ma *la.*

Vairocanarakṣita (eleventh century). *Commentary on the Difficult Points of Guide to the Bodhisattva Way. Bodhisattvacaryāvatārapañjikā. Byang chub sems dpa'i spyod pa la 'jug pa'i dka' 'grel.* Toh 3876, dbu ma *sha.*

———. *Flower Head of Training. Śikṣākusumamañjarī. Bslab pa me tog snye ma.* Toh 3943 Tengyur, dbu ma *khi.*

Vasubandhu (ca. fourth century). *Treasury of Abhidharma. Abhidharmakośa. Chos mngon pa mdzod.* Toh 4089, mngon pa *ku.*

———. *Treasury of Abhidharma Autocommentary. Abhidharmakośabhāṣya. Chos mngon pa mdzod kyi bshad pa.* Toh 4090, mngon pa *ku.*

———. *Twenty Verses. Viṃśatikā. Nyi shu pa.* Toh 4056, sems tsam *shi.*

Vibhūticandra (early thirteenth century). *A Distinctive Illumination: Commentary on the Intent of Guide to the Bodhisattva Way. Bodhicaryāvatāratātparyapañjikāviśeṣadyotanī. Byang chub spyod pa la 'jug pa'i dgongs pa'i 'grel pa khyad par gsal byed.* Toh 3880, dbu ma *sha.*

## Works Cited by the Editor

Appleton, Naomi. *Many Buddhas, One Buddha.* Sheffield, UK: Equinox Publishing, 2000.

Engle, Artemus, trans. *The Bodhisattva Path to Unsurpassed Enlightenment: A Complete Translation of the "Bodhisattvabhūmi"* by Ārya Asaṅga. Boulder: Snow Lion, 2016.

Gendun Chopel (1903–51). *Grains of Gold: Tales of a Cosmopolitan Traveler.* Translated by Thupten Jinpa and Donald J. Lopez, Jr. Chicago: University of Chicago Press, 2014.

Gyaltsab Dharma Rinchen (a.k.a. Gyaltsab Jé, 1364–1432). *Entryway for the Conqueror's Children: An Exposition of Guide to the Bodhisattva Way. Byang chub sems dpa'i spyod pa la 'jug pa'i rnam bshad rgyal sras 'jug ngogs*. Collected Works, vol. *nga*, 1–240. Typeset comparative edition. Mundgod: Je Yabse Sungbum Project, 2019.

Jinpa, Thupten. "*Bodhicaryāvatāra* and Tibetan Mind Training (*Lojong*)." *Readings of Śāntideva's Guide to Bodhisattva Practice.* Edited by Jonathan C. Gold and Douglas S. Duckworth, 146–61. New York: Columbia University Press, 2019.

———, trans. *The Bodhisattva Ideal: Selected Key Texts.* The Library of Tibetan Classics 11. New York: Wisdom Publications, 2026.

———, trans. *Illuminating the Intent: An Exposition of Entering the Middle Way* by Tsongkhapa. Somerville, MA: Wisdom Publications, 2021.

———. "Introduction." *Rgyal sras kyi spyod pa la 'jug pa'i chos skor.* Delhi: The Institute of Tibetan Classics, 2006.

———, trans. *Mind Training: The Great Collection.* Compiled by Könchok Gyaltsen and Shönü Gyalchok. The Library of Tibetan Classics 1. Boston: Wisdom Publications, 2006.

———, trans. *Stages of the Path and the Oral Transmission: Selected Teachings of the Geluk School.* The Library of Tibetan Classics 6. Somerville, MA: Wisdom Publications, 2022.

Kunzang Pelden (1862–1943). *The Nectar of Manjushri's Speech: A Detailed Commentary on Shantideva's "Way of the Bodhisattva."* Boston: Shambhala Publications, 2007.

Künzang Sönam (1823–1905). *The Profound Reality of Interdependence: An Overview of the Wisdom Chapter of the "Way of the Bodhisattva."* Introduced and translated by Douglas S. Duckworth. New York: Oxford University Press, 2019.

Lamrim Chenmo Translation Committee, trans. *Great Treatise on the Stages of the Path to Enlightenment.* 3 vols. Ithaca, NY: Snow Lion Publications, 2000–2004.

Lechen Künga Gyaltsen (fifteenth century). *Lamp Illuminating the History of the Kadam Tradition. Bka' gdams chos 'byung gsal ba'i sgron me.* Typeset edition. Lhasa: Tibetan Nationalities Press, 2003.

Minkyak Kunzang Sönam (1823–1905). *The Great Hūṃ: A Commentary on Śāntideva's "Way of the Bodhisattva."* Translated by Douglas Duckworth. New York: Wisdom Publications, 2024.

Ngawang Tsultrim (b. 1930). *Golden Mirror: Unraveling the Terms. Brda dkrol gser gyi me long*. Beijing: Mi rigs dpe skrun khang, 1996.

Ngedön Tengyé (nineteenth century). *Theg pa chen po'i dga' ston*. In *The Collected Works of Sman-sdoṅ Mtshams-pa Rin-po-che Karma Nges-don Bstan-rgyas*. Bir: D. Tsondu Senghe, 1975. BDRC MW10982.

Palden Yeshé (fourteenth century). *Rgyal sras thogs med bzang po'i rnam thar bdud rtsi'i thig pa*. In *Rgyal sras thogs med kyi bka' 'bum thor bu*. Thimphu: Kun bzang stobs rgyal, 1975. BDRC MW2CZ6641.

Roerich, George N., trans. *Blue Annals [of 'Gos Lo tsā ba]*. Delhi: Motilal Banarsidass, 1976 [1949].

Rotman, Andy. *Divine Stories: Divyāvadāna, Part 2*. Somerville, MA: Wisdom Publications, 2017.

Śāntideva (eighth century). *The Bodhicaryāvatāra*. Translated by Kate Crosby and Andrew Skilton. Oxford: Oxford University Press, 1995.

———. *Bodhicaryāvatāra of Śāntideva*. [Sanskrit-Tibetan bilingual edition.] Edited by Vidhushekhara Bhattacharya. Calcutta: Asiatic Society, 1960.

———. *A Guide to the Bodhisattva Way of Life*. Translated by Vesna A. Wallace and B. Alan Wallace. Ithaca: Snow Lion, 1997.

Sönam Tsemo (1142–82). *Commentary on Guide to the Bodhisattva Way*. Collected Works, vol. 3. Xylograph edition. n.d.

Thokmé Sangpo (1295–1369). *Rgyal ba'i sras po thogs med chen po'i bka' 'bum*. Dergé edition, Sde dge dpar khang chen mo, n.d. BDRC W00EGS1016240.

———. *An Ocean of Excellent Discourses: A Commentary on "Guide to the Bodhisattva Way." Byang chub sems dpa'i spyod pa la 'jug pa'i 'grel pa legs par bshad pa'i rgya mtsho*. Typeset edition. Sarnath: Sakya Students' Welfare Committee, 1974.

Tsongkhapa (1357–1419). *Notes on the Wisdom Chapter. Shes rab le'u'i zin bris*. Collected Works, vol. *pha*, 525–84. Typeset comparative edition. Mundgod: Je Yabse Sungbum Project, 2019.

Yongzin Yeshé Gyaltsen (1713–93). *Biographies of the Masters of the Lineage of the Stages of the Path. Lam rim bla ma brgyud pa'i rnam thar*. Collected Works, vols. *nga* and *ca*. Reproduced from a set of Tshe mchog gling blocks. New Delhi: Tibet House, 1979.

———. *Theg pa chen po'i blo sbyong gi khrid yig blo bzang dgongs rgyan*. Typeset as *Blo sbyong don bdun ma'i snying po*. Xining: Mtsho sngon mi rigs dpe skrun khang, 1992.

# About the Contributors

THUPTEN JINPA was educated in the Tibetan monastic system, where he received the highest degree of *geshé lharam* at Shartse College of Ganden Monastery. Jinpa also holds a BA in philosophy and a PhD in religious studies, both from the University of Cambridge, England. Since 1985, he has been the principal translator to His Holiness the Dalai Lama, accompanying him on tours throughout the world and translating and editing many books. Jinpa's own works include *Self, Reality and Reason in Tibetan Thought*, several volumes of translations in *The Library of Tibetan Classics*, and the modern biography *Tsongkhapa: A Buddha in the Land of Snows*. He is currently the president and the editor-in-chief of the Institute of Tibetan Classics, based in Montreal, and he also chairs the Mind and Life Institute and the Compassion Institute.

JULIA STENZEL is an assistant professor at Rangjung Yeshe Institute, Centre for Buddhist Studies of Kathmandu University, Nepal. She received her PhD from McGill University, Montreal. Her research focuses on cross-cultural transformation processes of Buddhist contemplative traditions and their relevance in today's world. Julia examined compassion meditations in Indian and Tibetan contexts and their secular application in contemporary secular settings. Her publications include *The Sciencization of Compassion* (Springer, 2020) and *Buddhist Monasteries of the Thai Forest Tradition in Ontario* (Wilfried Laurier Press, 2015).

# Institute of Tibetan Classics

The Institute of Tibetan Classics is a nonprofit, charitable educational organization based in Montreal, Canada. It is dedicated to two primary objectives: (1) to preserve and promote the study and deep appreciation of Tibet's rich intellectual, spiritual, and artistic heritage, especially among the Tibetan-speaking communities worldwide; and (2) to make the classical Tibetan knowledge and literature a truly global heritage, its spiritual and intellectual resources open to all.

To learn more about the Institute of Tibetan Classics and its various projects, please visit www.tibetanclassics.org or write to this address:

Institute of Tibetan Classics
304 Aberdare Road
Montreal (Quebec) H3P 3K3
Canada

# Choose Your Next Inspiration

**Mind Training**
An Online Course with Thupten Jinpa

Through inspiring teaching videos, specially-curated readings (including a brand new translation from Jinpa, created for this course), guided practices, and live Q&As with Jinpa, you'll begin to see the vast potential of mind training for your own mind and life.

**Bodhicitta**
*Wisdom and Compassion as a Way of Life*
An Online Course with Karma Phuntsho

Bodhicitta is not one teaching among many. It is, as the Buddha taught, the one teaching that contains all others. It determines whether or not practice actually becomes a journey to awakening.

**The Great Hūṃ**
*A Commentary on Śāntideva's Way of the Bodhisattva*
Minyak Kunzang Sonam
Translated by Douglas Duckworth

Śāntideva's *Way of the Bodhisattva* (*Bodhicaryāvatāra*) is without a doubt one of the greatest masterpieces of Indian

Buddhism and the single most influential text on Mahāyāna ethical theory. Since it was composed in around the eighth century, it has continuously animated the living tradition, especially in Tibet but now in the West as well, as more translations have become available. Its poetic evocations of the spirit of awakening allow readers to enter the mind of the bodhisattva.

**The Bodhisattva Ideal**
*Key Selected Texts*
Thupten Jinpa and Julia Stenzel

The power and promise of enlightened altruism, a life lived for the benefit of all beings, is on full display in this collection of Buddhist works on the heroic way of the bodhisattva. *Bodhisattva Awakening* is an excerpt from this volume.

**Shantideva's Guide to Awakening**
*A Commentary on the Bodhicharyavatara*
Geshe Yeshe Tobden
Foreword by His Holiness the Dalai Lama

One of the great classics of Buddhist literature, the *Bodhicharyavatara*, or *Way of the Bodhisattva*, is required reading for understanding Tibetan Buddhism. Presented in the form of a personal meditation in verse, Shantideva, the seventh-century Buddhist master, outlines the path of the bodhisattvas—those who renounce the peace of their own liberation, vowing instead to attain enlightenment for the sake of all others. The Dalai Lama once remarked that his own understanding of the bodhisattva path is based entirely upon this text.